ABOUT THIS PUBLICATION

FOR SERVICE ASSISTANCE

Customer Service Department
704.898.0770

North Carolina General Statues is published by The Muliti-Media Group of Greater Charlotte in Charlotte, North Carolina. Copyright 2015 by the Multi-Media Group of Greater Charlotte. This book or parts thereof may not be reproduced in any form, stored in a retrieval system, or transmitted in any form by any means—electronic, mechanical, photocopy, recording or otherwise—without prior written permission of the publisher, except as provided by United States of America copyright law.

The records required by U.S. Code 2257(a) through (c) and the pertinent regulations 28 C.F.R. Cli. 1, Part 75 with respect to this publication and all materials associated with such records are maintained by The Multi-Media Group of Greater Charlotte, Publisher and available for review by Attorney General.

www.visionbooks.org

Copyright © 2015 by MMGGC
All rights reserved!

TID: 5001187
ISBN (10) digit: 1502387328
ISBN (13) digit: 978-1502387325

123-4-56789-01234-Paperback
123-4-56789-01234-Hardback

First Edition

090520140547

Printed in the United States of America

2015 EDITION

North Carolina Criminal Law And Procedure-Pamphlet # 14

Printed In conjunction with the Administration of the Courts

North Carolina Criminal Law and Procedure
Pamphlet Reference Guide

Chapters	Pamphlet
Chapter 1 Civil Procedure	1
Chapter 1 Civil Procedure (Continue)	2
Chapter 1A Rules of Civil Procedure	2
Chapter 1B Contribution.	2
Chapter 1C Enforcement of Judgments.	2
Chapter 1D Punitive Damages.	2
Chapter 1E Eastern Band of Cherokee Indians.	2
Chapter 1F North Carolina Uniform Interstate Depositions and Discovery Act.	2
Chapter 2 - Clerk of Superior Court [Repealed and Transferred.]	3
Chapter 3 - Commissioners of Affidavits and Deeds [Repealed.]	3
Chapter 4 - Common Law	3
Chapter 5 - Contempt [Repealed.]	3
Chapter 5A - Contempt	3
Chapter 6 - Liability for Court Costs	3
Chapter 7 - Courts [Repealed and Transferred.]	3
Chapter 7A – Judicial Department	3
Chapter 7A – Continuation (Judicial Department)	4
Chapter 7A – Continuation (Judicial Department)	5
Chapter 7B - Juvenile Code	5
Chapter 8 - Evidence	6
Chapter 8A - Interpreters for Deaf Persons [Recodified.]	6
Chapter 8B - Interpreters for Deaf Persons	6
Chapter 8C - Evidence Code	6
Chapter 9 - Jurors	6
Chapter 10 - Notaries [Repealed.]	6
Chapter 10A - Notaries [Recodified.]	6
Chapter 10B - Notaries	6
Chapter 11 - Oaths	6
Chapter 12 - Statutory Construction	6
Chapter 13 - Citizenship Restored	6
Chapter 14 - Criminal Law	7
Chapter 14 –Criminal Law (Continuation)	8
Chapter 15 - Criminal Procedure	9
Chapter 15A - Criminal Procedure Act (Continuation)	10
Chapter 15A - Criminal Procedure Act (Continuation)	11
Chapter 15B - Victims Compensation	11
Chapter 15C - Address Confidentiality Program	11
Chapter 16 - Gaming Contracts and Futures	11
Chapter 17 - Habeas Corpus	11

Chapter 17A - Law-Enforcement Officers [Recodified.]	11
Chapter 17B - North Carolina Criminal Justice Education and Training System [Recodified.] Chapter 17C - North Carolina Criminal Justice Education and Training Standards Commission	11
	11
Chapter 17D - North Carolina Justice Academy	11
Chapter 17E - North Carolina Sheriffs' Education and Training Standards Commission	11
Chapter 18 - Regulation of Intoxicating Liquors [Repealed.]	12
Chapter 18A - Regulation of Intoxicating Liquors [Repealed.]	12
Chapter 18B - Regulation of Alcoholic Beverages	12
Chapter 18C - North Carolina State Lottery	12
Chapter 19 - Offenses against Public Morals	12
Chapter 19A - Protection of Animals	12
Chapter 20 - Motor Vehicles	13
Chapter 20 - Motor Vehicles (Continuation)	14
Chapter 20 - Motor Vehicles (Continuation)	15
Chapter 20 - Motor Vehicles (Continuation)	16
Chapter 21 - Bills of Lading	17
Chapter 22 - Contracts Requiring Writing	17
Chapter 22A - Signatures	17
Chapter 22B - Contracts Against Public Policy	17
Chapter 22C - Payments to Subcontractors	17
Chapter 23 - Debtor and Creditor	17
Chapter 24 – Interest	17
Chapter 25 – Uniform Commercial Code	18
Chapter 25 – Uniform Commercial Code (Continuation)	19
Chapter 25A – Retail Installment Sales Act	20
Chapter 25B - Credit	20
Chapter 25C - Sales of Artwork	20
Chapter 26 - Suretyship	20
Chapter 27 - Warehouse Receipts [Repealed.]	20
Chapter 28 - Administration [Repealed.]	20
Chapter 28A - Administration of Decedents' Estates	20
Chapter 28B - Estates of Absentees in Military Service	20
Chapter 28C - Estates of Missing Persons	20
Chapter 29 - Intestate Succession	21
Chapter 30 - Surviving Spouses	21
Chapter 31 - Wills	21
Chapter 31A - Acts Barring Property Rights	21
Chapter 31B - Renunciation of Property and Renunciation of Fiduciary Powers Act	21
Chapter 31C - Uniform Disposition of Community Property Rights at Death Act	21
Chapter 32 - Fiduciaries	21
Chapter 32A - Powers of Attorney	21
Chapter 33 - Guardian and Ward [Repealed and Recodified.]	21

Chapter 33A - North Carolina Uniform Transfers to Minors Act	21
Chapter 33B - North Carolina Uniform Custodial Trust Act	21
Chapter 34 - Veterans' Guardianship Act	22
Chapter 35 - Sterilization Procedures	22
Chapter 35A - Incompetency and Guardianship	22
Chapter 36 - Trusts and Trustees [Repealed.]	22
Chapter 36A - Trusts and Trustees	22
Chapter 36B - Uniform Management of Institutional Funds Act [Repealed.]	22
Chapter 36C - North Carolina Uniform Trust Code	22
Chapter 36D - North Carolina Community Third Party Trusts, Pooled Trusts	23
Chapter 36E - Uniform Prudent Management of Institutional Funds Act	23
Chapter 37 - Allocation of Principal and Income [Repealed.]	23
Chapter 37A - Uniform Principal and Income Act	23
Chapter 38 - Boundaries	23
Chapter 38A - Landowner Liability	23
Chapter 39 - Conveyances	23
Chapter 39A - Transfer Fee Covenants Prohibited	23
Chapter 40 - Eminent Domain [Repealed.]	23
Chapter 40A - Eminent Domain	23
Chapter 41 - Estates	23
Chapter 41A - State Fair Housing Act	23
Chapter 42 - Landlord and Tenant	23
Chapter 42A - Vacation Rental Act	23
Chapter 43 - Land Registration	23
Chapter 44 - Liens	24
Chapter 44A - Statutory Liens and Charges	24
Chapter 45 - Mortgages and Deeds of Trust	24
Chapter 45A - Good Funds Settlement Act	24
Chapter 46 - Partition	24
Chapter 47 - Probate and Registration	25
Chapter 47A - Unit Ownership	25
Chapter 47B - Real Property Marketable Title Act	25
Chapter 47C - North Carolina Condominium Act	25
Chapter 47D - Notice of Settlement Act [Expired.]	25
Chapter 47E - Residential Property Disclosure Act	25
Chapter 47F - North Carolina Planned Community Act	25
Chapter 47G - Option to Purchase Contracts	25
Chapter 47H - Contracts for Deed	25
Chapter 48 - Adoptions +	26
Chapter 48A - Minors	26
Chapter 49 - Bastardy	26
Chapter 49A - Rights of Children	26
Chapter 50 - Divorce and Alimony	26
Chapter 50A - Uniform Child-Custody Jurisdiction and	

Enforcement Act	26
Chapter 50B - Domestic Violence	26
Chapter 50C - Civil No-Contact Orders	26
Chapter 51 - Marriage	26
Chapter 52 - Powers and Liabilities of Married Persons	27
Chapter 52A - Uniform Reciprocal Enforcement of Support Act [Repealed.]	27
Chapter 52B - Uniform Premarital Agreement Act	27
Chapter 52C - Uniform Interstate Family Support Act	27
Chapter 53 - Banks	27
Chapter 53A - Business Development Corporations and North Carolina Capital Resource Corporations	28
Chapter 53B - Financial Privacy Act	28
Chapter 54 - Cooperative Organizations	28
Chapter 54A - Capital Stock Savings and Loan Associations [Repealed.]	28
Chapter 54B - Savings and Loan Associations	29
Chapter 54C - Savings Banks	29
Chapter 55 - North Carolina Business Corporation Act	30
Chapter 55A - North Carolina Nonprofit Corporation Act	31
Chapter 55B - Professional Corporation Act	31
Chapter 55C - Foreign Trade Zones	31
Chapter 55D - Filings, Names, and Registered Agents for Corporations, Nonprofit Corporations, and Partnerships	31
Chapter 56 - Electric, Telegraph and Power Companies [Repealed.]	31
Chapter 57 - Hospital, Medical and Dental Service Corporations [Recodified.]	31
Chapter 57A - Health Maintenance Organization Act [Recodified.]	31
Chapter 57B - Health Maintenance Organization Act [Recodified.]	31
Chapter 57C - North Carolina Limited Liability Company Act.	31
Chapter 58 - Insurance.	32
Chapter 58 - Insurance (Continuation)	33
Chapter 58 - Insurance (Continuation)	34
Chapter 58 - Insurance (Continuation)	35
Chapter 58 - Insurance (Continuation)	36
Chapter 58 - Insurance (Continuation)	37
Chapter 58 - Insurance (Continuation)	38
Chapter 58A - North Carolina Health Insurance Trust Commission [Recodified.]	38
Chapter 59 - Partnership.	39
Chapter 59B - Uniform Unincorporated Nonprofit Association Act.	39
Chapter 60 - Railroads and Other Carriers [Repealed and Transferred.]	39
Chapter 61 - Religious Societies	39
Chapter 62 - Public Utilities	39

Chapter 62 - Public Utilities (Continuation)	40
Chapter 62A - Public Safety Telephone Service And Wireless Telephone Service	40
Chapter 63 - Aeronautics	40
Chapter 63A - North Carolina Global TransPark Authority	40
Chapter 64 - Aliens	40
Chapter 65 – Cemeteries	40
Chapter 66 - Commerce and Business	41
Chapter 67 - Dogs	41
Chapter 68 - Fences and Stock Law	41
Chapter 69 - Fire Protection	41
Chapter 70 - Indian Antiquities, Archaeological Resources and Unmarked Human Skeletal Remains Protection	42
Chapter 71 - Indians [Repealed.]	42
Chapter 71A - Indians	42
Chapter 72 - Inns, Hotels and Restaurants	42
Chapter 73 - Mills	42
Chapter 74 - Mines and Quarries	42
Chapter 74A - Company Police [Repealed.]	42
Chapter 74B - Private Protective Services Act [Repealed.]	42
Chapter 74C - Private Protective Services	42
Chapter 74D - Alarm Systems	42
Chapter 74E - Company Police Act	42
Chapter 74F - Locksmith Licensing Act	42
Chapter 74G - Campus Police Act	42
Chapter 75 - Monopolies, Trusts and Consumer Protection	42
Chapter 75A - Boating and Water Safety	43
Chapter 75B - Discrimination in Business	43
Chapter 75C - Motion Picture Fair Competition Act	43
Chapter 75D - Racketeer Influenced and Corrupt Organizations	43
Chapter 75E - Unlawful Activities in Connection With Certain Corporate Transactions	43
Chapter 76 - Navigation	43
Chapter 76A - Navigation and Pilotage Commissions	43
Chapter 77 - Rivers, Creeks, and Coastal Waters	43
Chapter 78 - Securities Law [Repealed.]	43
Chapter 78A - North Carolina Securities Act	43
Chapter 78B - Tender Offer Disclosure Act [Repealed.]	43
Chapter 78C - Investment Advisers	43
Chapter 78D - Commodities Act	43
Chapter 79 - Strays [Repealed.]	43
Chapter 80 - Trademarks, Brands, etc.	44
Chapter 81 - Weights and Measures [Recodified.]	44
Chapter 81A - Weights and Measures Act of 1975.	44
Chapter 82 - Wrecks [Repealed.]	44
Chapter 83 - Architects [Recodified.]	44

Chapter 83A - Architects	44
Chapter 84 - Attorneys-at-Law	44
Chapter 84A - Foreign Legal Consultants	44
Chapter 85 - Auctions and Auctioneers [Repealed.]	44
Chapter 85A - Bail Bondsmen and Runners [Recodified.]	44
Chapter 85B - Auctions and Auctioneers	44
Chapter 85C - Bail Bondsmen and Runners [Recodified.]	44
Chapter 86 - Barbers [Recodified.]	44
Chapter 86A - Barbers	44
Chapter 87 - Contractors	44
Chapter 88 - Cosmetic Art [Repealed.]	44
Chapter 88A - Electrolysis Practice Act	44
Chapter 88B - Cosmetic Art	45
Chapter 89 - Engineering and Land Surveying [Recodified.]	45
Chapter 89A - Landscape Architects	45
Chapter 89B - Foresters	45
Chapter 89C - Engineering and Land Surveying	45
Chapter 89D - Landscape Contractors	45
Chapter 89E - Geologists Licensing Act	45
Chapter 89F - North Carolina Soil Scientist Licensing Act	45
Chapter 89G - Irrigation Contractors	45
Chapter 90 - Medicine and Allied Occupations	45
Chapter 90 - Medicine and Allied Occupations (Continuation)	46
Chapter 90 - Medicine and Allied Occupations (Continuation)	47
Chapter 90 - Medicine and Allied Occupations (Continuation)	48
Chapter 90A - Sanitarians and Water and Wastewater Treatment Facility Operators	48
Chapter 90B - Social Worker Certification and Licensure Act	48
Chapter 90C - North Carolina Recreational Therapy Licensure Act	48
Chapter 90D - Interpreters and Transliterators	48
Chapter 91 - Pawnbrokers [Repealed.]	48
Chapter 91A - Pawnbrokers Modernization Act of 1989	48
Chapter 92 - Photographers [Deleted.]	48
Chapter 93 - Certified Public Accountants	48
Chapter 93A - Real Estate License Law	49
Chapter 93B - Occupational Licensing Boards	49
Chapter 93C - Watchmakers [Repealed.]	49
Chapter 93D - North Carolina State Hearing Aid Dealers and Fitters Board.	49
Chapter 93E - North Carolina Appraisers Act	49
Chapter 94 - Apprenticeship	49
Chapter 95 - Department of Labor and Labor Regulations	49
Chapter 95 - Department of Labor and Labor Regulations (Continuation)	50
Chapter 96 - Employment Security	50
Chapter 97 - Workers' Compensation Act	50
Chapter 97 - Workers' Compensation Act (Continuation)	51

Chapter 98 - Burnt and Lost Records	51
Chapter 99 - Libel and Slander	51
Chapter 99A - Civil Remedies for Criminal Actions	51
Chapter 99B - Products Liability	51
Chapter 99C - Actions Relating to Winter Sports Safety and Accidents	51
Chapter 99D - Civil Rights	51
Chapter 99E - Special Liability Provisions	51
Chapter 100 - Monuments, Memorials and Parks	51
Chapter 101 - Names of Persons	51
Chapter 102 - Official Survey Base	51
Chapter 103 - Sundays, Holidays and Special Days	51
Chapter 104 - United States Lands	51
Chapter 104A - Degrees of Kinship	51
Chapter 104B - Hurricanes or Other Acts of Nature	51
Chapter 104C - Atomic Energy, Radioactivity and Ionizing Radiation [Repealed and Recodified.]	51
Chapter 104D - Southern States Energy Compact	51
Chapter 104E - North Carolina Radiation Protection Act	51
Chapter 104F - Southeast Interstate Low-Level Radioactive Waste Management Compact [Repealed]	51
Chapter 104G - North Carolina Low-Level Radioactive Waste Management Authority Act of 1987 [Repealed]	51
Chapter 105 - Taxation	51
Chapter 105 - Taxation (Continuation)	52
Chapter 105 - Taxation (Continuation)	53
Chapter 105 - Taxation (Continuation)	54
Chapter 105A - Setoff Debt Collection Act	55
Chapter 105B - Defaulted Student Loan Recovery Act	55
Chapter 106 - Agriculture	55
Chapter 106 - Agriculture (Continue)	56
Chapter 106 - Agriculture (Continue)	57
Chapter 107 - Agricultural Development Districts [Repealed.]	57
Chapter 108 - Social Services [Repealed and Recodified.]	57
Chapter 108A - Social Services	57
Chapter 108B - Community Action Programs	58
Chapter 108C Medicaid and Health Choice Provider Requirements.	58
Chapter 108D Medicaid Managed Care for Behavioral Health Services.	58
Chapter 109 - Bonds [Recodified.]	58
Chapter 110 - Child Welfare	58
Chapter 111 - Aid to the Blind	58
Chapter 112 - Confederate Homes and Pensions [Repealed.]	58
Chapter 113 - Conservation and Development	58
Chapter 113 - Conservation and Development (Continuation)	59

Chapter 113A - Pollution Control and Environment	59
Chapter 113A - Pollution Control and Environment (Continuation)	60
Chapter 113B - North Carolina Energy Policy Act of 1975	60
Chapter 114 - Department of Justice	60
Chapter 115 - Elementary and Secondary Education [Repealed.]	60
Chapter 115A - Community Colleges, Technical Institutes, and Industrial Education Centers [Repealed.]	60
Chapter 115B - Tuition and Fee Waivers	60
Chapter 115C - Elementary and Secondary Education	60
Chapter 115C - Elementary and Secondary Education (Continuation)	61
Chapter 115C - Elementary and Secondary Education (Continuation)	62
Chapter 115C - Elementary and Secondary Education (Continuation)	63
Chapter 115D - Community Colleges	63
Chapter 115E - Private Educational Facilities Finance Act [Recodified]	63
Chapter 116 - Higher Education	63
Chapter 116 - Higher Education (Continuation)	63
Chapter 116A - Escheats and Abandoned Property [Repealed.]	64
Chapter 116B - Escheats and Abandoned Property	64
Chapter 116C - Continuum of Education Programs	64
Chapter 116D - Higher Education Bonds	64
Chapter 117 - Electrification	64
Chapter 118 - Firemen's and Rescue Squad Workers' Relief and Pension Funds [Recodified.]	64
Chapter 118A - Firemen's Death Benefit Act [Repealed.]	64
Chapter 118B - Members of a Rescue Squad Death Benefit Act [Repealed.]	64
Chapter 119 - Gasoline and Oil Inspection and Regulation	64
Chapter 120 - General Assembly	65
Chapter 120 - General Assembly (Continuation)	66
Chapter 120 - General Assembly (Continuation)	67
Chapter 120C - Lobbying	67
Chapter 121 - Archives and History	67
Chapter 122 - Hospitals for the Mentally Disordered [Repealed.]	67
Chapter 122A - North Carolina Housing Finance Agency	67
Chapter 122B - North Carolina Agricultural Facilities Finance Act [Repealed.]	67
Chapter 122C - Mental Health, Developmental Disabilities, and Substance Abuse Act of 1985	67
Chapter 122C - Mental Health, Developmental Disabilities, and Substance Abuse Act of 1985 (Continuation)	68
Chapter 122D - North Carolina Agricultural Finance Act	68

Chapter 122E - North Carolina Housing Trust and Oil Overcharge Act	68
Chapter 123 - Impeachment	69
Chapter 123A - Industrial Development [Repealed.]	69
Chapter 124 - Internal Improvements	69
Chapter 125 - Libraries	69
Chapter 126 - State Personnel System	69
Chapter 127 - Militia [Repealed.]	69
Chapter 127A - Militia	69
Chapter 127B - Military Affairs	69
Chapter 127C - Advisory Commission on Military Affairs	69
Chapter 128 - Offices and Public Officers	69
Chapter 128 - Offices and Public Officers (Continuation)	70
Chapter 129 - Public Buildings and Grounds	70
Chapter 130 - Public Health [Repealed.]	70
Chapter 130A - Public Health	70
Chapter 130A - Public Health (Continuation)	71
Chapter 130A - Public Health (Continuation)	72
Chapter 130B - Hazardous Waste Management Commission [Repealed.]	72
Chapter 131 - Public Hospitals [Repealed.]	72
Chapter 131A - Health Care Facilities Finance Act	72
Chapter 131B - Licensing of Ambulatory Surgical Facilities [Repealed.]	72
Chapter 131C - Charitable Solicitation Licensure Act [Repealed.]	72
Chapter 131D - Inspection and Licensing of Facilities	72
Chapter 131E - Health Care Facilities and Services	72
Chapter 131E - Health Care Facilities and Services (Continuation)	73
Chapter 131F - Solicitation of Contributions	73
Chapter 132 - Public Records	73
Chapter 133 - Public Works	74
Chapter 134 - Youth Development [Recodified.]	74
Chapter 134A - Youth Services [Repealed.]	74
Chapter 135 - Retirement System for Teachers and State Employees; Social Security; Health Insurance Program for Children	74
Chapter 135 - Retirement System for Teachers and State Employees; Social Security; Health Insurance Program for Children	75
Chapter 136 - Transportation	75
Chapter 136 - Transportation (Continuation)	76
Chapter 137 - Rural Rehabilitation [Repealed.]	76
Chapter 138 - Salaries, Fees and Allowances	76
Chapter 138A - State Government Ethics Act	76
Chapter 139 - Soil and Water Conservation Districts	76

Chapter 140 - State Art Museum; Symphony and Art Societies	76
Chapter 140A - State Awards System	76
Chapter 141 - State Boundaries	76
Chapter 142 - State Debt	76
Chapter 143 - State Departments, Institutions, and Commissions	77
Chapter 143 - State Departments, Institutions, and Commissions (Continuation)	78
Chapter 143 - State Departments, Institutions, and Commissions (Continuation)	79
Chapter 143 - State Departments, Institutions, and Commissions (Continuation)	80
Chapter 143A - State Government Reorganization	80
Chapter 143B - Executive Organization Act of 1973	80
Chapter 143B - Executive Organization Act of 1973 (Continuation)	81
Chapter 143B - Executive Organization Act of 1973 (Continuation)	82
Chapter 143C - State Budget Act	83
Chapter 143D - The State Governmental Accountability and Internal Control Act	83
Chapter 144 - State Flag, Official Governmental Flags, Motto, and Colors	83
Chapter 145 - State Symbols and Other Official Adoptions.	83
Chapter 146 - State Lands	83
Chapter 147 - State Officers	83
Chapter 148 - State Prison System	84
Chapter 149 - State Song and Toast	84
Chapter 150 - Uniform Revocation of Licenses [Repealed.]	84
Chapter 150A - Administrative Procedure Act [Recodified.]	84
Chapter 150B - Administrative Procedure Act	84
Chapter 151 - Constables [Repealed.]	84
Chapter 152 - Coroners	84
Chapter 152A - County Medical Examiner [Repealed.]	84
Chapter 152A - County Medical Examiner [Repealed.] (Continuation)	85
Chapter 153 - Counties and County Commissioners [Repealed.]	85
Chapter 153A - Counties	85
Chapter 153B - Mountain Resources Planning Act	85
Chapter 153C - Uwharrie Regional Resources Act	85
Chapter 154 - County Surveyor [Repealed.]	85
Chapter 155 - County Treasurer [Repealed.]	85
Chapter 156 - Drainage	85
Chapter 156 – Drainage (Continuation)	86

Chapter 157 - Housing Authorities and Projects	86
Chapter 157A - Historic Properties Commissions [Transferred.]	86
Chapter 158 - Local Development	86
Chapter 159 - Local Government Finance	86
Chapter 159 - Local Government Finance (Continuation)	87
Chapter 159A - Pollution Abatement and Industrial Facilities Financing Act [Unconstitutional.]	87
Chapter 159B - Joint Municipal Electric Power and Energy Act	87
Chapter 159C - Industrial and Pollution Control Facilities Financing Act	87
Chapter 159D - The North Carolina Capital Facilities Financing Act	87
Chapter 159E - Registered Public Obligations Act	87
Chapter 159F - North Carolina Energy Development Authority [Repealed.]	87
Chapter 159G - Water Infrastructure	87
Chapter 159H - [Reserved.]	87
Chapter 159I - Solid Waste Management Loan Program and Local Government Special Obligation Bonds	87
Chapter 160 - Municipal Corporations [Repealed And Transferred.]	87
Chapter 160A - Cities and Towns	88
Chapter 160A - Cities and Towns (Continuation)	89
Chapter 160B - Consolidated City-County Act	89
Chapter 160C - Baseball Park Districts [Repealed.]	90
Chapter 161 - Register of Deeds	90
Chapter 162 - Sheriff	90
Chapter 162A - Water and Sewer Systems	90
Chapter 162B Continuity of Local Government in Emergency.	90
Chapter 163 Elections and Election Laws.	90
Chapter 163 Elections and Election Laws. (Continuation)	91
Chapter 164 Concerning the General Statutes of North Carolina.	92
Chapter 165 Veterans.	92
Chapter 166 Civil Preparedness Agencies [Repealed.]	92
Chapter 166A North Carolina Emergency Management Act.	92
Chapter 167 State Civil Air Patrol [Repealed.]	92
Chapter 168 Persons with Disabilities.	92
Chapter 168A Persons With Disabilities Protection Act.	92

Chapter 7 – Courts [Repealed and Transferred.]

§ 20-63.01. Bonds required for commission contractors.

(a) A guaranty bond is required for each commission contractor that is not a governmental subdivision of this State that is granted a contract to issue license plates or conduct business pursuant to G.S. 20-63. Provided, however, a commission contractor that is unable to secure a bond may, with the consent of the Division, provide an alternative to a guaranty bond, as provided in subsection (c) of this section.

The Division may revoke, with cause, a contract with a commission contractor that fails to maintain a bond or an alternative to a bond, pursuant to this section.

(b) (1) When application is made for a contract or contract renewal, the applicant shall file a guaranty bond with the clerk of the superior court and/or the register of deeds of the county in which the commission contractor will be located. The bond shall be in favor of the Division. The bond shall be executed by the applicant as principal and by a bonding company authorized to do business in this State. The bond shall be conditioned to provide indemnification to the Division for a loss of revenue for any reason, including bankruptcy, employee embezzlement or theft, foreclosure, or ceasing to operate.

(2) The bond shall be in an amount determined by the Division to be adequate to provide indemnification to the Division under the terms of the bond. The bond amount shall be at least one hundred thousand dollars ($100,000).

(3) The bond shall remain in force and effect until cancelled by the guarantor. The guarantor may cancel the bond upon 30 days' notice to the Division. Cancellation of the bond shall not affect any liability incurred or accrued prior to the termination of the notice period.

(4) The Division may be able to negotiate bonds for contractors who qualify for bonds as a group under favorable rates or circumstances. If so, the Division may require those contractors who can qualify for the group bond to obtain their bond as part of a group of contractors. The Division may deduct the premiums for any bonds it may be able to negotiate at group rates from the commissioned contractors' compensation.

(c) An applicant that is unable to secure a bond may seek a waiver of the guaranty bond from the Division and approval of one of the guaranty bond alternatives set forth in this subsection. With the approval of the Division, an applicant may file with the clerk of the superior court and/or the register of deeds of the county in which the commission contractor will be located, in lieu of a bond:

(1) An assignment of a savings account in an amount equal to the bond required (i) which is in a form acceptable to the Division; (ii) which is executed by the applicant; (iii) which is executed by a state or federal savings and loan association, state bank, or national bank that is doing business in North Carolina and whose accounts are insured by a federal depositors corporation; and (iv) for which access to the account in favor of the State of North Carolina is subject to the same conditions as for a bond in subsection (b) of this section.

(2) A certificate of deposit (i) which is executed by a state or federal savings and loan association, state bank, or national bank which is doing business in North Carolina and whose accounts are insured by a federal depositors corporation; (ii) which is either payable to the State of North Carolina, unrestrictively endorsed to the Division of Motor Vehicles; in the case of a negotiable certificate of deposit, is unrestrictively endorsed to the Division of Motor Vehicles; or in the case of a nonnegotiable certificate of deposit, is assigned to the Division of Motor Vehicles in a form satisfactory to the Division; and (iii) for which access to the certificate of deposit in favor of the State of North Carolina is subject to the same conditions as for a bond in subsection (b) of this section. (2007-488, s. 1.)

§ 20-63.02. Advisory committee of commission contractors.

(a) Committee and Duties. - An advisory committee is established and is designated the License Plate Agent (LPA) Advisory Committee. The Division and the LPA Advisory Committee are directed to work together to ensure excellent and efficient customer service with respect to vehicle titling and registration services provided through commission contracts awarded under G.S. 20-63. As part of this effort, the Division and the Committee must periodically review all forms and instructions used in the vehicle titling and registration process to ensure that they are readily understandable and not duplicative. The Committee must meet at least quarterly.

(b) Membership and Terms. - The LPA Advisory Committee consists of persons who are on the staff of the Division of Motor Vehicles and six persons appointed by the North Carolina Association of Motor Vehicle Registration Contractors. The Commissioner determines the number of Division staff persons to appoint to the Committee and designates the chair of the Committee. Members of the Committee appointed by the Commissioner serve ex officio. Members of the Committee appointed by the Association serve two-year terms beginning on July 1 of an odd-numbered year. A member who serves for a specific term continues to serve after the expiration of the member's term until a successor is appointed.

(c) Expenses. - Members of the LPA Advisory Committee are allowed the per diem, subsistence, and travel allowances established under G.S. 138-5 for service on State boards and commissions. (2013-372, s. 1(a).)

§ 20-63.1. Division may cause plates to be reflectorized.

The Division of Motor Vehicles is hereby authorized to cause vehicle license plates for 1968 and future years to be completely treated with reflectorized materials designed to increase visibility and legibility of license plates at night. (1967, c. 8; 1975, c. 716, s. 5.)

§ 20-64. Transfer of registration plates to another vehicle.

(a) Except as otherwise provided in this Article, registration plates shall be retained by the owner thereof upon disposition of the vehicle to which assigned, and may be assigned to another vehicle, belonging to such owner and of a like vehicle category within the meaning of G.S. 20-87 and 20-88, upon proper application to the Division and payment of a transfer fee and such additional fees as may be due because the vehicle to which the plates are to be assigned requires a greater registration fee than that vehicle to which the license plates were last assigned. In cases where the plate is assigned to another vehicle belonging to such owner, and is not of a like vehicle category within the meaning of G.S. 20-87 and 20-88, the owner shall surrender the plate to the Division and receive therefor a plate of the proper category, and the unexpired portion of the fee originally paid by the owner for the plate so surrendered shall be a credit toward the fee charged for the new plate of the proper category. Provided, that the owner shall not be entitled to a cash refund when the registration fee for the vehicle to which the plates are to be assigned is less than the registration fee for that vehicle to which the license plates were last assigned. An owner assigning or transferring plates to another vehicle as provided herein shall be subject to the same assessments and penalties for use of the plates on another vehicle or for improper use of the plates, as he could have been for the use of the plates on the vehicle to which last assigned. Provided, however, that upon compliance with the requirements of this section, the registration plates of vehicles owned by and registered in the name of a corporation may be transferred and assigned to a like vehicle category within the meaning of G.S. 20-87 and 20-88, upon the showing that the vehicle to which the transfer and assignment is to be made is owned by a corporation which is a wholly owned subsidiary of the corporation applying for such transfer and assignment.

(b)   Upon a change of the name of a corporation or a change of the name under which a proprietorship or partnership is doing business, the corporation, partnership or proprietorship shall forthwith apply for correction of the certificate of title of all vehicles owned by such corporation, partnership or proprietorship so as to correctly reflect the name of the corporation or the name under which the proprietorship or partnership is doing business, and pay the fees required by law.

(c)   Upon a change in the composition of a partnership, ownership of vehicles belonging to such partnership shall not be deemed to have changed so long as one partner of the predecessor partnership remains a partner in the reconstituted partnership, but the reconstituted partnership shall forthwith apply for correction of the certificate of title of all vehicles owned by such partnership so as to correctly reflect the composition of the partnership and the name under which it is doing business, if any, and pay the fees required by law.

(d)   When a proprietorship or partnership is incorporated, the corporation shall retain license plates assigned to vehicles belonging to it and may use the same, provided the corporation applies for and obtains transfers of the certificates of title of all vehicles and pays the fees required by law.

(e)   Upon death of the owner of a registered vehicle, such registration shall continue in force as a valid registration until the end of the year for which the license is issued unless ownership of the vehicle passes or is transferred to any person other than the surviving spouse before the end of the year.

(f)   The owner or transferor of a registered vehicle who surrenders the registration plate to the division may secure a refund for the unexpired portion of such plate prorated on a monthly basis, beginning the first day of the month following surrender of the plate to the division, provided the annual fee of such surrendered plate is sixty dollars ($60.00) or more. This refund may not exceed one half of the annual license fee. No refund shall be made unless the owner or transferor furnishes proof of financial responsibility on the registered vehicle effective until the date of the surrender of the plate. Proof of financial responsibility shall be furnished in a manner prescribed by the Commissioner.

(g)   The Commissioner of Motor Vehicles shall have the power to make such rules and regulations as he may deem necessary for the administration of transfers of license plates and vehicles under this Article. (1937, c. 407, s. 28; 1945, c. 576, s. 1; 1947, c. 914, s. 1; 1951, c. 188; c. 819, s. 1; 1961, c. 360, s. 5; 1963, cc. 1067, 1190; 1967, c. 995; 1973, c. 1134; 1975, c. 716, s. 5; 1981, c. 227; 2004-167, s. 1; 2004-199, s. 59; 2007-491, s. 5.)

§ 20-64.1: Repealed by Session Laws 1995 (Regular Session, 1996), c. 756, s. 6.

§ 20-64.2: Repealed by Session Laws 2010-132, s. 4, effective December 1, 2010.

§ 20-65. Repealed by Session Laws 1979, 2nd Session, c. 1280, s. 1.

§ 20-66. Renewal of vehicle registration.

(a)   Annual Renewal. - The registration of a vehicle must be renewed annually. To renew the registration of a vehicle, the owner of the vehicle must file an application with the Division and pay the required registration fee. The Division may receive and grant an application for renewal of registration at any time before the registration expires.

(b)   Method of Renewal. - When the Division renews the registration of a vehicle, it must issue a new registration card for the vehicle and either a new registration plate or a registration renewal sticker. The Division may renew a registration plate for any type of vehicle by means of a renewal sticker.

(b1)   Repealed by Session Laws 1993, c. 467, s. 2.

(c)   Renewal Stickers. - A registration renewal sticker issued by the Division must be displayed on the registration plate that it renews in the place prescribed by the Commissioner and must indicate the period for which it and the registration plate on which it is displayed are valid. Except where physical differences between a registration renewal sticker and a registration plate render a provision of this Chapter inapplicable, the provisions of this Chapter relating to registration plates apply to registration renewal stickers.

(d),   (e) Repealed by Session Laws 1993 (Reg. Sess., 1994), c. 761, s. 5.

(f)   Repealed by Session Laws 1993, c. 467, s. 2.

(g)   When Renewal Sticker Expires. - The registration of a vehicle that is renewed by means of a registration renewal sticker expires at midnight on the last day of the month designated on the sticker. It is lawful, however, to operate the vehicle on a highway until midnight on the fifteenth day of the month following the month in which the sticker expired.

The Division may vary the expiration dates of registration renewal stickers issued for a type of vehicle so that an approximately equal number expires at the end of each month, quarter, or other period consisting of one or more months. When the Division implements registration renewal for a type of vehicle by means of a renewal sticker, it may issue a registration renewal sticker that expires at the end of any monthly interval.

(h)   Repealed by Session Laws 2004-167, s. 3, as amended by Session Laws 2004-199, s. 59, effective January 1, 2006.

(i)   Property Tax Consolidation. - When the Division receives an application under subsection (a) for the renewal of registration before the current registration expires, the Division shall grant the application if it is made for the purpose of consolidating the property taxes payable by the applicant on classified motor vehicles, as defined in G.S. 105-330. The registration fee for a motor vehicle whose registration cycle is changed under this subsection shall be reduced by a prorated amount. The prorated amount is one-twelfth of the registration fee in effect when the motor vehicle's registration was last renewed multiplied by the number of full months remaining in the motor vehicle's current registration cycle, rounded to the nearest multiple of twenty-five cents (25¢).

(j)   Inspection Prior to Renewal of Registration. - The Division shall not renew the registration of a vehicle unless it has a current safety or emissions inspection.

(k)   Repealed by Session Laws 2008-190, s. 1, effective October 1, 2008. (1937, c. 407, s. 30; 1955, c. 554, s. 3; 1973, c. 1389, s. 1; 1975, c. 716, s. 5; 1977, c. 337; 1979, 2nd Sess., c. 1280, ss. 2, 3; 1981 (Reg. Sess., 1982), c. 1258, s. 1; 1985 (Reg. Sess., 1986), c. 982, s. 24; 1991, c. 624, ss. 6, 7; c. 672, s. 7; c. 726, s. 23; 1993, c. 467, s. 2; 1993 (Reg. Sess., 1994), c. 761, s. 5; 2004-167, ss. 2, 3; 2004-199, s. 59; 2007-503, s. 1; 2008-190, s. 1.)

§ 20-66.1. Repealed by Session Laws 1973, c. 1389, s. 2.

§ 20-67. Notice of change of address or name.

(a)   Address. - A person whose address changes from the address stated on a certificate of title or registration card must notify the Division of the change within 60 days after the change occurs. The person may obtain a duplicate certificate of title or registration card stating the new address but is not required to do so. A person who does not move but whose address changes due to governmental action may not be charged with violating this subsection.

(b)   Name. - A person whose name changes from the name stated on a certificate of title or registration card must notify the Division of the change within 60 days after the change occurs. The person may obtain a duplicate certificate of title or registration card but is not required to do so.

(c)   Fee. - G.S. 20-85 sets the fee for a duplicate certificate of title or registration card. (1937, c. 407, s. 31; 1955, c. 554, s. 4; 1975, c. 716, s. 5; 1979, c. 106; 1997-122, s. 7.)

§ 20-68. Replacement of lost or damaged certificates, cards and plates.

(a)   In the event any registration card or registration plate is lost, mutilated, or becomes illegible, the owner or legal representative of the owner of the vehicle for which the same was issued, as shown by the records of the Division, shall immediately make application for and may obtain a duplicate or a substitute or a new registration under a new registration number, as determined to be most advisable by the Division, upon the applicant's furnishing under oath information satisfactory to the Division and payment of required fee.

(b) If a certificate of title is lost, stolen, mutilated, destroyed or becomes illegible, the first lienholder or, if none, the owner or legal representative of the owner named in the certificate, as shown by the records of the Division, shall promptly make application for and may obtain a duplicate upon furnishing information satisfactory to the Division. It shall be mailed to the first lienholder named in it or, if none, to the owner. The Division shall not issue a new certificate of title upon application made on a duplicate until 15 days after receipt of the application. A person recovering an original certificate of title for which a duplicate has been issued shall promptly surrender the original certificate to the Division. (1937, c. 407, s. 32; 1961, c. 360, s. 7; c. 835, s. 7; 1975, c. 716, s. 5.)

§ 20-69. Division authorized to assign new engine number.

The owner of a motor vehicle upon which the engine number or serial number has become illegible or has been removed or obliterated shall immediately make application to the Division for a new engine or serial number for such motor vehicle. The Division, when satisfied that the applicant is the lawful owner of the vehicle referred to in such application is hereby authorized to assign a new engine or serial number thereto, and shall require that such number, together with the name of this State, or a symbol indicating this State, be stamped upon the engine, or in the event such number is a serial number, then upon such portion of the motor vehicle as shall be designated by the Division. (1937, c. 407, s. 33; 1975, c. 716, s. 5.)

§ 20-70. Division to be notified when another engine is installed or body changed.

(a) Whenever a motor vehicle registered hereunder is altered by the installation of another engine in place of an engine, the number of which is shown in the registration records, or the installation of another body in place of a body, the owner of such motor vehicle shall immediately give notice to the Division in writing on a form prepared by it, which shall state the number of the former engine and the number of the newly installed engine, the registration number of the motor vehicle, the name of the owner and any other information which the Division may require. Whenever another engine has been substituted as provided in this section, and the notice given as required hereunder, the Division shall insert the number of the newly installed engine upon the registration card and certificate of title issued for such motor vehicle.

(b) Whenever a new engine or serial number has been assigned to and stamped upon a motor vehicle as provided in G.S. 20-69, or whenever a new engine has been installed or body changed as provided in this section, the Division shall require the owner to surrender to the Division the registration card and certificate of title previously issued for said vehicle. The Division shall also require the owner to make application for a duplicate registration card and a duplicate certificate of title showing the new motor or serial number thereon or new style of body, and upon receipt of such application and fee, as for any other duplicate title, the Division shall issue to said owner a duplicate registration and a duplicate certificate of title showing thereon the new number in place of the original number or the new style of body.

(c) The notification and registration requirements contained in subsections (a) and (b) of this section regarding an engine change shall be required only if the motor vehicle into which a new engine is installed uses an engine number as the sole means to identify the vehicle. (1937, c. 407, s. 34; 1943, c. 726; 1975, c. 716, s. 5; 2009-405, s. 3.)

§ 20-71. Altering or forging certificate of title, registration card or application, a felony; reproducing or possessing blank certificate of title.

(a) Any person who, with fraudulent intent, shall alter any certificate of title, registration card issued by the Division, or any application for a certificate of title or registration card, or forge or counterfeit any certificate of title or registration card purported to have been issued by the Division under the provisions of this Article, or who, with fraudulent intent, shall alter, falsify or forge any assignment thereof, or who shall hold or use any such certificate, registration card, or application, or assignment, knowing the same to have been altered, forged or falsified, shall be guilty of a felony and upon conviction thereof shall be punished in the discretion of the court.

(b) It shall be unlawful for any person with fraudulent intent to reproduce or possess a blank North Carolina certificate of title or facsimile thereof. Any person, firm or corporation violating the provisions of this section shall be guilty of a Class I felony. (1937, c. 407, s. 35; 1959, c. 1264, s. 2; 1971, c. 99; 1975, c. 716, s. 5; 1979, c. 499; 1993, c. 539, s. 1251; 1994, Ex. Sess., c. 24, s. 14(c).)

§ 20-71.1. Registration evidence of ownership; ownership evidence of defendant's responsibility for conduct of operation.

(a)   In all actions to recover damages for injury to the person or to property or for the death of a person, arising out of an accident or collision involving a motor vehicle, proof of ownership of such motor vehicle at the time of such accident or collision shall be prima facie evidence that said motor vehicle was being operated and used with the authority, consent, and knowledge of the owner in the very transaction out of which said injury or cause of action arose.

(b)   Proof of the registration of a motor vehicle in the name of any person, firm, or corporation, shall for the purpose of any such action, be prima facie evidence of ownership and that such motor vehicle was then being operated by and under the control of a person for whose conduct the owner was legally responsible, for the owner's benefit, and within the course and scope of his employment. (1951, c. 494; 1961, c. 975.)

Part 3A.

Salvage Titles.

§ 20-71.2. Declaration of purpose.

The titling of salvage motor vehicles constitutes a problem in North Carolina because members of the public are sometimes misled into believing a motor vehicle has not been damaged by collision, fire, flood, accident, or other cause or that the vehicle has not been altered, rebuilt, or modified to such an extent that it impairs or changes the original components of the motor vehicle. It is therefore in the public interest that the Commissioner of Motor Vehicles issue rules to give public notice of the titling of such vehicles and to carry out the provisions of this Part of the motor vehicle laws of North Carolina. (1987, c. 607, s. 1.)

§ 20-71.3. Salvage and other vehicles - titles and registration cards to be branded.

(a)   Motor vehicle certificates of title and registration cards issued pursuant to G.S. 20-57 shall be branded in accordance with this section.

As used in this section, "branded" means that the title and registration card shall contain a designation that discloses if the vehicle is classified as any of the following:

(1) Salvage Motor Vehicle.

(2) Salvage Rebuilt Vehicle.

(3) Reconstructed Vehicle.

(4) Flood Vehicle.

(5) Non-U.S.A. Vehicle.

(6) Any other classification authorized by law.

(a1) Any motor vehicle that is declared a total loss by an insurance company licensed and approved to conduct business in North Carolina, in addition to the designations noted in subsection (a) of this section, shall:

(1) Have the title and registration card marked "TOTAL LOSS CLAIM".

(2) Have a tamperproof permanent marker inserted into the doorjamb of that vehicle by the Division, at the time of the final inspection of the reconstructed vehicle, that states "TOTAL LOSS CLAIM VEHICLE". Should that vehicle be later reconstructed, repaired, or rebuilt, a permanent tamperproof marker shall be inserted in the doorjamb of the reconstructed, repaired, or rebuilt vehicle.

(b) Any motor vehicle up to and including six model years old damaged by collision or other occurrence, that is to be retitled in this State, shall be subject to preliminary and final inspections by the Enforcement Section of the Division. For purposes of this section, the term "six model years" shall be calculated by counting the model year of the vehicle's manufacture as the first model year and the current calendar year as the final model year.

These inspections serve as antitheft measures and do not certify the safety or road-worthiness of a vehicle.

(c) The Division shall not retitle a vehicle described in subsection (b) of this section that has not undergone the preliminary and final inspections required by that subsection.

(d) Any motor vehicle up to and including six model years old that has been inspected pursuant to subsection (b) of this section may be retitled with an unbranded title based upon a title application by the rebuilder with a supporting affidavit disclosing all of the following:

(1) The parts used or replaced.

(2) The major components replaced.

(3) The hours of labor and the hourly labor rate.

(4) The total cost of repair.

(5) The existence, if applicable, of the doorjamb "TOTAL LOSS CLAIM VEHICLE" marker.

The unbranded title shall be issued only if the cost of repairs, including parts and labor, does not exceed seventy-five percent (75%) of its fair market retail value.

(e) Any motor vehicle more than six model years old damaged by collision or other occurrence that is to be retitled by the State may be retitled, without inspection, with an unbranded title based upon a title application by the rebuilder with a supporting affidavit disclosing all of the following:

(1) The parts used or replaced.

(2) The major components replaced.

(3) The hours of labor and the hourly labor rate.

(4) The total cost of repair.

(5) The existence, if applicable, of the doorjamb "TOTAL LOSS CLAIM VEHICLE" marker.

(6) The cost to replace the air bag restraint system.

The unbranded title shall be issued only if the cost of repairs, including parts and labor and excluding the cost to replace the air bag restraint system, does not exceed seventy-five percent (75%) of its fair market retail value.

(f) The Division shall maintain the affidavits required by this section and make them available for review and copying by persons researching the salvage and repair history of the vehicle.

(g) Any motor vehicle that has been branded in another state shall be branded with the nearest applicable brand specified in this section, except that no junk vehicle or vehicle that has been branded junk in another state shall be titled or registered.

(h) A branded title for a salvage motor vehicle damaged by collision or other occurrence shall be issued as follows:

(1) For motor vehicles up to and including six model years old, a branded title shall be issued if the cost of repairs, including parts and labor, exceeds seventy-five percent (75%) of its fair market value at the time of the collision or other occurrence.

(2) For motor vehicles more than six model years old, a branded title shall be issued if the cost of repairs, including parts and labor and excluding the cost to replace the air bag restraint system, exceeds seventy-five percent (75%) of its fair market value at the time of the collision or other occurrence.

(i) Once the Division has issued a branded title for a motor vehicle all subsequent titles for that motor vehicle shall continue to reflect the branding.

(j) The Division shall prepare necessary forms and doorjamb marker specifications and may adopt rules required to carry out the provisions of this Part. (1987, c. 607, s. 1; 1987 (Reg. Sess., 1988), c. 1105, s. 2; 1989, c. 455, ss. 2, 3; 1989 (Reg. Sess., 1990), c. 916, s. 1; 1997-443, s. 32.26; 1998-212, s. 27.8(a); 2003-258, s. 1.)

§ 20-71.4. Failure to disclose damage to a vehicle shall be a misdemeanor.

(a) It shall be unlawful for any transferor of a motor vehicle to do any of the following:

(1) Transfer a motor vehicle up to and including five model years old when the transferor has knowledge that the vehicle has been involved in a collision or other occurrence to the extent that the cost of repairing that vehicle, excluding the cost to replace the air bag restraint system, exceeds twenty-five percent (25%) of its fair market retail value at the time of the collision or other occurrence, without disclosing that fact in writing to the transferee prior to the transfer of the vehicle.

(2) Transfer a motor vehicle when the transferor has knowledge that the vehicle is, or was, a flood vehicle, a reconstructed vehicle, or a salvage motor vehicle, without disclosing that fact in writing to the transferee prior to the transfer of the vehicle.

(a1) For purposes of this section, the term "five model years" shall be calculated by counting the model year of the vehicle's manufacture as the first model year and the current calendar year as the final model year. Failure to disclose any of the information required under subsection (a) of this section that is within the knowledge of the transferor will also result in civil liability under G.S. 20-348. The Commissioner may prepare forms to carry out the provisions of this section.

(b) It shall be unlawful for any person to remove the title or supporting documents to any motor vehicle from the State of North Carolina with the intent to conceal damage (or damage which has been repaired) occurring as a result of a collision or other occurrence.

(c) It shall be unlawful for any person to remove, tamper with, alter, or conceal the "TOTAL LOSS CLAIM VEHICLE" tamperproof permanent marker that is affixed to the doorjamb of any total loss claim vehicle. It shall be unlawful for any person to reconstruct a total loss claim vehicle and not include or affix a "TOTAL LOSS CLAIM VEHICLE" tamperproof permanent marker to the doorjamb of the rebuilt vehicle. Violation of this subsection shall constitute a Class I felony, punishable by a fine of not less than five thousand dollars ($5,000) for each offense.

(d) Violation of subsections (a) and (b) of this section shall constitute a Class 2 misdemeanor.

(e) The provisions of this section shall not apply to a State agency that assists the United States Department of Defense with purchasing, transferring, or titling a vehicle to another State agency, a unit of local government, a volunteer fire department, or a volunteer rescue squad. (1987, c. 607, s. 1; 1987 (Reg. Sess., 1988), c. 1105, s. 3; 1989, c. 455, s. 4; 1989 (Reg. Sess., 1990), c. 916, s. 2; 1993, c. 539, s. 337; 1994, Ex. Sess., c. 24, s. 14(c); 1998-212, s. 27.8(b); 2003-258, s. 2; 2009-550, s. 2(a).)

Part 4. Transfer of Title or Interest.

§ 20-72. Transfer by owner.

(a) Whenever the owner of a registered vehicle transfers or assigns his title or interests thereto, he shall remove the license plates. The registration card and plates shall be forwarded to the Division unless the plates are to be transferred to another vehicle as provided in G.S. 20-64. If they are to be transferred to and used with another vehicle, then the endorsed registration card and the plates shall be retained and preserved by the owner. If such registration plates are to be transferred to and used with another vehicle, then the owner shall make application to the Division for assignment of the registration plates to such other vehicle under the provisions of G.S. 20-64. Such application shall be made within 20 days after the date on which such plates are last used on the vehicle to which theretofore assigned.

(b) In order to assign or transfer title or interest in any motor vehicle registered under the provisions of this Article, the owner shall execute in the presence of a person authorized to administer oaths an assignment and warranty of title on the reverse of the certificate of title in form approved by the Division, including in such assignment the name and address of the transferee; and no title to any motor vehicle shall pass or vest until such assignment is executed and the motor vehicle delivered to the transferee. The provisions of this section shall not apply to any foreclosure or repossession under a chattel mortgage or conditional sales contract or any judicial sale. The provisions of this subsection shall not apply to (i) any transfer to an insurer pursuant to G.S. 20-109.1(b)(2) or (ii) any transfer to a used motor vehicle dealer pursuant to G.S. 20-109.1(e1).

When a manufacturer's statement of origin or an existing certificate of title on a motor vehicle is unavailable, a motor vehicle dealer licensed under Article 12 of this Chapter may also transfer title to another by certifying in writing in a sworn statement to the Division that all prior perfected liens on the vehicle have been paid and that the motor vehicle dealer, despite having used reasonable diligence, is unable to obtain the vehicle's statement of origin or certificate of title. The Division is authorized to develop a form for this purpose. The filing of a false sworn certification with the Division pursuant to this paragraph shall constitute a Class H felony.

Any person transferring title or interest in a motor vehicle shall deliver the certificate of title duly assigned in accordance with the foregoing provision to the transferee at the time of delivering the vehicle, except that where a security interest is obtained in the motor vehicle from the transferee in payment of the purchase price or otherwise, the transferor shall deliver the certificate of title to the lienholder and the lienholder shall forward the certificate of title together with the transferee's application for new title and necessary fees to the Division within 20 days. Any person who delivers or accepts a certificate of title assigned in blank shall be guilty of a Class 2 misdemeanor.

The title to a salvage vehicle shall be forwarded to the Division as provided in G.S. 20-109.1, except with respect to the title of any salvage vehicle transferred pursuant to G.S. 20-109.1(b)(2) or G.S. 20-109.1(e1).

(c) When the Division finds that any person other than the registered owner of a vehicle has in his possession a certificate of title to the vehicle on which there appears an endorsement of an assignment of title but there does not appear in the assignment any designation to show the name and address of the assignee or transferee, the Division shall be authorized and empowered to seize and hold said certificate of title until the assignor whose name appears in the assignment appears before the Division to complete the execution of the assignment or until evidence satisfactory to the Division is presented to the Division to show the name and address of the transferee. (1937, c. 407, s. 36; 1947, c. 219, ss. 4, 5; 1955, c. 554, ss. 5, 6; 1961, c. 360, s. 8; c. 835, s. 8; 1963, c. 552, ss. 3, 4; 1971, c. 678; 1973, c. 1095, s. 2; 1975, c. 716, s. 5; 1993, c. 539, s. 338; 1994, Ex. Sess., c. 24, s. 14(c); 2000-182, s. 4; 2013-400, s. 2.)

§ 20-73. New owner must get new certificate of title.

(a) Time Limit. - A person to whom a vehicle is transferred, whether by purchase or otherwise, must apply to the Division for a new certificate of title. An application for a certificate of title must be submitted within 28 days after the vehicle is transferred. A person who must follow the procedure in G.S. 20-76 to get a certificate of title and who applies for a title within the required 20-day time limit is considered to have complied with this section even when the Division issues a certificate of title to the person after the time limit has elapsed.

A person may apply directly for a certificate of title or may allow another person, such as the person from whom the vehicle is transferred or a person who has a lien on the vehicle, to apply for a certificate of title on that person's behalf. A person to whom a vehicle is transferred is responsible for getting a certificate of title within the time limit regardless of whether the person allowed another to apply for a certificate of title on the person's behalf.

(b) Exceptions. - This section does not apply to any of the following:

(1) A dealer or an insurance company to whom a vehicle is transferred when the transfer meets the requirements of G.S. 20-75.

(2) A State agency that assists the United States Department of Defense with purchasing, transferring, or titling a vehicle to another State agency, a unit of local government, a volunteer fire department, or a volunteer rescue squad.

(c) Penalties. - A person to whom a vehicle is transferred who fails to apply for a certificate of title within the required time is subject to a civil penalty of fifteen dollars ($15.00) and is guilty of a Class 2 misdemeanor. A person who undertakes to apply for a certificate of title on behalf of another person and who fails to apply for a title within the required time is subject to a civil penalty of fifteen dollars ($15.00). When a person to whom a vehicle is transferred fails to obtain a title within the required time because a person who undertook to apply for the certificate of title did not do so within the required time, the Division may impose a civil penalty only on the person who undertook to apply for the title. Civil penalties collected under this subsection shall be credited to the Highway Fund. (1937, c. 407, s. 37; 1939, c. 275; 1947, c. 219, s. 6; 1961, c. 360, s. 9; 1975, c. 716, s. 5; 1991, c. 689, s. 332; 1993, c. 539, s. 339; 1994, Ex. Sess., c. 24, s. 14(c); 2005-276, s. 44.1(j); 2009-81, s. 1; 2009-550, s. 2(b).)

§ 20-74. Penalty for making false statement about transfer of vehicle.

A dealer or another person who, in an application required by this Division, knowingly makes a false statement about the date a vehicle was sold or acquired shall be guilty of a Class 3 misdemeanor. (1937, c. 407, s. 38; 1939, c. 275; 1961, c. 360, s. 10; 1975, c. 716, s. 5; 1979, c. 801, s. 8; 1981, c. 690, s. 21; 1991, c. 689, s. 333; 1993, c. 539, s. 340; 1994, Ex. Sess., c. 24, s. 14(c).)

§ 20-75. When transferee is dealer or insurance company.

When the transferee of a vehicle registered under this Article is:

(1)   A dealer who is licensed under Article 12 of this Chapter and who holds the vehicle for resale; or

(2)   An insurance company taking the vehicle for sale or disposal for salvage purposes where the title is taken or requested as a part of a bona fide claim settlement transaction and only for the purpose of resale,

the transferee shall not be required to register the vehicle nor forward the certificate of title to the Division as provided in G.S. 20-73.

To assign or transfer title or interest in the vehicle, the dealer or insurance company shall execute, in the presence of a person authorized to administer oaths, a reassignment and warranty of title on the reverse of the certificate of title in the form approved by the Division, which shall include the name and address of the transferee. The title to the vehicle shall not pass or vest until the reassignment is executed and the motor vehicle delivered to the transferee.

The dealer transferring title or interest in a motor vehicle shall deliver the certificate of title duly assigned in accordance with the foregoing provision to the transferee at the time of delivering the vehicle, except:

(1)   Where a security interest in the motor vehicle is obtained from the transferee in payment of the purchase price or otherwise, the dealer shall deliver the certificate of title to the lienholder and the lienholder shall forward the certificate of title together with the transferee's application for new certificate of title and necessary fees to the Division within 20 days; or

(2)   Where the transferee has the option of cancelling the transfer of the vehicle within 10 days of delivery of the vehicle, the dealer shall deliver the certificate of title to the transferee at the end of that period. Delivery need not be made if the contract for sale has been rescinded in writing by all parties to the contract.

Any person who delivers or accepts a certificate of title assigned in blank shall be guilty of a Class 2 misdemeanor.

The title to a salvage vehicle shall be forwarded to the Division as provided in G.S. 20-109.1, except with respect to the title of any salvage vehicle transferred pursuant to G.S. 20-109.1(b)(2) or G.S. 20-109.1(e1). (1937, c. 407, s. 39; 1961, c. 835, s. 9; 1963, c. 552, s. 5; 1967, c. 760; 1973, c. 1095, s. 3; 1975, c. 716, s. 5; 1993, c. 440, s. 12; c. 539, s. 341; 1994, Ex. Sess., c. 24, s. 14(c); 1997-327, s. 2.1; 2013-400, s. 3.)

§ 20-75.1. Conditional delivery of motor vehicles.

Notwithstanding G.S. 20-52.1, 20-72, and 20-75, nothing contained in those sections prohibits a dealer from entering into a contract with any purchaser for the sale of a vehicle and delivering the vehicle to the purchaser under terms by which the dealer's obligation to execute the manufacturer's certificate of origin or the certificate of title is conditioned on the purchaser obtaining financing for the purchase of the vehicle. Liability, collision, and comprehensive insurance on a vehicle sold and delivered conditioned on the purchaser obtaining financing for the purchaser of the vehicle shall be covered by the dealer's insurance policy until such financing is finally approved and execution of the manufacturer's certificate of origin or execution of the certificate of title. Upon final approval and execution of the manufacturer's certificate of origin or the certificate of title, and upon the purchaser having liability insurance on another vehicle, the delivered vehicle shall be covered by the purchaser's insurance policy beginning at the time of final financial approval and execution of the manufacturer's certificate of origin or the certificate of title. The dealer shall notify the insurance agency servicing the purchaser's insurance policy or the purchaser's insurer of the purchase on the day of, or if the insurance agency or insurer is not open for business, on the next business day following approval of the purchaser's financing and execution of the manufacturer's certificate of origin or the certificate of title. This subsection is in addition to any other provisions of law or insurance policies and does not repeal or supersede those provisions. (1993, c. 328, s. 1.)

§ 20-76. Title lost or unlawfully detained; bond as condition to issuance of new certificate.

(a)   Whenever the applicant for the registration of a vehicle or a new certificate of title thereto is unable to present a certificate of title thereto by reason of the same being lost or unlawfully detained by one in possession, or the same is otherwise not available, the Division is hereby authorized to receive such application and to examine into the circumstances of the case, and may require the filing of affidavits or other information; and when the Division is satisfied that the applicant is entitled thereto and that G.S. 20-72 has been complied with, it is hereby authorized to register such vehicle and issue a new registration card, registration plate or plates and certificates of title to the person entitled thereto, upon payment of proper fees.

(b)   Whenever the applicant for a new certificate of title is unable to satisfy the Division that he is entitled thereto as provided in subsection (a) of this section, the applicant may nevertheless obtain issuance of a new certificate of title by filing a bond with the Division as a condition to the issuance thereof. The bond shall be in the form prescribed by the Division and shall be executed by the applicant. It shall be accompanied by the deposit of cash with the Division, be executed as surety by a person, firm or corporation authorized to conduct a surety business in this State or be in the nature of a real estate bond as described in G.S. 20-279.24(a). The bond shall be in an amount equal to one and one-half times the value of the vehicle as determined by the Division and conditioned to indemnify any prior owner or lienholder, any subsequent purchaser of the vehicle or person acquiring any security interest therein, and their respective successors in interest, against any expense, loss or damage, reason of the issuance of the certificate of title to the vehicle or on account of any defect in or undisclosed security interest in the right, title and interest of the applicant in and to the vehicle. Any person damaged by issuance of the certificate of title shall have a right of action to recover on the bond for any breach of its conditions, but the aggregate liability of the surety to all persons shall not exceed the amount of the bond. The bond, and any deposit accompanying it, shall be returned at the end of three years or prior thereto if the vehicle is no longer registered in this State and the currently valid certificate of title is surrendered to the Division, unless the Division has been notified of the pendency of an action to recover on the bond. (1937, c. 407, s. 40; 1947, c. 219, s. 7; 1961, c. 360, s. 11; c. 835, s. 10; 1975, c. 716, s. 5.)

§ 20-77. Transfer by operation of law; sale under mechanic's or storage lien; unclaimed vehicles.

(a)   Whenever the title or interest of an owner in or to a vehicle shall pass to another by operation of law, as upon order in bankruptcy, execution sale, repossession upon default in performing the terms of a lease or executory sales contract, or otherwise than by voluntary transfer, the transferee shall secure a new certificate of title upon proper application, payment of the fees provided by law, and presentation of the last certificate of title, if available and such instruments or documents of authority or certified copies thereof as may be sufficient or required by law to evidence or effect a transfer of interest in or to chattels in such cases.

(b) In the event of transfer as upon inheritance or devise, the Division shall, upon a receipt of a certified copy of a will, letters of administration and/or a certificate from the clerk of the superior court showing that the motor vehicle registered in the name of the decedent owner has been assigned to the owner's surviving spouse as part of the spousal year's allowance, transfer both title and license as otherwise provided for transfers. If a decedent dies intestate and no administrator has qualified or the clerk of superior court has not issued a certificate of assignment as part of the spousal year's allowance, or if a decedent dies testate with a small estate and leaving a purported will, which, in the opinion of the clerk of superior court, does not justify the expense of probate and administration and probate and administration is not demanded by any interested party entitled by law to demand same, and provided that the purported will is filed in the public records of the office of the clerk of the superior court, the Division may upon affidavit executed by all heirs effect such transfer. The affidavit shall state the name of the decedent, date of death, that the decedent died intestate or testate and no administration is pending or expected, that all debts have been paid or that the proceeds from the transfer will be used for that purpose, the names, ages and relationship of all heirs and devisees (if there be a purported will), and the name and address of the transferee of the title. A surviving spouse may execute the affidavit and transfer the interest of the decedent's minor or incompetent children where such minor or incompetent does not have a guardian. A transfer under this subsection shall not affect the validity nor be in prejudice of any creditor's lien.

(c) Mechanic's or Storage Lien. - In any case where a vehicle is sold under a mechanic's or storage lien, or abandoned property, the Division shall be given a 20-day notice as provided in G.S. 20-114.

(d) An operator of a place of business for garaging, repairing, parking or storing vehicles for the public in which a vehicle remains unclaimed for 10 days, or the landowners upon whose property a motor vehicle has been abandoned for more than 30 days, shall, within five days after the expiration of that period, report the vehicle as unclaimed to the Division. Failure to make such report shall constitute a Class 3 misdemeanor. Persons who are required to make this report and who fail to do so within the time period specified may collect other charges due but may not collect storage charges for the period of time between when they were required to make this report and when they actually did send the report to the Division by certified mail.

Any vehicle which remains unclaimed after report is made to the Division may be sold by such operator or landowner in accordance with the provisions relating to the enforcement of liens and the application of proceeds of sale of Article 1 of Chapter 44A.

(e) Any person, who shall sell a vehicle to satisfy a mechanic's or storage lien or any person who shall sell a vehicle as upon order in bankruptcy, execution sale, repossession upon default in performing the terms of a lease or executory sales contract, or otherwise by operation of law, shall remove any license plates attached thereto and return them to the Division. (1937, c. 407, s. 41; 1943, c. 726; 1945, cc. 289, 714; 1955, c. 296, s. 1; 1959, c. 1264, s. 3; 1961, c. 360, ss. 12, 13; 1967, c. 562, s. 8; 1971, cc. 230, 512, 876; 1973, c. 1386, ss. 1, 2; c. 1446, s. 21; 1975, c. 438, s. 2; c. 716, s. 5; 1993, c. 539, s. 342; 1994, Ex. Sess., c. 24, s. 14(c); 1995 (Reg. Sess., 1996), c. 635, s. 1; 2003-336, s. 1; 2011-284, s. 14.)

§ 20-78. When Division to transfer registration and issue new certificate; recordation.

(a) The Division, upon receipt of a properly endorsed certificate of title, application for transfer thereof and payment of all proper fees, shall issue a new certificate of title as upon an original registration. The Division, upon receipt of an application for transfer of registration plates, together with payment of all proper fees, shall issue a new registration card transferring and assigning the registration plates and numbers thereon as upon an original assignment of registration plates. The Division, upon receipt of an application for transfer thereof and payment of all proper fees, but without receipt of a properly endorsed certificate of title, shall issue a salvage certificate of title pursuant to G.S. 20-109.1(b)(2) or G.S. 20-109.1(e1).

(b) The Division shall maintain a record of certificates of title issued by the Division for a period of 20 years. After 20 years, the Division shall maintain a record of the last two owners.

The Commissioner is hereby authorized and empowered to provide for the photographic or photostatic recording of certificate of title records in such manner as he may deem expedient. The photographic or photostatic copies herein authorized shall be sufficient as evidence in tracing of titles of the motor vehicles designated therein, and shall also be admitted in evidence in all actions and proceedings to the same extent that the originals would have been admitted. (1937, c. 407, s. 42; 1943, c. 726; 1947, c. 219, s. 8; 1961, c. 360, s. 14; 1971, c. 1070, s. 4; 1975, c. 716, s. 5; 1999-452, s. 15; 2013-400, s. 4.)

§ 20-78.1. Terminal rental adjustment clauses; vehicle leases that are not sales or security interests.

Notwithstanding any other provision of law, a lease transaction does not create a sale or security interest in a motor vehicle or trailer merely because the lease contains a terminal rental adjustment clause that provides that the rental price is permitted or required to be adjusted up or down by reference to the amount of money realized upon the sale or other disposition of the motor vehicle or trailer. (2011-223, s. 1.)

Part 5. Issuance of Special Plates.

§ 20-79. Dealer license plates.

(a) How to Get a Dealer Plate. - The Division may issue a person licensed under Article 12 of this Chapter the appropriate classification of dealer license plate. A person eligible for a dealer license plate may obtain one by filing an application with the Division and paying the required fee. An application must be filed on a form provided by the Division. The required fee is the amount set by G.S. 20-87(7).

(b) Number of Plates. - A dealer who was licensed under Article 12 of this Chapter for the previous 12-month period ending December 31 may obtain the number of dealer license plates allowed by the following table; the number allowed is based on the number of motor vehicles the dealer sold during the relevant 12-month period and the average number of qualifying sales representatives the dealer employed during that same 12-month period:

Vehicles Sold In Relevant 12-Month Period	Maximum Number of Plates
Fewer than 12	3

At least 12 but less than 25	6
At least 25 but less than 37	7
At least 37 but less than 49	8
49 or more	At least 8, but no more than 5 times the average number of qualifying sales representatives employed by the dealer during the relevant 12-month period.

A dealer who was not licensed under Article 12 of this Chapter for part or all of the previous 12-month period ending December 31 may obtain the number of dealer license plates that equals four times the number of qualifying sales representatives employed by the dealer on the date the dealer files the application. A "qualifying sales representative" is a sales representative who works for the dealer at least 25 hours a week on a regular basis and is compensated by the dealer for this work.

A dealer who sold fewer than 49 motor vehicles the previous 12-month period ending December 31 but has sold at least that number since January 1 may apply for additional dealer license plates at any time. The maximum number of dealer license plates the dealer may obtain is the number the dealer could have obtained if the dealer had sold at least 49 motor vehicles in the previous 12-month period ending December 31.

A dealer who applies for a dealer license plate must certify to the Division the number of motor vehicles the dealer sold in the relevant period. Making a material misstatement in an application for a dealer license plate is grounds for the denial, suspension, or revocation of a dealer's license under G.S. 20-294.

A dealer engaged in the alteration and sale of specialty vehicles may apply for up to two dealer plates in addition to the number of dealer plates that the dealer would otherwise be entitled to under this section.

This subsection does not apply to manufacturers licensed under Article 12 of this Chapter.

(c)   Form and Duration. - A dealer license plate is subject to G.S. 20-63, except for the requirement that the plate display the registration number of a motor vehicle and the requirement that the plate be a "First in Flight" plate. A dealer license plate must have a distinguishing symbol identifying the plate as a dealer license plate. The symbol may vary depending upon the classification of dealer license plate issued. The Division must provide suitably reduced sized license plates for motorcycle dealers and manufacturers.

A dealer license plate is issued for a period of one year. The Division shall vary the expiration dates of dealer registration renewals so that an approximately equal number expires at the end of each month, quarter, or other period consisting of one or more months. A dealer license plate may be transferred from one vehicle to another. When the Division issues a dealer plate, it may issue a registration that expires at the end of any monthly interval. When one of the following occurs, a dealer must surrender to the Division all dealer license plates issued to the dealer:

(1)   The dealer surrenders the license issued to the dealer under Article 12 of this Chapter.

(2)   The Division suspends or revokes the license issued to the dealer under Article 12 of this Chapter.

(3)   The Division rescinds the dealer license plates because of a violation of the restrictions on the use of a dealer license plate.

To obtain a dealer license plate after it has been surrendered, the dealer must file a new application for a dealer license plate and pay the required fee for the plate.

(d)   Restrictions on Use. - A dealer license plate may be displayed only on a motor vehicle that meets all of the following requirements:

(1)   Is part of the inventory of the dealer.

(2)   Is not consigned to the dealer.

(3)   Is covered by liability insurance that meets the requirements of Article 9A of this Chapter.

(4)   Is not used by the dealer in another business in which the dealer is engaged.

(5) Is driven on a highway by a person who meets one of the following descriptions:

a. Has a demonstration permit to test-drive the motor vehicle and carries the demonstration permit while driving the motor vehicle.

b. Is an officer or sales representative of the dealer and is driving the vehicle for a business purpose of the dealer.

c. Is an employee of the dealer and is driving the vehicle in the course of employment.

d. Is an employee of the dealer or of a contractor of the dealer and is driving the vehicle within a 20-mile radius of a place where the vehicle is being repaired or otherwise prepared for sale.

e. Is an employee of the dealer or of a contractor of the dealer and is transporting the vehicle to or from a vehicle auction or to the dealer's established salesroom.

f. Is an officer, sales representative, or other employee of a franchised motor vehicle dealer or is an immediate family member of an officer, sales representative, or other employee of a franchised motor vehicle dealer.

(6) A copy of the registration card for the dealer plate issued to the dealer is carried by the person operating the motor vehicle or, if the person is operating the motor vehicle in this State, the registration card is maintained on file at the dealer's address listed on the registration card, and the registration card must be able to be produced within 24 hours upon request of any law enforcement officer.

A dealer may issue a demonstration permit for a motor vehicle to a person licensed to drive that type of motor vehicle. A demonstration permit authorizes each person named in the permit to drive the motor vehicle described in the permit for up to 96 hours after the time the permit is issued. A dealer may, for good cause, renew a demonstration permit for one additional 96-hour period.

A dealer may not lend, rent, lease, or otherwise place a dealer license plate at the disposal of a person except as authorized by this subsection.

(e) Sanctions. - The following sanctions apply when a motor vehicle displaying a dealer license plate is driven in violation of the restrictions on the use of the plate:

(1) The individual driving the motor vehicle is responsible for an infraction and is subject to a penalty of one hundred dollars ($100.00).

(2) The dealer to whom the plate is issued is subject to a civil penalty imposed by the Division of two hundred fifty dollars ($250.00).

(3) The Division may rescind all dealer license plates issued to the dealer whose plate was displayed on the motor vehicle.

A penalty imposed under subdivision (1) of this subsection is payable to the county where the infraction occurred, as required by G.S. 14-3.1. A civil penalty imposed under subdivision (2) of this subsection shall be credited to the Highway Fund as nontax revenue.

(f) Transfer of Dealer Registration. - No change in the name of a firm, partnership or corporation, nor the taking in of a new partner, nor the withdrawal of one or more of the firm, shall be considered a new business; but if any one or more of the partners remain in the firm, or if there is change in ownership of less than a majority of the stock, if a corporation, the business shall be regarded as continuing and the dealers' plates originally issued may continue to be used.

(g) Penalties. - The clear proceeds of all civil penalties, civil forfeitures, and civil fines that are collected by the Department of Transportation pursuant to this section shall be remitted to the Civil Penalty and Forfeiture Fund in accordance with G.S. 115C-457.2.

(h) Definition. - For purposes of this section, the term "dealer" means a person who is licensed under Article 12 of this Chapter. (1937, c. 407, s. 43; 1947, c. 220, s. 2; 1949, c. 583, s. 3; 1951, c. 985, s. 2; 1959, c. 1264, s. 3.5; 1961, c. 360, s. 15; 1975, c. 716, s. 5; 1979, c. 239; c. 612, s. 1; 1985, c. 764, s. 21; 1985 (Reg. Sess., 1986), c. 852, s. 17; 1989, c. 770, s. 74.1(a); 1993, c. 321, s. 169.4; c. 440, s. 2; c. 539, s. 343; 1993 (Reg. Sess., 1994), c. 697, ss. 1, 2; c. 761, s. 6; 1994, Ex. Sess., c. 24, s. 14(c); 1997-335, s. 1; 2001-212, s. 1; 2004-167, s. 4; 2004-199, s. 59; 2005-276, s. 6.37(q); 2007-291, s. 1; 2007-481, s. 1; 2010-132, s. 5; 2011-318, s. 2.)

§ 20-79.01. Special sports event temporary license plates.

(a) Application. - A dealer who is licensed under Article 12 of this Chapter and who agrees to loan to another for use at a special sports event a vehicle that could display a dealer license plate if driven by an officer or employee of the dealer may obtain a temporary special sports event license plate for that vehicle by filing an application with the Division and paying the required fee. A "special sports event" is a sports event that is held no more than once a year and is open to the public. An application must be filed on a form provided by the Division and contain the information required by the Division. The fee for a temporary special sports event license plate is five dollars ($5.00).

(b) Form and Duration. - A temporary special sports event license plate must state on the plate the date it was issued, the date it expires, and the make, model, and serial number of the vehicle for which it is issued. A temporary special sports event license plate may be issued for no more than 45 days. The dealer to whom the plate is issued must destroy the plate on or before the date it expires.

(c) Restrictions on Use. - A temporary special sports event license plate may be displayed only on the vehicle for which it is issued. A vehicle displaying a temporary special sports event license plate may be driven by anyone who is licensed to drive the type of vehicle for which the plate is issued and may be driven for any purpose. (1993, c. 440, s. 13.)

§ 20-79.1. Use of temporary registration plates or markers by purchasers of motor vehicles in lieu of dealers' plates.

(a) The Division may, subject to the limitations and conditions hereinafter set forth, deliver temporary registration plates or markers designed by said Division to a dealer duly registered under the provisions of this Article who applies for at least 25 such plates or markers and who encloses with such application a fee of one dollar ($1.00) for each plate or marker for which application is made. Such application shall be made upon a form prescribed and furnished by the Division. Dealers, subject to the limitations and conditions hereinafter set forth, may issue such temporary registration plates or markers to owners of vehicles, provided that such owners shall comply with the pertinent provisions of this section.

(b) Every dealer who has made application for temporary registration plates or markers shall maintain in permanent form a record of all temporary registration plates or markers delivered to him, and shall also maintain in permanent form a record of all temporary registration plates or markers issued by him, and in addition thereto, shall maintain in permanent form a record of any other information pertaining to the receipt or the issuance of temporary registration plates or markers that the Division may require. Each record shall be kept for a period of at least one year from the date of entry of such record. Every dealer shall allow full and free access to such records during regular business hours, to duly authorized representatives of the Division and to peace officers.

(c) Every dealer who issues temporary registration plates or markers shall also issue a temporary registration certificate upon a form furnished by the Division and deliver it with the registration plate or marker to the owner.

(d) A dealer shall:

(1) Not issue, assign, transfer, or deliver temporary registration plates or markers to anyone other than a bona fide purchaser or owner of a vehicle which he has sold.

(2) Not issue a temporary registration plate or marker without first obtaining from the purchaser or owner a written application for titling and registration of the vehicle and the applicable fees.

(3) Within 10 working days, mail or deliver the application and fees to the Division or deliver the application and fees to a local license agency for processing. Delivery need not be made if the contract for sale has been rescinded in writing by all parties to the contract.

(4) Not deliver a temporary registration plate to anyone purchasing a vehicle that has an unexpired registration plate that is to be transferred to the purchaser.

(5) Not lend to anyone, or use on any vehicle that he may own, any temporary registration plates or markers.

A dealer may issue temporary markers, without obtaining the written application for titling and registration or collecting the applicable fees, to nonresidents for the purpose of removing the vehicle from the State.

(e) Every dealer who issues temporary plates or markers shall write clearly and indelibly on the face of the temporary registration plate or marker:

(1) The dates of issuance and expiration;

(2) The make, motor number, and serial numbers of the vehicle; and

(3) Any other information that the Division may require.

It shall be unlawful for any person to issue a temporary registration plate or marker containing any misstatement of fact or to knowingly write any false information on the face of the plate or marker.

(f) If the Division finds that the provisions of this section or the directions of the Division are not being complied with by the dealer, the Division may suspend, after a hearing, the right of a dealer to issue temporary registration plates or markers. Nothing in this section shall be deemed to require a dealer to collect or receive property taxes from any person.

(g) Every person to whom temporary registration plates or markers have been issued shall permanently destroy such temporary registration plates or markers immediately upon receiving the limited registration plates or the annual registration plates from the Division: Provided, that if the limited registration plates or the annual registration plates are not received within 30 days of the issuance of the temporary registration plates or markers, the owner shall, notwithstanding, immediately upon the expiration of such 30-day period, permanently destroy the temporary registration plates or markers.

(h) Temporary registration plates or markers shall expire and become void upon the receipt of the limited registration plates or the annual registration plates from the Division, or upon the rescission of a contract to purchase a motor vehicle, or upon the expiration of 30 days from the date of issuance, depending upon whichever event shall first occur. No refund or credit or fees paid by dealers to the Division for temporary registration plates or markers shall be allowed, except in the event that the Division discontinues the issuance of temporary registration plates or markers or unless the dealer discontinues business. In this event the unissued registration plates or markers with the unissued registration certificates shall be returned to the Division and the dealer may petition for a refund. Upon the expiration of the 30 days from the date of issuance, a second 30-day temporary registration plate or marker may be issued by the dealer upon showing the vehicle has been sold, a temporary lien has been filed as provided in G.S. 20-58, and that the dealer, having used reasonable diligence, is unable to obtain the vehicle's statement of origin or certificate of title so that the lien may be perfected.

(i) A temporary registration plate or marker may be used on the vehicle for which issued only and may not be transferred, loaned, or assigned to another. In the event a temporary registration plate or marker or temporary registration certificate is lost or stolen, the owner shall permanently destroy the remaining plate or marker or certificate and no operation of the vehicle for which the lost or stolen registration certificate, registration plate or marker has been issued shall be made on the highways until the regular license plate is received and attached thereto.

(j) The Commissioner of Motor Vehicles shall have the power to make such rules and regulations, not inconsistent herewith, as he shall deem necessary for the purpose of carrying out the provisions of this section.

(k) The provisions of G.S. 20-63, 20-71, 20-110 and 20-111 shall apply in like manner to temporary registration plates or markers as is applicable to nontemporary plates. (1957, c. 246, s. 1; 1963, c. 552, s. 8; 1975, c. 716, s. 5; 1985, c. 95; c. 263; 1997-327, ss. 1, 2; 2000-182, s. 5; 2007-471, s. 1; 2009-445, s. 25(a); 2010-95, s. 22(d); 2013-414, s. 70(c).)

§ 20-79.1A. Limited registration plates.

A limited registration plate is issuable to a person who applies, either directly or through a dealer licensed under Article 12 of this Chapter, for a title to a motor vehicle and a registration plate for the vehicle and who submits payment for the applicable title and registration fees but does not submit payment for any municipal corporation property taxes on the vehicle. A person who submits payment for municipal corporation property taxes receives an annual registration plate.

A limited registration plate must be clearly and visibly designated as "temporary." The plate expires on the last day of the second month following the date of application of the limited registration plate. The plate may be used only on the vehicle for which it is issued and may not be transferred, loaned, or assigned to another. If the plate is lost or stolen, the vehicle for which the plate was issued may not be operated on a highway until a replacement limited registration plate or a regular license plate is received and attached to the vehicle.

The Division is not required to issue a registration certificate for a limited registration plate. A combined tax and registration notice issued under G.S. 105-330.5 serves as the registration certificate for the plate. (2007-471, s. 2; 2009-445, ss. 24(b), 25(a); 2010-95, ss. 22(c), (d); 2013-414, s. 70(b), (c).)

§ 20-79.2. Transporter plates.

(a) Who Can Get a Plate. - The Division may issue a transporter plate authorizing the limited operation of a motor vehicle in the circumstances listed in this subsection. A person who receives a transporter plate must have proof of financial responsibility that meets the requirements of Article 9A of this Chapter. The person to whom a transporter plate may be issued and the circumstances in which the vehicle bearing the plate may be operated are as follows:

(1) To a business or a dealer to facilitate the manufacture, construction, rebuilding, or delivery of new or used truck cabs or bodies between manufacturer, dealer, seller, or purchaser.

(2) To a financial institution that has a recorded lien on a motor vehicle to repossess the motor vehicle.

(3) To a dealer or repair facility to pick up and deliver a motor vehicle that is to be repaired, is to undergo a safety or emissions inspection, or is to otherwise be prepared for sale by a dealer, to road-test the vehicle, if it is repaired or inspected within a 20-mile radius of the place where it is repaired or inspected, and to deliver the vehicle to the dealer. A repair facility may not receive more than two transporter plates for this purpose.

(4) To a business that has at least 10 registered vehicles to move a motor vehicle that is owned by the business and is a replaced vehicle offered for sale.

(5) To a dealer or a business that contracts with a dealer and has a business privilege license to take a motor vehicle either to or from a motor vehicle auction where the vehicle will be or was offered for sale. The title to the vehicle, a bill of sale, or written authorization from the dealer or auction must be inside the vehicle when the vehicle is operated with a transporter plate.

(6) To a business or dealer to road-test a repaired truck whose GVWR is at least 15,000 pounds when the test is performed within a 10-mile radius of the place where the truck was repaired and the truck is owned by a person who has a fleet of at least five trucks whose GVWRs are at least 15,000 pounds and who maintains the place where the truck was repaired.

(7) To a business or dealer to move a mobile office, a mobile classroom, or a mobile or manufactured home, or to transport a newly manufactured travel trailer, fifth-wheel trailer, or camping trailer between a manufacturer and a dealer. Any transporter plate used under this subdivision may not be used on the power unit.

(8) To a business to drive a motor vehicle that is registered in this State and is at least 35 years old to and from a parade or another public event and to drive the motor vehicle in that event. A person who owns one of these motor vehicles is considered to be in the business of collecting those vehicles.

(9) To a dealer to drive a motor vehicle that is part of the inventory of a dealer to and from a motor vehicle trade show or exhibition or to, during, and from a parade in which the motor vehicle is used.

(10) To drive special mobile equipment in any of the following circumstances:

a. From the manufacturer of the equipment to a facility of a dealer.

b. From one facility of a dealer to another facility of a dealer.

c. From a dealer to the person who buys the equipment from the dealer.

(b) How to Get a Plate. - A business or a dealer may obtain a transporter plate by filing an application with the Division and paying the required fee. An application must be on a form provided by the Division and contain the information required by the Division. The fee for a transporter plate is one-half the fee set in G.S. 20-87(5) for a passenger motor vehicle of not more than 15 passengers.

(b1) Number of Plates. - The total number of Dealer-Transporter or dealer plates issued to a dealer may not exceed the total number of plates that can be issued to the dealer under G.S. 20-79(b). Transporter plates issued to a dealer shall bear the words "Dealer-Transporter." This subsection does not apply to a person who is not a dealer.

(b2)   Sanctions. - The following sanctions apply when a motor vehicle displaying a "Dealer-Transporter" or "Transporter" license plate is driven in violation of the restrictions on the use of the plate or of the requirement to have proof of financial responsibility:

(1)   The individual driving the motor vehicle is responsible for an infraction and is subject to a penalty of one hundred dollars ($100.00).

(2)   The dealer or business to whom the plate is issued is subject to a civil penalty imposed by the Division of two hundred fifty dollars ($250.00) per occurrence.

(3)   The Division may rescind all dealer license plates, dealer transporter plates, or transporter plates issued to the dealer or business whose plate was displayed on the motor vehicle.

(4)   A person who sells, rents, leases, or otherwise provides a transporter plate to another person in exchange for the money or any other thing of value is guilty of a Class I felony. A conviction for a violation of this subdivision is considered a felony involving moral turpitude for purposes of G.S. 20-294.

A penalty imposed under subdivision (1) of this subsection is payable to the county where the infraction occurred, as required by G.S. 14-3.1. A civil penalty imposed under subdivision (2) of this subsection shall be credited to the Highway Fund as nontax revenue. A law enforcement officer having probable cause to believe that a transporter plate is being used in violation of this section may seize the plate.

(c)   Form, Duration, and Transfer. - A transporter plate is subject to G.S. 20-63, except for the requirement that the plate display the registration number of a motor vehicle and the requirement that the plate be a "First in Flight" plate. A transporter plate shall have a distinguishing symbol identifying the plate as a transporter plate. The symbol may vary depending upon the classification of transporter plate issued. A transporter plate is issued for a period of one year. The Division shall vary the expiration dates of transporter registration renewals so that an approximately equal number expires at the end of each month, quarter, or other period consisting of one or more months. When the Division issues a transporter plate, it may issue a registration that expires at the end of any monthly interval. During the year for which it is issued, a business or dealer may transfer a transporter plate from one vehicle to another as long as the vehicle is driven only for a purpose authorized by subsection (a) of this section.

The Division must rescind a transporter plate that is displayed on a motor vehicle driven for a purpose that is not authorized by subsection (a) of this section.

(d)   County. - A county may obtain one transporter plate, without paying a fee, by filing an application with the Division on a form to be provided by the Division. A transporter plate issued pursuant to this subsection may only be used to transport motor vehicles as part of a program established by the county to receive donated motor vehicles and make them available to low-income individuals.

If a motor vehicle is operated on the highways of this State using a transporter plate authorized by this section, all of the following requirements shall be met:

(1)   The driver of the vehicle shall have in his or her possession the certificate of title for the motor vehicle, which has been properly reassigned by the previous owner to the county or the affected donor program.

(2)   The vehicle shall be covered by liability insurance that meets the requirements of Article 9A of this Chapter.

The form and duration of the transporter plate shall be as provided in subsection (c) of this section.

(e)   Any vehicle being operated on the highways of this State using a transporter plate shall have proof of financial responsibility that meets the requirement of Article 9A of this Chapter. (1961, c. 360, s. 21; 1969, c. 600, s. 1; 1975, c. 222; 1979, c. 473, ss. 1, 2; c. 627, ss. 1-3; 1981, c. 727, ss. 1, 2; 1983, c. 426; 1987, c. 520; 1993, c. 440, s. 4; 1995, c. 50, s. 1; 1997-335, s. 2; 2001-147, s. 1; 2010-132, s. 6.)

§ 20-79.3: Repealed by Session Laws 1993, c. 440, s. 5.

§ 20-79.4. Special registration plates.

(a)   General. - Upon application and payment of the required registration fees, a person may obtain from the Division a special registration plate for a motor vehicle registered in that person's name if the person qualifies for the registration plate. A holder of a special registration plate who becomes ineligible for the plate, for whatever reason, must return the special plate within 30 days. A special registration plate may not be issued for a vehicle registered under the International Registration Plan. A special registration plate may be issued for a commercial vehicle that is not registered under the International Registration Plan. A special registration plate may not be developed using a name or logo for which a trademark has been issued unless the holder of the trademark licenses, without charge, the State to use the name or logo on the special registration plate.

(a1)   Qualifying for a Special Plate. - In order to qualify for a special plate, an applicant shall meet all of the qualifications set out in this section. The Division of Motor Vehicles shall verify the qualifications of an individual to whom any special plate is issued to ensure only qualified applicants receive the requested special plates.

(a2)   Special Plates Based Upon Military Service. - The Division of Veterans Affairs shall be responsible for verifying and maintaining all verification documentation for all special plates that are based upon military service. The Division shall not issue a special plate that is based on military service unless the application is accompanied by a motor vehicle registration (MVR) verification form signed by the Director of the Division of Veterans Affairs, or the Director's designee, showing that the Division of Veterans Affairs has verified the applicant's credentials and qualifications to hold the special plate applied for.

(1)   Unless a qualifying condition exists requiring annual verification, no additional verification shall be required to renew a special registration plate either in person or through an online service.

(2)   If the Division of Veterans Affairs determines a special registration plate has been issued due to an error on the part of the Division of Motor Vehicles, the plate shall be recalled and canceled.

(3)   If the Division of Veterans Affairs determines a special registration plate has been issued to an applicant who falsified documents or has fraudulently applied for the special registration plate, the Division of Motor Vehicles shall revoke the special plate and take appropriate enforcement action.

(a3)   The Division shall develop, in consultation with the State Highway Patrol and the Division of Adult Correction, a standardized format for special license plates. The format shall allow for the name of the State and the license plate number to be reflective and to contrast with the background so it may be easily read by the human eye and by cameras installed along roadways as part of tolling and speed enforcement. A designated segment of the plate shall be set aside for unique design representing various groups and interests. Nothing in this subsection shall be construed to require the recall of existing special license plates.

(b) Types. - The Division shall issue the following types of special registration plates:

(1) 82nd Airborne Division Association Member. - Issuable to a member of the 82nd Airborne Division Association, Inc. The plate shall bear the insignia of the 82nd Airborne Division Association, Inc. The Division may not issue the plate authorized by this subdivision unless it receives at least 300 applications for the plate.

(2) Administrative Officer of the Courts. - Issuable to the Director of the Administrative Office of the Courts. The plate shall bear the phrase "J-20".

(3) AIDS Awareness. - Issuable to the registered owner of a motor vehicle in accordance with G.S. 20-81.12. The plate shall bear the phrase "Find a Cure" beside the logo of a red ribbon on the left side of the plate.

(4) Air Medal Recipient. - Issuable to the recipient of the Air Medal. The plate shall bear the emblem of the Air Medal and the words "Air Medal".

(5) Alpha Kappa Alpha Sorority. - Issuable to the registered owner of a motor vehicle. The plate shall bear the sorority's symbol and name. The Division may not issue the plate authorized by this subdivision unless it receives at least 300 applications for the plate.

(6) Alpha Phi Alpha Fraternity. - Issuable to a member or supporter of the Alpha Phi Alpha Fraternity in accordance with G.S. 20-81.12. The plate shall bear the fraternity's symbol and name.

(7) ALS Research. - Issuable to the registered owner of a motor vehicle in accordance with G.S. 20-81.12. The plate shall bear the phrase "Nothing Less, Cure ALS" and the logo of the nonprofit group the ALS Association, Jim "Catfish" Hunter Chapter.

(8) Alternative Fuel Vehicles. - Issuable to the registered owner of an alternative fuel vehicle. The plate shall bear the words "Alternative Fuel

Vehicle". The Division must receive 300 or more applications for the plate before it may be developed.

(9) Amateur Radio Operator. - Issuable to an amateur radio operator who holds an unexpired and unrevoked amateur radio license issued by the Federal Communications Commission and who asserts to the Division that a portable transceiver is carried in the vehicle. The plate shall bear the phrase "Amateur Radio". The plate shall bear the operator's official amateur radio call letters, or call letters with numerical or letter suffixes so that an owner of more than one vehicle may have the call letters on each.

(10) American Legion. - Issuable to a member of the American Legion. The plate shall bear the words "American Legion" and the emblem of the American Legion. The Division may not issue the plate authorized by this subdivision unless it receives at least 300 applications for the plate.

(11) American Red Cross. - Issuable to the registered owner of a motor vehicle in accordance with G.S. 20-81.12. The plate shall bear the phrases "Proud Supporter," "American Red Cross," and the official American Red Cross logo.

(12) Animal Lovers. - Issuable to the registered owner of a motor vehicle in accordance with G.S. 20-81.12. The plate may bear a picture of a dog and cat and the phrase "I Care."

(13) ARC of North Carolina. - Issuable to the registered owner of a motor vehicle in accordance with G.S. 20-81.12. The plate shall bear the logo of The ARC of North Carolina, Inc., and the phrase "The ARC".

(14) Armed Forces Expeditionary Medal Recipient. - Issuable to a recipient of the Armed Forces Expeditionary Medal. The plate shall bear the phrase "Armed Forces Expeditionary Medal" and a representation of the Armed Forces Expeditionary Medal. The Division may not issue the plate authorized by this subdivision unless it receives at least 300 applications for the plate.

(15) Arthritis Foundation. - Issuable to the registered owner of a motor vehicle in accordance with G.S. 20-81.12. The plate shall bear the phrase "Let's Move Together" and a logo selected by The Arthritis Foundation, Inc.

(16) ARTS NC. - Issuable to the registered owner of a motor vehicle in accordance with G.S. 20-81.12. The plate shall bear the phrase "The Creative State" with a logo designed by ARTS North Carolina, Inc.

(17) Audubon North Carolina. - Issuable to the registered owner of a motor vehicle in accordance with G.S. 20-81.12. The plate shall bear the National Audubon Society, Inc., logo and a representation of a bird native to North Carolina.

(18) Autism Society of North Carolina. - Issuable to the registered owner of a motor vehicle in accordance with G.S. 20-81.12. The plate shall bear the phrase "Autism Society of North Carolina", and the logo of the Autism Society.

(19) Aviation Maintenance Technician. - Issuable to a person who is a Federal Aviation Authority certified Aviation Maintenance Technician. The plate shall bear the logo of the F.A.A. Airworthiness Program and the initials "A.M.T." The Division may not issue the plate authorized by this subdivision unless it receives at least 300 applications for the plate.

(20) Back Country Horsemen of North Carolina. - Issuable to the registered owner of a motor vehicle in accordance with G.S. 20-81.12. The plate shall bear a picture of a horseman trail riding and bear the phrase "Back Country Horsemen of NC."

(21) Battle of Kings Mountain. - Issuable to the registered owner of a motor vehicle in accordance with G.S. 20-81.12. The plate shall bear the phrase "Battle of Kings Mountain" with a representation of Kings Mountain on it.

(22) Be Active NC. - Issuable to the registered owner of a motor vehicle in accordance with G.S. 20-81.12. The plate shall bear the phrase "Be Active NC" and a representation of the "Be Active NC" logo.

(23) Blue Knights. - Issuable to a member of the Blue Knights International Law Enforcement Officers Motorcycle Club, Inc. The plate shall bear the emblem of the Blue Knights International Law Enforcement Officers Motorcycle Club, Inc. The Division must receive 300 or more applications for the plate before this plate may be developed. A person may obtain a special registration plate under this subdivision for a motor vehicle or motorcycle registered in that person's name. The registration fees and the restrictions on the issuance of a specialized registration plate for a motorcycle are the same as for any motor vehicle.

(24) Boy Scouts of America. - Issuable to the registered owner of a motor vehicle in accordance with G.S. 20-81.12. The plate shall bear the phrase "Boy Scouts of America" and an emblem representing the Boy Scouts of America.

(25) Brain Injury Awareness. - Issuable to the registered owner of a motor vehicle in accordance with G.S. 20-81.12. The plate shall bear the phrase "Brain Injury Awareness" and the logo of the nonprofit group Brain Injury Association of North Carolina, Inc.

(26) Breast Cancer Awareness. - Issuable to the registered owner of a motor vehicle. The plate shall bear the phrase "Early Detection Saves Lives" and a representation of a pink ribbon. The Division must receive 300 or more applications for the plate before it may be developed.

(27) Breast Cancer Earlier Detection. - Issuable to the registered owner of a motor vehicle in accordance with G.S. 20-81.12. The plate shall bear the phrase "Friends for An Earlier Breast Cancer Test."

(28) Brenner Children's Hospital. - Issuable to the registered owner of a motor vehicle in accordance with G.S. 20-81.12. The plate shall bear the emblem of Wake Forest University Baptist Medical Center's Brenner Children's Hospital.

(29) Bronze Star Recipient. - Issuable to a recipient of the Bronze Star. The plate shall bear the emblem of the Bronze Star and the words "Bronze Star".

(30) Bronze Star Valor Recipient. - Issuable to a recipient of the Bronze Star Medal for valor in combat. The plate shall bear the emblem of the Bronze Star with a "Combat V" emblem and the words "Bronze Star." To be eligible for this plate, the applicant must provide documentation that the medal was issued for valor in combat.

(31) Buddy Pelletier Surfing Foundation. - Issuable to the registered owner of a motor vehicle in accordance with G.S. 20-81.12. The plate shall bear the words "Buddy Pelletier Surfing Foundation" and bear the logo of the Foundation.

(32) Buffalo Soldiers. - Issuable to the registered owner of a motor vehicle in accordance with G.S. 20-81.12. The plate shall bear the words "The Buffalo Soldiers" and the logo of the 9th & 10th (Horse) Cavalry Association of the Buffalo Soldiers North Carolina Chapter (BSNCC).

(33) Carolina Raptor Center. - Issuable to the registered owner of a motor vehicle in accordance with G.S. 20-81.12. The plate shall bear the words "Imagination in Flight" and the emblem of the Carolina Raptor Center.

(34) Carolina Regional Volleyball Association. - Issuable to the registered owner of a motor vehicle in accordance with G.S. 20-81.12. The plate shall bear a phrase and logo selected by the Association.

(35) Carolina's Aviation Museum. - This plate is issuable to the registered owner of a motor vehicle in accordance with G.S. 20-81.12. The plate shall bear the phrase "Carolina's Aviation Museum" and a logo provided by the museum.

(36) Carolinas Credit Union Foundation. - Issuable to the registered owner of a motor vehicle in accordance with G.S. 20-81.12. The plate shall bear the phrase "Carolinas Credit Union Foundation" with an emblem of the Carolinas Credit Union Foundation, Inc.

(37) Carolinas Golf Association. - Issuable to the registered owner of a motor vehicle in accordance with G.S. 20-81.12. The plate shall bear the phrase "Carolinas Golf Association" and an emblem of the Carolinas Golf Association.

(38) Celebrate Adoption. - Issuable to the registered owner of a motor vehicle. The plate shall bear the phrase "Celebrate Adoption" and a representation of a white ribbon with a red heart on it. The Division must receive 300 or more applications for the plate before it may be developed.

(39) Charlotte Checkers. - Issuable to the registered owner of a motor vehicle in accordance with G.S. 20-81.12. The plate shall bear the phrase "GOCHECKERS.COM" and the logo of the Charlotte Checkers.

(40) Childhood Cancer Awareness. - Issuable to the registered owner of a motor vehicle. The plate shall bear the phrase "Childhood Cancer Hurts" beside the logo of a gold ribbon on the left side of the plate. The Division may not issue the plate authorized by this subdivision unless it receives at least 300 applications for the plate.

(41) Choose Life. - Issuable to a registered owner of a motor vehicle in accordance with G.S. 20-81.12. The plate shall bear the phrase "Choose Life."

(42) Civic Club. - Issuable to a member of a nationally recognized civic organization whose member clubs in the State are exempt from State corporate

income tax under G.S. 105-130.11(a)(5). Examples of these clubs include Jaycees, Kiwanis, Optimist, Rotary, Ruritan, and Shrine. The plate shall bear a word or phrase identifying the civic club and the emblem of the civic club. A person may obtain from the Division a special registration plate under this subdivision for the registered owner of a motor vehicle or a motorcycle. The registration fees and the restrictions on the issuance of a specialized registration plate for a motorcycle are the same as for any motor vehicle. The Division may not issue a civic club plate authorized by this subdivision unless it receives at least 300 applications for that civic club plate.

(43) Civil Air Patrol Member. - Issuable to an active member of the North Carolina Wing of the Civil Air Patrol. The plate shall bear the phrase "Civil Air Patrol". A plate issued to an officer member shall begin with the number "201" and the number shall reflect the seniority of the member; a plate issued to an enlisted member, a senior member, or a cadet member shall begin with the number "501".

(44) Class D Citizen's Radio Station Operator. - Issuable to a Class D citizen's radio station operator. For an operator who has been issued Class D citizen's radio station call letters by the Federal Communications Commission, the plate shall bear the operator's official Class D citizen's radio station call letters. For an operator who has not been issued Class D citizen's radio station call letters by the Federal Communications Commission, the plate shall bear the phrase "Citizen's Band Radio".

(45) Clerk of Superior Court. - Issuable to a current or retired clerk of superior court. A plate issued to a current clerk shall bear the phrase "Clerk Superior Court" and the letter "C" followed by a number that indicates the county the clerk serves. A plate issued to a retired clerk shall bear the phrase "Clerk Superior Court, Retired", the letter "C" followed by a number that indicates the county the clerk served, and the letter "X" indicating the clerk's retired status.

(46) Coast Guard Auxiliary Member. - Issuable to an active member of the United States Coast Guard Auxiliary. The plate shall bear the phrase "Coast Guard Auxiliary".

(47) Coastal Conservation Association. - Issuable to the registered owner of a motor vehicle in accordance with G.S. 20-81.12. The plate shall bear the logo and name of the Coastal Conservation Association.

(48) Coastal Land Trust. - Issuable to the registered owner of a motor vehicle in accordance with G.S. 20-81.12. The plate shall bear the phrase "Coastal Land Trust" with a logo designed by the North Carolina Coastal Land Trust.

(49) Cold War Veteran. - Issuable to a veteran of the Armed Forces of the United States who served during the Cold War era, September 2, 1945, through December 26, 1991, and who was separated from the Armed Forces of the United States under honorable conditions. The plate shall bear the words "Cold War Veteran" and an insignia representing the Cold War era. The Division may not issue the plate authorized by this subdivision unless it receives at least 300 applications for the plate.

(50) Collegiate Insignia Plate. - Issuable to the registered owner of a motor vehicle in accordance with G.S. 20-81.12. The plate may bear a phrase or an insignia representing a public or private college or university.

(51) Combat Infantry Badge Recipient. - Issuable to a recipient of the Combat Infantry Badge. The plate shall bear the phrase "Combat Infantry Badge " and a representation of the Combat Infantry Badge. The Division may not issue the plate authorized by this subdivision unless it receives at least 300 applications for the plate.

(52) Combat Veteran. - Issuable to a veteran of the Armed Forces of the United States who served in a combat zone, or in waters adjacent to a combat zone, during a period of war and who was separated from the Armed Forces of the United States under honorable conditions. The Division may not issue the plate authorized by this subdivision unless it receives at least 300 applications for the plate. A "period of war" is any of the following:

a. World War I, which began April 16, 1917, and ended November 11, 1918.

b. World War II, which began December 7, 1941, and ended December 31, 1946.

c. The Korean Conflict, which began June 27, 1950, and ended January 31, 1955.

d. The Vietnam Era, which began August 5, 1964, and ended May 7, 1975.

e. The Persian Gulf War.

f. Any other campaign, expedition, or engagement for which the United States Department of Defense authorizes a campaign badge or medal.

(53) Commercial Fishing. - Issuable to the registered owner of a motor vehicle in accordance with G.S. 20-81.12. The plate may bear a phrase and picture appropriate to the subject of commercial fishing in North Carolina. The Division may not issue the plate authorized by this subdivision unless it receives at least 300 applications for the plate.

(54) Concerned Bikers Association/ABATE of North Carolina. - Issuable to the registered owner of a motor vehicle or a motorcycle in accordance with G.S. 20-81.12. The plate shall bear the Concerned Bikers Association logo with the phrase "Concerned Bikers Association." The Division must receive 300 or more applications for the plate before this plate may be developed. A person may obtain a special registration plate under this subdivision for a motor vehicle or motorcycle registered in that person's name. The registration fees and the restrictions on the issuance of a specialized registration plate for a motorcycle are the same as for any motor vehicle.

(55) Corvette Club. - Issuable to the registered owner of a motor vehicle. The plate shall bear the flags logo of the Chevrolet Corvette. The Division may not issue the plate authorized by this subdivision unless it receives at least 300 applications for the plate.

(56) County Commissioner. - Issuable to a county commissioner of a county in this State. The plate shall bear the words "County Commissioner" followed first by a number representing the commissioner's county and then by a letter or number that distinguishes plates issued to county commissioners of the same county. The number of a county shall be the order of the county in an alphabetical list of counties that assigns number one to the first county in the list and a letter or number to distinguish different cars owned by the county commissioners in that county. The Division may not issue the plate authorized by this subdivision unless it receives at least 100 applications for the plate.

(57) Crystal Coast. - Issuable to the registered owner of a motor vehicle in accordance with G.S. 20-81.12. The plate shall bear the words "Crystal Coast Artificial Reef Association" and a representation of a SCUBA diving flag.

(58) Daniel Stowe Botanical Garden. - Issuable to the registered owner of a motor vehicle in accordance with G.S. 20-81.12. The plate shall bear the phrase

"Daniel Stowe Botanical Garden" with a logo designed by the Daniel Stowe Botanical Garden Foundation, Inc.

(59) Daughters of the American Revolution. - Issuable to the registered owner of a motor vehicle. The plate may bear a phrase and picture appropriate to the organization. The Division may not issue the plate authorized by this subdivision unless it receives at least 300 applications for the plate.

(60) Delta Sigma Theta Sorority. - Issuable to the registered owner of a motor vehicle. The plate shall bear the sorority's name and symbol. The Division must receive 300 or more applications for the plate before it may be developed.

(61) Disabled Veteran. - Issuable to a veteran of the Armed Forces of the United States who suffered a 100% service-connected disability.

(62) Distinguished Flying Cross. - Issuable to a recipient of the Distinguished Flying Cross. The plate shall bear the emblem of the Distinguished Flying Cross and the words "Distinguished Flying Cross".

(63) District Attorney. - Issuable to a North Carolina or United States District Attorney. The plate issuable to a North Carolina district attorney shall bear the letters "DA" followed by a number that represents the prosecutorial district the district attorney serves. The plate for a United States attorney shall bear the phrase "U.S. Attorney" followed by a number that represents the district the attorney serves, with 1 being the Eastern District, 2 being the Middle District, and 3 being the Western District.

(64) Donate Life. - Issuable to the registered owner of a motor vehicle in accordance with G.S. 20-81.12. The plate shall bear the phrase "Donate Life" with a logo designed by Donate Life North Carolina.

(65) Don't Tread on Me. - Issuable to a registered owner of a motor vehicle. The plate shall bear the phrase "Don't Tread on Me" under the representation of the Gadsden Flag. The Division may not issue the plate authorized by this subdivision unless it receives at least 300 applications for the plate.

(66) Ducks Unlimited. - Issuable to the registered owner of a motor vehicle in accordance with G.S. 20-81.12. The plate shall bear the logo of Ducks Unlimited, Inc., and shall bear the words: "Ducks Unlimited".

(67) E-911 Telecommunicator. - Issuable to an active E-911 Telecommunicator. An active E-911 Telecommunicator is an individual employed by a public safety agency whose primary responsibility is to receive, process, transmit, or dispatch emergency and nonemergency calls for police, fire, emergency medical, and other public safety services via telephone and other communication devices. The plate shall bear the phrase "E-911 Telecommunicator." The Division may not issue the plate authorized by this subdivision unless it receives at least 300 applications for the plate.

(68) Eagle Scout. - Issuable to a young man who has been certified as an Eagle Scout by the Boy Scouts of America, or to his parents or guardians. The plate shall bear the insignia of the Boy Scouts of America and shall bear the words "Eagle Scout". The Division may not issue the plate authorized by this subdivision unless it receives at least 300 applications for the plate.

(69) El Pueblo. - Issuable to the registered owner of a motor vehicle in accordance with G.S. 20-18.12. The plate shall bear the El Pueblo logo and the words "El Pueblo". The Division may not issue the plate authorized by this subdivision unless it receives at least 300 applications for the plate.

(70) Emergency Medical Technician. - Issuable to an emergency medical technician, as defined in G.S. 131E-155. The plate shall bear the Star of Life logo and the letters "EMT". The Division may not issue the plate authorized by this subdivision unless it receives at least 300 applications for the plate.

(71) Farmland Preservation. - Issuable to the registered owner of a motor vehicle in accordance with G.S. 20-81.12. The plate shall bear a phrase and picture provided by the Department of Agriculture and Consumer Services appropriate to the subject of farmland preservation.

(72) Fire Department or Rescue Squad Member. - Issuable to an active regular member or volunteer member of a fire department, rescue squad, or both a fire department and rescue squad. The plate shall bear the words "Firefighter", "Rescue Squad", or "Firefighter-Rescue Squad".

(73) First in Forestry. - Issuable to the registered owner of a motor vehicle. The plate shall bear the words "First in Forestry". The Division may not issue the plate authorized by this subdivision unless it receives at least 300 applications for the plate.

(74) First in Turf. - Issuable to the registered owner of a motor vehicle in accordance with G.S. 20-81.12. The plate shall bear the words "First in Turf."

(75) First Tee. - Issuable to the registered owner of a motor vehicle in accordance with G.S. 20-81.12. The plate may bear a phrase and logo representing youth golf or The First Tee, Inc.

(76) Flag of the United States of America. - Issuable to the registered owner of a motor vehicle. The plate shall bear an image of a waving American flag. The Division may not issue the plate authorized by this subdivision unless it receives at least 300 applications for the plate.

(77) Fox Hunting. - Issuable to the registered owner of a motor vehicle. The plate may bear a phrase and a picture representing fox hunting. The Division may not issue the plate authorized by this subdivision unless it receives at least 300 applications for the plate.

(78) Fraternal Order of Police. - The plate authorized by this subdivision shall bear a representation of the Fraternal Order of Police emblem containing the letters "FOP". The Division must receive 300 applications for the plate before it may be developed. The plate is issuable to one of the following:

a. A person who presents proof of active membership in the State Lodge, Fraternal Order of Police for the year in which the license plate is sought.

b. The surviving spouse of a person who was a member of the State Lodge, Fraternal Order of Police, so long as the surviving spouse continues to renew the plate and does not remarry.

(79) Future Farmers of America. - Issuable to a member or a supporter of the National Future Farmers of America Organization. The plate shall bear the emblem of the organization and the letters "FFA". The Division may not issue the plate authorized by this subdivision unless it receives at least 300 applications for the plate.

(80) Girl Scout Gold Award recipient. - Issuable to a young woman who has been certified as a Girl Scout Gold Award recipient by the Girl Scouts of the U.S.A., or to her parents or guardians. The plate shall bear the insignia of the Girl Scouts of the U.S.A. and shall bear the words "Girl Scout Gold Award". The Division may not issue the plate authorized by this subdivision unless it receives at least 300 applications for the plate.

(81) Girl Scouts. - Issuable to the owner of a registered vehicle in accordance with G.S. 20-81.12. The plate shall bear the phrase "Girl Scouts" with an emblem representing the Girl Scouts of the U.S.A.

(82) Gold Star Lapel Button. - Issuable to the recipient of the Gold Star lapel button. The plate shall bear the emblem of the Gold Star lapel button and the words "Gold Star".

(83) Goodness Grows. - Issuable to the registered owner of a motor vehicle in accordance with G.S. 20-81.12. The plate shall bear the "Goodness Grows in North Carolina" logo and the phrase "Agriculture: NC's #1 Industry".

(84) Greensboro Symphony Guild. - Issuable to the registered owner of a motor vehicle in accordance with G.S. 20-81.12. The plate shall bear the logo of the Greensboro Symphony Guild and the phrase "Music Matters".

(85) Greyhound Friends of North Carolina. - Issuable to the registered owner of a motor vehicle in accordance with G.S. 20-81.12. The plate shall bear the phrase "Greyhound Friends of North Carolina" and a picture of a greyhound.

(86) Guilford Battleground Company. - Issuable to the registered owner of a motor vehicle in accordance with G.S. 20-81.12. The plate shall bear the phrase "Revolutionary" used by the Guilford Battleground Company and an image that depicts General Nathaniel Greene.

(87) Harley Owners' Group. - Issuable to the registered owner of a motor vehicle in accordance with G.S. 20-81.12. The plate shall be designed in consultation with and approved by the Harley-Davidson Motor Company, Inc., and shall bear the words and trademark of the "Harley Owners' Group".

(88) High Point Furniture Market 100th Anniversary. - Issuable to the registered owner of a motor vehicle. The plate shall bear the phrase "High Point Furniture Market 100th Anniversary" and the emblem of the High Point Market. The Division may not issue the plate authorized by this subdivision unless it receives at least 300 applications for the plate.

(89) High School Insignia Plate. - Issuable to the registered owner of a motor vehicle in accordance with G.S. 20-81.12. The plate may bear a phrase or an insignia representing a public high school in North Carolina.

(90) Historic Vehicle Owner. - Issuable for a motor vehicle that is at least 35 years old measured from the date of manufacture. The plate for an historic vehicle shall bear the word "Antique" unless the vehicle is a model year 1943 or older. The plate for a vehicle that is a model year 1943 or older shall bear the word "Antique" or the words "Horseless Carriage", at the option of the vehicle owner.

(91) Historical Attraction Plate. - Issuable to the registered owner of a motor vehicle in accordance with G.S. 20-81.12. The plate may bear a phrase or an insignia representing a publicly owned or nonprofit historical attraction located in North Carolina.

(92) Hollerin'. - Issuable to the registered owner of a motor vehicle. The plate shall bear the phrase "Hollerin" under a representation of a person hollering on the left side of the plate. The Division may not issue the plate authorized by this subdivision unless it receives at least 300 applications for the plate.

(93) Home Care and Hospice. - Issuable to the registered owner of a motor vehicle in accordance with G.S. 20-81.12. The plate shall bear the phrase "Home Care and Hospice" and the letters "HH" on the right side of the plate.

(94) Home of American Golf. - Issuable to the registered owner of a motor vehicle in accordance with G.S. 20-81.12. The plate shall bear the phrase "Home of American Golf" and include the Pinehurst logo and a representation relating to golf.

(95) HOMES4NC Plate. - Issuable to the registered owner of a motor vehicle in accordance with G.S. 20-81.12. The plate shall bear "HOMES4NC", the logo of the North Carolina Association of Realtors Housing Opportunity Foundation, and shall be developed in conjunction with that organization. The Division may not issue the plate authorized by this subdivision unless it receives at least 300 applications for the plate.

(96) Honorary Plate. - Issuable to a member of the Honorary Consular Corps, who has been certified by the U. S. State Department, the plate shall bear the words "Honorary Consular Corps" and a distinguishing number based on the order of issuance.

(97) Hospice Care. - Issuable to the registered owner of a motor vehicle in accordance with G.S. 20-81.12. The plate shall bear the phrase "Hospice Care" and the letters "HC" on the right side of the plate.

(98) I.B.P.O.E.W. - Issuable to the registered owner of a motor vehicle in accordance with G.S. 20-81.12. The plate shall bear the phrase "The Improved Benevolent and Protective Order of Elks of the World" and the logo of the Improved Benevolent and Protective Order of Elks of the World.

(99) In God We Trust. - Issuable to the registered owner of a motor vehicle in accordance with G.S. 20-81.12. The plate shall bear the phrase "In God We Trust."

(100) International Association of Fire Fighters. - The plate authorized by this subdivision shall bear the logo of the International Association of Fire Fighters. The Division may not issue the plate unless it receives at least 300 applications for the plate. The plate is issuable to one of the following:

a. A person who presents proof of active membership in the International Association of Fire Fighters for the year in which the license plate is sought.

b. The surviving spouse of a person who was a member of the International Association of Fire Fighters, so long as the surviving spouse continues to renew the plate and does not remarry.

(101) Jaycees. - Issuable to the registered owner of a motor vehicle in accordance with G.S. 20-81.12. The plate shall bear the phrase "Jaycees" and a logo designed by the North Carolina Jaycees.

(102) Judge or Justice. - Issuable to a sitting or retired judge or justice in accordance with G.S. 20-79.6.

(103) Juvenile Diabetes Research Foundation. - Issuable to the registered owner of a motor vehicle in accordance with G.S. 20-81.12. The plate shall bear the phrase "Juvenile Diabetes Research" and the "sneaker" logo of the nonprofit group Juvenile Diabetes Research Foundation International, Inc.

(104) Kappa Alpha Order. - Issuable to the registered owner of a motor vehicle. The plate shall bear the fraternity's symbol and name. The Division may not issue the plate authorized by this subdivision unless it receives at least 300 applications for the plate.

(105) Kappa Alpha Psi Fraternity. - Issuable to the registered owner of a motor vehicle. The plate shall bear the fraternity's symbol and name. The Division may

not issue the plate authorized by this subdivision unless it receives at least 300 applications for the plate.

(106) Kids First. - Issuable to the registered owner of a motor vehicle in accordance with G.S. 20-81.12. The plate may bear the phrase "Kids First" and a logo of children's hands.

(107) Legion of Merit. - Issuable to a recipient of the Legion of Merit award. The plate shall bear the emblem and name of the Legion of Merit decoration.

(108) Legion of Valor. - Issuable to a recipient of one of the following military decorations: the Congressional Medal of Honor, the Distinguished Service Cross, the Navy Cross, the Air Force Cross, or the Coast Guard Cross. The plate shall bear the emblem and name of the recipient's decoration.

(109) Legislator. - Issuable to a member of the North Carolina General Assembly. The plate shall bear "The Great Seal of the State of North Carolina" and, as appropriate, the word "Senate" or "House" followed by the Senator's or Representative's assigned seat number.

(110) Leukemia & Lymphoma Society. - Issuable to the registered owner of a motor vehicle in accordance with G.S. 20-81.12. The plate shall bear the phrase and logo provided by The Leukemia & Lymphoma Society that reflects "TEAM IN TRAINING".

(111) Lifetime Sportsman. - Issuable to the registered owner of a motor vehicle. The plate shall bear a picture representing North Carolina Wildlife Resources Commission emblem for a "Lifetime Sportsman." The Division must receive 300 or more applications for a Lifetime Sportsman plate before the plate may be developed.

(112) Litter Prevention. - Issuable to the registered owner of a motor vehicle in accordance with G.S. 20-81.12. The plate may bear a phrase and picture appropriate to the subject of litter prevention in North Carolina.

(113) Lung Cancer Research. - Issuable to the registered owner of a motor vehicle in accordance with G.S. 20-81.12. The plate shall bear the phrase "Lung Cancer Research" and a representation of the American Lung Association's Red Cross.

(114) Maggie Valley Trout Festival. - Issuable to the registered owner of a motor vehicle in accordance with G.S. 20-81.12. The plate shall bear the Trout Festival logo.

(115) Magistrate. - Issuable to a current or retired North Carolina magistrate. A plate issued to a current magistrate shall bear the letters "MJ" followed by a number indicating the district court district the magistrate serves, then by a hyphen, and then by a number indicating the seniority of the magistrate. The Division shall use the number "9" to designate District Court Districts 9 and 9B. A plate issued to a retired magistrate shall bear the phrase "Magistrate, Retired", the letters "MJX " followed by a hyphen and the number that indicates the district court district the magistrate served, followed by a letter based on the order of issuance of the plates.

(116) March of Dimes. - Issuable to the registered owner of a motor vehicle in accordance with G.S. 20-81.12. The plate may bear a phrase or an insignia representing the March of Dimes Foundation.

(117) Marine Corps League. - Issuable to a member of the Marine Corps League. The plate shall bear the words "Marine Corps League" or the letters "MCL" and the emblem of the Marine Corps League. The Division may not issue the plate authorized by this subdivision unless it receives at least 150 applications for the plate.

(118) Marshal. - Issuable to a United States Marshal. The plate shall bear the phrase "U.S. Marshal" followed by a number that represents the district the Marshal serves, with 1 being the Eastern District, 2 being the Middle District, and 3 being the Western District.

(119) Mayor. - Issuable to the mayor of a municipality in this State. The plate shall bear the phrase "Mayor" and the letter "M" followed by a number that indicates the municipality the mayor serves. The number of a municipality shall be the order of the municipality in an alphabetical list of municipalities that assigns number one to the first municipality in the list, except that municipalities incorporated with an effective date after July 1, 2009, shall be placed at the end of the list in order of date of incorporation. The Division may not issue the plate authorized by this subdivision unless it receives at least 300 applications for the plate.

(120) Military Reservist. - Issuable to a member of a reserve component of the Armed Forces of the United States. The plate shall bear the name and insignia

of the appropriate reserve component. Plates shall be numbered sequentially for members of a component with the numbers 1 through 5000 reserved for officers, without regard to rank.

(121) Military Retiree. - Issuable to an individual who has retired from the Armed Forces of the United States. The plate shall bear the word "Retired" and the name and insignia of the branch of service from which the individual retired.

(122) Military Veteran. - Issuable to an individual who served honorably in the Armed Forces of the United States. The plate shall bear the words "U.S. Military Veteran" and the name and insignia of the branch of service in which the individual served. The Division may not issue the plate authorized by this subdivision unless it receives at least 300 applications for the plate.

(123) Military Wartime Veteran. - Issuable to either a member or veteran of the Armed Forces of the United States who served during a period of war who received a campaign or expeditionary ribbon or medal for their service. If the person is a veteran of the Armed Forces of the United States, then the veteran must be separated from the Armed Forces of the United States under honorable conditions. The plate shall bear a word or phrase identifying the period of war and a replica of the campaign badge or medal awarded for that war. The Division may not issue the plate authorized by this subdivision unless it receives a total of 300 applications for all periods of war, combined, to be represented on this plate. A "period of war" is any of the following:

a. World War I, meaning the period beginning April 16, 1917, and ending November 11, 1918.

b. World War II, meaning the period beginning December 7, 1941, and ending December 31, 1946.

c. The Korean Conflict, meaning the period beginning June 27, 1950, and ending January 31, 1955.

d. The Vietnam Era, meaning the period beginning August 5, 1964, and ending May 7, 1975.

e. Desert Storm, meaning the period beginning August 2, 1990, and ending April 11, 1991.

f. Operation Enduring Freedom, meaning the period beginning October 24, 2001, and ending at a date to be determined.

g. Operation Iraqi Freedom, meaning the period beginning March 19, 2003, and ending at a date to be determined.

h. Any other campaign, expedition, or engagement for which the United States Department of Defense authorizes a campaign badge or medal.

(124) Mission Foundation. - Issuable to the registered owner of a motor vehicle in accordance with G.S. 20-81.12. The plate may bear a phrase and logo selected by Mission Healthcare Foundation, Inc.

(125) Morehead Planetarium. - Issuable to the registered owner of a motor vehicle in accordance with G.S. 20-81.12. The plate shall bear a phrase and logo selected by the Morehead Planetarium and Science Center.

(126) Morgan Horse Club. - Issuable to the registered owner of a motor vehicle in accordance with G.S. 20-81.12. The plate shall bear a picture of a Morgan horse and bear the phrase "Morgan Horse".

(127) Mothers Against Drunk Driving. - Issuable to the registered owner of a motor vehicle. The plate shall bear the letters "M.A.D.D." and the words "Mothers Against Drunk Driving". The Division must receive 300 or more applications for the plate before it may be developed.

(128) Mountains-to-Sea Trail. - Issuable to the registered owner of a motor vehicle in accordance with G.S. 20-81.12. The plate shall bear the phrase "Mountains-to-Sea Trail" with a background designed by the Friends of the Mountains-to-Sea Trail, Inc.

(129) Municipal Council. - Issuable to a municipal council member, commissioner, or alderman of a municipality in this State. The plate shall bear the words "Council Member," "Commissioner," or "Alderman," followed first by a number representing the council member's municipality and then by a letter or number that distinguishes plates issued to council members of the same municipality. The number of a municipality shall be the order of the municipality in an alphabetical list of municipalities that assigns number one to the first municipality in the list, except that municipalities incorporated with an effective date after July 1, 2009, shall be placed at the end of the list in order of date of

incorporation. The Division may not issue the plate authorized by this subdivision unless it receives at least 300 applications for the plate.

(130) Municipality Plate. - Issuable to the registered owner of a motor vehicle in accordance with G.S. 20-81.12. The plate shall bear a graphic selected by the municipality represented by the plate and approved by the Division.

(131) National Defense Service Medal. - Issuable to a recipient of the National Defense Service Medal. The plate shall bear a replica of the National Defense Service Medal and the phrase "National Defense Service Medal." The Division may not issue the plate authorized by this subdivision unless it receives at least 300 applications for the plate.

(132) National Guard Member. - Issuable to an active or a retired member of the North Carolina National Guard. The plate shall bear the phrase "National Guard". A plate issued to an active member shall bear a number that reflects the seniority of the member; a plate issued to a commissioned officer shall begin with the number "1"; a plate issued to a noncommissioned officer with a rank of E7, E8, or E9 shall begin with the number "1601"; a plate issued to an enlisted member with a rank of E6 or below shall begin with the number "3001". The plate issued to a retired or separated member shall indicate the member's retired status.

(133) National Kidney Foundation. - Issuable to the registered owner of a motor vehicle in accordance with G.S. 20-81.12. The plate shall bear a phrase and logo selected by the Foundation.

(134) National Law Enforcement Officers Memorial. - Issuable to the registered owner of a motor vehicle in accordance with G.S. 20-81.12. The plate shall bear the phrase "National Law Enforcement Officers Memorial" and the logo of the National Law Enforcement Officers Memorial.

(135) National Multiple Sclerosis Society. - Issuable to the registered owner of a motor vehicle in accordance with G.S. 20-81.12. The plate shall have the logo of the National Multiple Sclerosis Society and the telephone number "1-800-FIGHT MS" on the plate.

(136) National Rifle Association. - Issuable to the registered owner of a motor vehicle. The plate shall bear a phrase or insignia representing the National Rifle Association of America. The Division must receive 300 or more applications for the plate before it may be developed.

(137) National Wild Turkey Federation. - Issuable to the registered owner of a motor vehicle. The plate shall bear the design of a strutting wild turkey and dogwood blossoms and the words "Working For The Wild Turkey." The Division must receive 300 or more applications for the plate before it may be developed.

(138) Native American. - Issuable to the registered owner of a motor vehicle in accordance with G.S. 20-81.12. The plate may bear a phrase or an insignia representing Native Americans. The Division must receive 300 or more applications for the plate before it may be developed.

(139) Native Brook Trout. - Issuable to the registered owner of a motor vehicle in accordance with G.S. 20-81.12. The plate shall bear the phrase "Native Brook Trout" with a picture of a brook trout native to North Carolina in the background.

(140) NC Agribusiness. - Issuable to the registered owner of a motor vehicle in accordance with G.S. 20-81.12. The plate shall bear the logo of the North Carolina Agribusiness Council, Inc., and the phrase "NC's #1 Industry".

(141) NCAMCCACC Clerk. - Issuable to a clerk of a municipal governing board or a clerk of a county board of commissioners of a municipality or county in this State. For a municipal clerk, the plate shall bear the words "NCAMC Clerk" followed by a number representing the municipal clerk's city or town. The number of a city shall be the order of the city in an alphabetical list of cities that assigns number one to the first city in the list. For a county clerk, the plate shall bear the words "NCACC Clerk" followed by a number representing the county clerk's county. The number of a county shall be the order of the county in an alphabetical list of counties that assigns number one to the first county in the list. The Division may not issue the plate authorized by this subdivision unless it receives at least 300 applications for the plate.

(142) NC Beekeepers. - Issuable to the registered owner of a motor vehicle in accordance with G.S. 20-81.12. The plate shall bear the phrase "NC Beekeepers" with a logo designed by the North Carolina Beekeepers Association, Inc.

(143) NC Children's Promise. - Issuable to the registered owner of a motor vehicle in accordance with G.S. 20-81.12. The plate shall bear the phrase "N.C. Children's Promise" and a logo representing the North Carolina Children's Promise organization.

(144) NC Civil War. - This plate is issuable to the registered owner of a motor vehicle in accordance with G.S. 20-81.12. The plate shall bear the phrase "Freedom-Sacrifice-Memory" and a logo provided by the North Carolina Department of Cultural Resources.

(145) NC Coastal Federation. - Issuable to the registered owner of a motor vehicle in accordance with G.S. 20-81.12. The plate shall bear a phrase used by the North Carolina Coastal Federation and an image that depicts the coastal area of the State.

(146) NC FIRST Robotics. - Issuable to the registered owner of a motor vehicle in accordance with G.S. 20-81.12. The plate shall bear the logo of NC FIRST Robotics and the phrase "NC FIRST Robotics."

(147) NC Fisheries Association. - Issuable to the registered owner of a motor vehicle in accordance with G.S. 20-81.12. The plate shall bear the phrase "Our Oldest Industry" and the logo of the North Carolina Fisheries Association.

(148) NC Horse Council. - Issuable to the registered owner of a motor vehicle in accordance with G.S. 20-81.12. The plate shall bear the phrase "NC Horse Council" and a logo designed by the North Carolina Horse Council, Inc.

(149) NC Mining. - Issuable to the registered owner of a motor vehicle in accordance with G.S. 20-81.12. The plate shall bear the phrase "NC Mining" with a logo designed by the North Carolina Gold Foundation, Inc.

(150) NCSC. - Issuable to the registered owner of a motor vehicle in accordance with G.S. 20-81.12. The plate shall bear the phrase "NC Sportsmen's Caucus" and a logo provided by the Congressional Sportsmen's Foundation.

(151) NC Tennis Foundation. - Issuable to the registered owner of a motor vehicle in accordance with G.S. 20-81.12. The plate shall bear the phrase "Play Tennis" and the image of an implement of the tennis sport.

(152) NC Trout Unlimited. - Issuable to the registered owner of a motor vehicle in accordance with G.S. 20-81.12. The plate shall bear the phrase "Back the Brookie" and an image that depicts a North Carolina brook trout.

(153) NC Veterinary Medical Association. - Issuable to a member of the NC Veterinary Medical Association in accordance with G.S. 20-81.12. The plate

shall bear the phrase "NC Veterinary Medical Association" with an emblem of the North Carolina Veterinary Medical Association.

(154) NC Victim Assistance Network. - Issuable to the registered owner of a motor vehicle in accordance with G.S. 20-81.12. The plate shall bear the emblem of the North Carolina Victim Assistance Network.

(155) NC Wildlife Federation. - Issuable to the registered owner of a motor vehicle in accordance with G.S. 20-81.12. The plate shall bear a logo designed by the North Carolina Wildlife Federation, Inc.

(156) NC Youth Soccer Association. - Issuable to the registered owner of a motor vehicle in accordance with G.S. 20-81.12. The plate shall bear a logo designed by the NC Youth Soccer Association.

(157) North Carolina 4-H Development Fund. - Issuable to the registered owner of a motor vehicle in accordance with G.S. 20-81.12. The plate may bear a phrase or insignia representing The North Carolina 4-H Development Fund.

(158) North Carolina Bluegrass Association. - Issuable to the registered owner of a motor vehicle in accordance with G.S. 20-81.12. The plate shall bear a graphic selected by the NC Bluegrass Association.

(159) North Carolina Cattlemen's Association. - Issuable to the registered owner of a motor vehicle in accordance with G.S. 20-81.12. The plate shall bear the seal of the North Carolina Cattlemen's Association.

(160) North Carolina Emergency Management Association. - Issuable to the registered owner of a motor vehicle in accordance with G.S. 20-81.12. The plate shall bear the phrase "North Carolina Emergency Management" and "www.readync.org."

(161) North Carolina Green Industry Council. - Issuable to the registered owner of a motor vehicle in accordance with G.S. 20-81.12. The plate may bear the words "NC Green Industry Council" and the phrase "The Authentic Green" along with a logo designed by The North Carolina Green Industry Council.

(162) North Carolina Libraries. - Issuable to the registered owner of a motor vehicle in accordance with G.S. 20-81.12. The plate shall bear the words "North Carolina Libraries" and bear the international logo for libraries. The Division must receive 300 or more applications for the plate before it may be developed.

(163) North Carolina Master Gardener. - Issuable to the registered owner of a motor vehicle in accordance with G.S. 20-81.12. The plate shall bear the letters "MG" with a logo representing the North Carolina Master Gardeners.

(164) North Carolina Paddle Festival. - Issuable to the registered owner of a motor vehicle in accordance with G.S. 20-81.12. The plate may bear a phrase and logo representing the North Carolina Paddle Festival.

(165) North Carolina State Flag. - Issuable to the registered owner of a motor vehicle. The plate shall bear the image of the flag of the Great State of North Carolina. The letters and numbers shall be black. The Division may not issue the plate authorized by this subdivision unless it receives at least 300 applications for the plate.

(166) North Carolina Wildlife Habitat Foundation. - Issuable to the owner of a motor vehicle in accordance with G.S. 20-81.12. The plate shall bear the logo of the North Carolina Wildlife Habitat Foundation on the left side. The numbers or other writing on the plate shall be black and the border shall be black. The plate shall be developed by the Division in consultation with and approved by the North Carolina Wildlife Habitat Foundation. The Division may not issue the plate authorized by this subdivision unless it receives at least 300 applications for the plate.

(167) Nurses. - Issuable to the registered owner of a motor vehicle in accordance with G.S. 20- 81.12. The plate shall bear the phrase "First in Nursing" and a representation relating to nursing.

(168) Olympic Games. - Issuable to the registered owner of a motor vehicle in accordance with G.S. 20-81.12. The plate may bear a phrase or insignia representing the Olympic Games.

(169) Omega Psi Phi Fraternity. - Issuable to the registered owner of a motor vehicle in accordance with G.S. 20-81.12. The plate shall bear the fraternity's symbol and name.

(170) Operation Coming Home. - Issuable to the registered owner of a motor vehicle in accordance with G.S. 20-81.12. The plate shall bear the phrase "Operation Coming Home" with a logo designed by Operation Coming Home Foundation, Inc.

(171) Order of the Long Leaf Pine. - Issuable to a person who has received the award of membership in the Order of the Long Leaf Pine from the Governor. The plate shall bear the phrase "Order of the Long Leaf Pine."

(172) Outer Banks Preservation Association. - Issuable to the registered owner of a motor vehicle in accordance with G.S. 20-81.12. The plate shall bear a logo designed by the Outer Banks Preservation Association, Inc.

(173) Pamlico-Tar River Foundation. - Issuable to the registered owner of a motor vehicle in accordance with G.S. 20-81.12. The plate shall bear the name of the Pamlico-Tar River Foundation.

(174) Pancreatic Cancer Awareness. - Issuable to the registered owner of a motor vehicle in accordance with G.S. 20-81.12. The plate shall bear a representation of a purple ribbon on the right side of the plate.

(175) Paramedics. - Issuable to an emergency medical technician-paramedic, as defined in G.S. 131E-155. The plate shall bear the Star of Life logo and the phrase "Professional Paramedic". The Division may not issue the plate authorized by this subdivision unless it receives at least 300 applications for the plate.

(176) Partially Disabled Veteran. - Issuable to a veteran of the Armed Forces of the United States who suffered a service connected disability of less than 100%.

(177) Pearl Harbor Survivor. - Issuable to a veteran of the Armed Forces of the United States who was present at and survived the attack on Pearl Harbor on December 7, 1941. The plate will bear the phrase "Pearl Harbor Survivor" and the insignia of the Pearl Harbor Survivors' Association.

(178) P.E.O. Sisterhood. - Issuable to the registered owner of a motor vehicle in accordance with G.S. 20-81.12. The plate shall bear the phrase "P.E.O." and a logo designed by P.E.O. International.

(179) Personalized. - Issuable to the registered owner of a motor vehicle. The plate will bear the letters or letters and numbers requested by the owner. The Division may refuse to issue a plate with a letter combination that is offensive to good taste and decency. The Division may not issue a plate that duplicates another plate.

(180) Piedmont Airlines. - This plate is issuable to the registered owner of a motor vehicle in accordance with G.S. 20-81.12. The plate authorized by this subdivision shall bear the phrase "PA" and the Piedmont Speed Bird logo.

(181) POWIA. - Issuable to the owner of a motor vehicle. The plate shall bear the official POWIA logo. The Division must receive 300 or more applications for the plate before it may be developed.

(182) Prince Hall Mason. - This plate is issuable to the registered owner of a motor vehicle in accordance with G.S. 20-81.12. The plate shall bear the phrase "Prince Hall Mason" and a picture of the Masonic symbol.

(183) Prisoner of War. - Issuable to the following:

a. A member or veteran member of the Armed Forces of the United States who has been captured and held prisoner by forces hostile to the United States while serving in the Armed Forces of the United States.

b. The surviving spouse of a person who had a prisoner of war plate at the time of death so long as the surviving spouse continues to renew the plate and does not remarry.

(184) Professional Engineer. - Issuable to the registered owner of a motor vehicle in accordance with G.S. 20-81.12. The plate may bear a phrase and logo representing the Professional Engineers of North Carolina.

(185) Professional Sports Fan. - Issuable to the registered owner of a motor vehicle. The plate shall bear the logo of a professional sports team located in North Carolina. The Division shall receive 300 or more applications for a professional sports fan plate before a plate may be issued.

(186) Prostate Cancer Awareness. - Issuable to the registered owner of a motor vehicle. The plate shall bear the phrase "Prostate Cancer Awareness" and a representation of a blue ribbon. The Division must receive 300 or more applications for the plate before it may be developed.

(187) Purple Heart Recipient. - Issuable to a recipient of the Purple Heart award. The plate shall bear the phrase "Purple Heart Veteran, Combat Wounded." A person may obtain from the Division a special registration plate under this subdivision for the registered owner of a motor vehicle or a motorcycle. A motorcycle plate issued under this subdivision shall bear a

depiction of the Purple Heart Medal and the phrase "Purple Heart Veteran, Combat Wounded."

(188) Red Drum. - Issuable to the registered owner of a motor vehicle in accordance with G.S. 20-81.12. The plate shall bear the phrase "Red Drum" with a picture of a red drum native to North Carolina in the background.

(189) Red Hat Society. - Issuable to the registered owner of a motor vehicle. The plate shall bear a representation of The Red Hat Society. The Division must receive 300 or more applications for the plate before it may be developed.

(190) Register of Deeds. - Issuable to a register of deeds. The plate shall bear the words "Register of Deeds" and the letter "R" followed by a number representing the county of the register of deeds. The number of a county shall be the order of the county in an alphabetical list of counties that assigns number one to the first county in the list. A plate issued to a retired register of deeds shall bear the phrase "Register of Deeds, Retired," followed by a number that indicates the county where the register of deeds served and a designation indicating the retired status of the register of deeds.

(191) Relay for Life. - Issuable to the registered owner of a motor vehicle. The plate shall bear the phrase "Relay for Life" with a logo designed by the American Cancer Society. The Division may not issue the plate authorized by this subdivision unless it receives at least 300 applications for the plate.

(192) Retired Law Enforcement Officers. - The plate authorized by this subdivision shall bear the phrase "Retired Law Enforcement Officer" and a representation of a law enforcement badge. The Division must receive 300 or more applications for the plate before it may be developed. The plate is issuable to one of the following:

a. A retired law enforcement officer presenting to the Division, along with the application for the plate, a copy of the officer's retired identification card or letter of retirement.

b. The surviving spouse of a person who had a retired law enforcement officer plate at the time of death so long as the surviving spouse continues to renew the plate and does not remarry.

(193) Retired Legislator. - Issuable to a retired member of the North Carolina General Assembly in accordance with G.S. 20-81.12. A person who has served

in the North Carolina General Assembly is a retired member for purposes of this subdivision. The plate shall bear "The Great Seal of the State of North Carolina" and, as appropriate, the phrase "Retired Senate Member" or "Retired House Member" followed by a number representing the retired member's district with the letters "RM". If more than one retired member is from the same district, then the number shall be followed by a letter from A through Z. The plates shall be issued in the order applications are received.

(194)   Retired State Highway Patrol. - The plate authorized by this subdivision shall bear the phrase "SHP, Retired." The Division may not issue the plate authorized by this subdivision unless it receives at least 300 applications for the plate. The plate is issuable to one of the following:

a.   An individual who has retired from the North Carolina State Highway Patrol, presenting to the Division, along with the application for the plate, a copy of the retiree's retired identification card or letter of retirement.

b.   The surviving spouse of a person who had retired from the State Highway Patrol who, along with the application for the plate, presents a copy of the deceased retiree's identification card or letter of retirement and certifies in writing that the retiree is deceased and that the applicant is not remarried.

(195)   RiverLink. - Issuable to the registered owner of a motor vehicle in accordance with G.S. 20-81.12. The plate shall bear the phrase "RiverLink.org" and a logo representing RiverLink, Inc.

(196)   Rocky Mountain Elk Foundation. - Issuable to the registered owner of a motor vehicle in accordance with G.S. 20-81.12. The plate shall bear the phrase "Rocky Mountain Elk Foundation" and a logo approved by the Rocky Mountain Elk Foundation, Inc.

(197)   Ronald McDonald House. - Issuable to the registered owner of a motor vehicle in accordance with G.S. 20-81.12. The plate shall bear the phrase "House and Hands" with the words "Ronald McDonald House Charities" below the emblem and the letters "RH".

(198)   Save the Sea Turtles. - Issuable to the registered owner of a motor vehicle in accordance with G.S. 20-81.12. The plate may bear the phrase "Save the Sea Turtles" and a representation related to sea turtles.

(199) Scenic Rivers. - Issuable to the registered owner of a motor vehicle in accordance with G.S. 20-81.12. The plate shall bear the words "Scenic Rivers" and a picture representing the unique beauty of the scenic rivers of North Carolina.

(200) School Board. - Issuable to a school board member in this State. The plate shall bear the words "School Board" followed first by a number representing the school board and then by a letter or number that distinguishes plates issued to members of the same board. The number of a school board shall be the order of the school board in an alphabetical list of school boards that assigns number one to the first school board in the list. The Division may not issue the plate authorized by this subdivision unless it receives at least 300 applications for the plate.

(201) School Technology. - Issuable to the registered owner of a motor vehicle in accordance with G.S. 20-81.12. The plate may bear a phrase or an insignia representing the public school system in North Carolina.

(202) SCUBA. - Issuable to the registered owner of a motor vehicle in accordance with G.S. 20-81.12. The plate shall bear the phrase "SCUBA" and a logo of the Diver Down Flag.

(203) Shag Dancing. - Issuable to the registered owner of a motor vehicle in accordance with G.S. 20-81.12. The plate may bear the phrase "I'd Rather Be Shaggin'" and a picture representing shag dancing.

(204) Share the Road. - Issuable to the registered owner of a motor vehicle in accordance with G.S. 20-81.12. The plate shall bear a representation of a bicycle and the phrase "Share the Road".

(205) Sheriff. - Issuable to a current sheriff or to a retired sheriff who served as sheriff for at least 10 years before retiring. A plate issued to a current sheriff shall bear the word "Sheriff" and the letter "S" followed by a number that indicates the county the sheriff serves. A plate issued to a retired sheriff shall bear the phrase "Sheriff, Retired", the letter "S" followed by a number that indicates the county the sheriff served, and the letter "X" indicating the sheriff's retired status.

(206) Sigma Gamma Rho Sorority. - Issuable to the registered owner of a motor vehicle. The plate shall bear the sorority's symbol and name. The Division

may not issue the plate authorized by this subdivision unless it receives at least 300 applications for the plate.

(207) Silver Star Recipient. - Issuable to a recipient of the Silver Star. The plate shall bear the emblem of the Silver Star and the words "Silver Star".

(208) Silver Star Recipient/Disabled Veteran. - Issuable to a recipient of the Silver Star who is also a veteran of the Armed Forces of the United States who suffered a one hundred percent (100%) service-connected disability. The plate shall bear the emblem of the Silver Star laid over the universal symbol for the handicapped and the words "Silver Star." For the purposes of a fee for this plate, it shall be treated as a one hundred percent (100%) Disabled Veteran plate.

(209) Sneads Ferry Shrimp Festival. - Issuable to the registered owner of a motor vehicle in accordance with G.S. 20-81.12. The plate may bear a phrase and logo representing the Sneads Ferry Shrimp Festival.

(210) Soil and Water Conservation. - Issuable to the registered owner of a motor vehicle in accordance with G.S. 20-81.12. The plate may bear a phrase and picture appropriate to the subject of water quality and environmental protection in North Carolina.

(211) Special Forces Association. - Issuable to the registered owner of a motor vehicle in accordance with G.S. 20-81.12. The plate shall bear a representation of the Special Forces Association shoulder patch with tabs and shall bear the words "Special Forces Association."

(212) Special Olympics. - Issuable to the registered owner of a motor vehicle in accordance with G.S. 20-81.12. The plate may bear a phrase or an insignia representing the North Carolina Special Olympics.

(213) Sport Fishing. - Issuable to the registered owner of a motor vehicle in accordance with G.S. 20-81.12. The plate may bear a phrase and picture appropriate to the subject of sport fishing in North Carolina. The Division may not issue the plate authorized by this subdivision unless it receives at least 300 applications for the plate.

(214) Square Dance Clubs. - Issuable to a member of a recognized square dance organization exempt from corporate income tax under G.S. 105-130.11(a)(5). The plate shall bear a word or phrase identifying the club and the

emblem of the club. The Division shall not issue a dance club plate authorized by this subdivision unless it receives at least 300 applications for that dance club plate.

(215) S.T.A.R. - Issuable to the registered owner of a motor vehicle in accordance with G.S. 20-81.12. The plate shall bear the phrase "For the Love of Horses" and a logo depicting a horse rearing up on its hind legs.

(216) State Attraction. - Issuable to the registered owner of a motor vehicle in accordance with G.S. 20-81.12. The plate may bear a phrase or an insignia representing a publicly owned or nonprofit State or federal attraction located in North Carolina.

(217) State Government Official. - Issuable to elected and appointed members of State government in accordance with G.S. 20-79.5.

(218) Stock Car Racing Theme. - Issuable to the registered owner of a motor vehicle pursuant to G.S. 20-81.12. This is a series of plates bearing an emblem, seal, other symbol or design displaying themes of professional stock car auto racing, or professional stock car auto racing drivers. The Division shall not develop any plate in the series without a license to use copyrighted or registered words, symbols, trademarks, or designs associated with the plate. The plate shall be designed in consultation with and approved by the person authorized to provide the State with the license to use the words, symbols, trademarks, or designs associated with the plate. The Division shall not pay a royalty for the license to use the copyrighted or registered words, symbols, trademarks, or designs associated with the plate.

(219) Street Rod Owner. - Issuable to the registered owner of a modernized private passenger motor vehicle manufactured prior to the year 1949 or designed to resemble a vehicle manufactured prior to the year 1949. The plate shall bear the phrase "Street Rod". The Division may not issue the plate authorized by this subdivision unless it receives at least 300 applications for the plate.

(220) Support NC Education. - Issuable to the registered owner of a motor vehicle in accordance with G.S. 20-81.12. The plate shall bear the phrase "Support NC Education" with a picture of a mortar board hat and a diploma.

(221) Support Our Troops. - Issuable to the registered owner of a motor vehicle in accordance with G.S. 20-81.12. The plate shall bear a picture of a soldier and a child and shall bear the words: "Support Our Troops".

(222) Support Soccer. - Issuable to the registered owner of a motor vehicle in accordance with G.S. 20-81.12. The plate shall bear the phrase "Support Soccer" and a logo designed by the North Carolina Soccer Hall of Fame, Inc.

(223) Surveyor Plate. - Issuable to the registered owner of a motor vehicle in accordance with G.S. 20-81.12. The plate shall bear the words "Following In Their Footsteps" and shall bear a picture of a transit.

(224) Sustainable Fisheries. - Issuable to the registered owner of a motor vehicle in accordance with G.S. 20-81.12. The plate may bear a phrase and picture appropriate to the subject of sustainable fisheries in North Carolina.

(225) Sweet Potato. - Issuable to the registered owner of a motor vehicle. The plate may bear a phrase and picture representing the State's official vegetable, the sweet potato. The Division may not issue the plate authorized by this subdivision unless it receives at least 300 applications for the plate.

(226) Tarheel Classic Thunderbird Club. - Issuable to the registered owner of a motor vehicle. The plate shall bear the logo of the Tarheel Classic Thunderbird Club and the phrase "Tarheel Classic Thunderbird Club". The Division may not issue the plate authorized by this subdivision unless it receives at least 300 applications for the plate.

(227) Toastmasters Club. - Issuable to the registered owner of a motor vehicle in accordance with G.S. 20-81.12. The plate shall bear the phrase "Toastmasters" and a logo designed by Toastmasters International.

(228) Tobacco Heritage. - Issuable to the registered owner of a motor vehicle. The plate shall bear a picture of a tobacco leaf and plow. The Division may not issue the plate authorized by this subdivision unless it receives at least 300 applications for the plate.

(229) Topsail Island Shoreline Protection. - Issuable to the registered owner of a motor vehicle in accordance with G.S. 20-81.12. The plate shall bear a phrase and graphic selected by the Topsail Island Shoreline Protection Committee.

(230) Town of Oak Island. - Issuable to the registered owner of a motor vehicle. The plate shall bear the seal of the Town of Oak Island and the letters "OKI." The Division may not issue the plate authorized by this subdivision unless it receives at least 300 applications for the plate.

(231) Transportation Personnel. - Issuable to various members of the Divisions of the Department of Transportation. The plate shall bear the letters "DOT" followed by a number from 1 to 85, as designated by the Governor.

(232) Travel and Tourism. - Issuable to the registered owner of a motor vehicle in accordance with G.S. 20-81.12. The plate shall bear the phrase "www.visitnc.com."

(233) Turtle Rescue Team. - Issuable to the registered owner of a motor vehicle in accordance with G.S. 20-81.12. The plate shall bear a phrase and logo selected by the North Carolina State University College of Veterinary Medicine Turtle Rescue Team.

(234) United States Service Academy. - Issuable to a graduate of one of the service academies, upon furnishing to the Division proof of graduation. The plate shall bear the name of the specific service academy with an emblem that designates the specific service academy being represented. The Division, with the cooperation of each service academy, shall develop a special plate for each of the service academies. The Division must receive a combined total of 300 or more applications for all the plates authorized by this subdivision before a specific service academy plate may be developed.

(235) University Health Systems of Eastern Carolina. - Issuable to the registered owner of a motor vehicle in accordance with G.S. 20-81.12. The plate may bear a phrase or insignia representing the University Health Systems of Eastern Carolina.

(236) US Equine Rescue League. - Issuable to the registered owner of a motor vehicle in accordance with G.S. 20-81.12. The plate shall bear the phrase "United States Equine Rescue League", and a depiction of two horses in a circle.

(237) U.S. Navy Submarine Veteran. - Issuable to a veteran of the United States Navy Submarine Service. The plate shall bear the phrase "United States Navy Submarine Veteran" and shall bear a representation of the Submarine Service Qualification insignia overlaid upon a representation of the State of

North Carolina. The Division may not issue the plate authorized by this subdivision unless it receives at least 150 applications for the plate.

(238) U.S. Representative. - Issuable to a United States Representative for North Carolina. The plate shall bear the phrase "U.S. House" and shall be issued on the basis of Congressional district numbers.

(239) U.S. Senator. - Issuable to a United States Senator for North Carolina. The plates shall bear the phrase "U.S. Senate" and shall be issued on the basis of seniority represented by the numbers 1 and 2.

(240) USA Triathlon. - Issuable to the registered owner of a motor vehicle in accordance with G.S. 20-81.12. The plate may bear the USA Triathlon logo. The Division may not issue the plate authorized by this subdivision unless it receives at least 300 applications for the plate.

(241) USO of NC. - Issuable to the registered owner of a motor vehicle in accordance with G.S. 20-81.12. The plate shall bear the emblem of the USO of NC.

(242) The V Foundation for Cancer Research. - Issuable to the registered owner of a motor vehicle in accordance with G.S. 20-81.12. The plate shall bear a phrase and insignia representing The V Foundation for Cancer Research.

(243) Veterans of Foreign Wars. - Issuable to a member or a supporter of the Veterans of Foreign Wars. The plate shall bear the words "Veterans of Foreign Wars" or "VFW" and the emblem of the VFW. The Division may not issue the plate authorized by this subdivision unless it receives at least 300 applications for the plate.

(244) Victory Junction Gang Camp. - Issuable to the registered owner of a motor vehicle. The plate may bear the phrase "Victory Junction Gang Camp." The Division must receive 300 or more applications for the plate before it may be developed.

(245) Vietnam Veterans of America. - Issuable to a member of the Vietnam Veterans of America. The plate shall bear the words "Vietnam Veterans of America" or "VVA" and the emblem of the VVA. A person may obtain from the Division a special registration plate under this subdivision for a motor vehicle or a motorcycle registered in that person's name. The registration fees and the restrictions on the issuance of a specialized registration plate for a motorcycle

are the same as for any motor vehicle. The Division may not issue either type of the plate authorized by this subdivision unless it receives at least 300 applications for the plate.

(246) Volunteers in Law Enforcement. - Issuable to a volunteer member of a State or local law enforcement agency. The plate shall bear the phrase "Volunteers in Law Enforcement."

(247) Watermelon. - Issuable to the registered owner of a motor vehicle. The plate shall bear a picture representing a slice of watermelon. The Division may not issue the plate authorized by this subdivision unless it receives at least 300 applications for the plate.

(248) Wildlife Resources. - Issuable to the registered owner of a motor vehicle in accordance with G.S. 20-81.12. The plate shall bear a picture representing a native wildlife species occurring in North Carolina.

(249) YMCA. - Issuable to the registered owner of a motor vehicle in accordance with G.S. 20-81.12. The plate shall bear the logo of the YMCA on the right side of the plate.

(250) Zeta Phi Beta Sorority. - Issuable to the registered owner of a motor vehicle in accordance with G.S. 20-81.12. The plate shall bear the sorority's name and symbol.

(c) Repealed by Session Laws 1991 (Regular Session, 1992), c. 1042, s. 1. (1991, c. 672, s. 2; c. 726, s. 23; 1991 (Reg. Sess., 1992), c. 1042, s. 1; 1993, c. 543, s. 2; 1995, c. 326, ss. 1-3; c. 433, ss. 1, 4.1; 1997-156, s. 1; 1997-158, s. 1; 1997-339, s. 1; 1997-427, s. 1; 1997-461, ss. 2-4; 1997-477, s. 1; 1997-484, ss. 1-3; 1998-155, s. 1; 1998-160, ss. 1, 2; 1998-163, ss. 3-5; 1999-220, s. 3.1; 1999-277, s. 1; 1999-314, s. 1; 1999-403, s. 1; 1999-450, s. 1; 1999-452, s. 16; 2000-159, ss. 1, 2; 2001-40, s. 1; 2001-483, s. 1; 2001-498, ss. 1(a), 1(b), 2; 2002-134, ss. 1-4; 2002-159, s. 68; 2003-10, s. 1; 2003-11, s. 1; 2003-68, s. 1; 2003-424, s. 2; 2004-131, s. 2; 2004-182, s. 1; 2004-185, s. 2; 2004-200, s. 1; 2005-216, ss. 2, 3; 2006-209, ss. 2, 7; 2007-400, s. 2; 2007-470, s. 1; 2007-483, ss. 2, 8(d); 2007-522, s. 1; 2009-121, s. 1; 2009-274, s. 4; 2009-376, s. 1; 2010-39, s. 1; 2011-145, ss. 2, 19.1(h); 2011-183, s. 23; 2011-392, ss. 2, 3; 2012-194, ss. 45.7, 57; 2013-376, ss. 1, 2, 9(e); 2013-414, s. 57(a).)

§ 20-79.5. Special registration plates for elected and appointed State government officials.

(a) Plates. - The State government officials listed in this section are eligible for a special registration plate under G.S. 20-79.4. The plate shall bear the number designated in the following table for the position held by the official.

Position   Number on Plate

Governor
1

Lieutenant Governor
2

Speaker of the House of Representatives
3

President Pro Tempore of the Senate
4

Secretary of State
5

State Auditor
6

State Treasurer
7

Superintendent of Public Instruction
8

Attorney General
9

Commissioner of Agriculture
10

Commissioner of Labor
11

Commissioner of Insurance
12

Speaker Pro Tempore of the House
13

Legislative Services Officer
14

Secretary of Administration
15

Secretary of Environment and Natural Resources
16

Secretary of Revenue
17

Secretary of Health and Human Services
18

Secretary of Commerce
19

Secretary of Public Safety
20

Secretary of Cultural Resources
21

Governor's Staff
22-29

State Budget Officer
30

State Personnel Director
31

Chair of the State Board of Education
32

President of the U.N.C. System
33

President of the Community Colleges System
34

State Board Member, Commission Member,

or State Employee Not Named in List   35-43

Alcoholic Beverage Control Commission   44-46

Assistant Commissioners of Agriculture   47-48

Deputy Secretary of State
49

Deputy State Treasurer
50

Assistant State Treasurer
51

Deputy Commissioner for the Department of Labor
52

Chief Deputy for the Department of Insurance
53

Assistant Commissioner of Insurance
54

Deputies and Assistant to the Attorney General   55-65

Board of Economic Development Nonlegislative Member   66-88

State Ports Authority Nonlegislative Member   89-96

Utilities Commission Member   97-103

State Board Member, Commission Member,

or State Employee Not Named in List   104

Post-Release Supervision and Parole Commission Member 105-107

State Board Member, Commission Member,

or State Employee Not Named in List   108-200".

(b) Designation. - When the table in subsection (a) designates a range of numbers for certain officials, the number given an official in that group shall be assigned. The Governor shall assign a number for members of the Governor's staff, nonlegislative members of the Board of Economic Development, nonlegislative members of the State Ports Authority, members of State boards and commissions, and for State employees. The Attorney General shall assign a number for the Attorney General's deputies and assistants.

The first number assigned to the Alcoholic Beverage Control Commission is reserved for the Chair of that Commission. The remaining numbers shall be assigned to the Alcoholic Beverage Control Commission members on the basis of seniority. The first number assigned to the Utilities Commission is reserved for the Chair of that Commission. The remaining numbers shall be assigned to the Utilities Commission members on the basis of seniority. The first number assigned to the Post-Release Supervision and Parole Commission is reserved for the Chair of that Commission. The remaining numbers shall be assigned to the Post-Release Supervision and Parole Commission members on the basis of seniority. (1991, c. 672, s. 2; c. 726, s. 23; 1991 (Reg. Sess., 1992), c. 959, s. 1; 1996, 2nd Ex. Sess., c. 18, s. 8(a); 1997-443, ss. 11A.118(a), 11A.119(a); 2000-137, s. 4.(e); 2006-203, s. 14; 2007-483, s. 3(a); 2011-145, s. 19.1(g), (i), (m); 2012-83, s. 4; 2013-382, s. 9.1(c).)

§ 20-79.6. Special registration plates for members of the judiciary.

(a) Supreme Court. - A special plate issued to a Justice of the North Carolina Supreme Court shall bear the words "Supreme Court" and the Great Seal of North Carolina and a number from 1 through 7. The Chief Justice of the Supreme Court of North Carolina shall be issued the plate bearing the number 1 and the remaining plates shall be issued to the Associate Justices on the basis of seniority.

Special plates issued to retired members of the Supreme Court shall bear a number indicating the member's position of seniority at the time of retirement followed by the letter "X" to indicate the member's retired status.

(a1) Court of Appeals. - A special plate issued to a Judge of the North Carolina Court of Appeals shall bear the words "Court of Appeals" and the Great Seal of North Carolina and a number beginning with the number 1. The Chief Judge of the North Carolina Court of Appeals shall be issued a plate with the number 1 and the remaining plates shall be issued to the Associate Judges with the numbers assigned on the basis of seniority.

Special plates issued to retired members of the Court of Appeals shall bear a number indicating the member's position of seniority at the time of retirement followed by the letter "X" to indicate the member's retired status.

(b) Superior Court. - A special plate issued to a resident superior court judge shall bear the letter "J" followed by a number indicative of the judicial district the judge serves. The number issued to the senior resident superior court judge shall be the numerical designation of the judge's judicial district, as defined in G.S. 7A-41.1(a)(1). If a district has more than one regular resident superior court judge, a special plate for a resident superior court judge of that district shall bear the number issued to the senior resident superior court judge followed by a hyphen and a letter of the alphabet beginning with the letter "A" to indicate the judge's seniority.

For any grouping of districts having the same numerical designation, other than districts where there are two or more resident superior court judges, the number issued to the senior resident superior court judge shall be the number the districts in the set have in common. A special plate issued to the other regular resident superior court judges of the set of districts shall bear the number issued to the senior resident superior court judge followed by a hyphen and a letter of the alphabet beginning with the letter "A" to indicate the judge's seniority among all of the regular resident superior court judges of the set of districts. The letter assigned to a resident superior court judge will not necessarily correspond with the letter designation of the district the judge serves.

Where there are two or more regular resident superior court judges for the district or set of districts, the registration plate with the letter "A" shall be issued to the judge who, from among all the regular resident superior court judges of the district or set of districts, has the most continuous service as a regular resident superior court judge; provided if two or more judges are of equal service, the oldest of those judges shall receive the next letter registration plate. Thereafter, registration plates shall be issued based on seniority within the district or set of districts.

A special judge, emergency judge, or retired judge of the superior court shall be issued a special plate bearing the letter "J" followed by a number designated by the Administrative Office of the Courts with the approval of the Chief Justice of the Supreme Court of North Carolina. The plate for a retired judge shall have the letter "X" after the designated number to indicate the judge's retired status.

(c)   District Court. - A special plate issued to a North Carolina district court judge shall bear the letter "J" followed by a number. For the chief judge of the district court district, the number shall be equal to the sum of the numerical designation of the district court district the chief judge serves, plus 100. The number for all other judges of the district courts serving within the same district court district shall be the same number as appears on the special plate issued to the chief district judge followed by a letter of the alphabet beginning with the letter "A" to indicate the judge's seniority. A retired district court judge shall be issued a similar plate except that the numerical designation shall be followed by the letter "X" to indicate the judge's retired status.

(d)   United States. - A special plate issued to a Justice of the United States Supreme Court, a Judge of the United States Circuit Court of Appeals, or a District Judge of the United States District Court residing in North Carolina shall bear the words "U.S. J" followed by a number beginning with "1". The number shall reflect the judge's seniority based on continuous service as a United States Judge as designated by the Secretary of State. A judge who has retired or taken senior status shall be issued a similar plate except that the number shall be based on the date of the judge's retirement or assumption of senior status and shall follow the numerical designation of active justices and judges. (1991, c. 672, s. 2; c. 726, s. 23; 1999-403, s. 5; 1999-456, s. 67.1.)

§ 20-79.7. Fees for special registration plates and distribution of the fees.

(a) Free of Charge. - Upon request, the Division shall annually provide and issue free of charge a single special registration plate listed in this subsection to a person qualified to receive the plate in accordance with G.S. 20-79.4(a2). This subsection does not apply to a special registration plate issued for a vehicle that has a registered weight greater than 6,000 pounds. The regular motor vehicle registration fees in G.S. 20-88 apply if the registered weight of the vehicle is greater than 6,000 pounds:

(1) A Legion of Valor registration plate to a recipient of the Legion of Valor award.

(2) A 100% Disabled Veteran registration plate to a 100% disabled veteran.

(3) An Ex-Prisoner of War registration plate to an ex-prisoner of war.

(4) A Bronze Star Valor registration plate to a recipient of the Bronze Star Medal for valor in combat award.

(5) A Silver Star registration plate to a recipient of the Silver Star award.

(a1) Fees. - All other special registration plates are subject to the regular motor vehicle registration fee in G.S. 20-87 or G.S. 20-88 plus an additional fee in the following amount:

Special Plate	Additional Fee Amount
American Red Cross	$30.00
Animal Lovers	$30.00
Arthritis Foundation	$30.00
ARTS NC	$30.00
Back Country Horsemen of NC	$30.00

Boy Scouts of America	$30.00
Brenner Children's Hospital	$30.00
Carolina Raptor Center	$30.00
Carolinas Credit Union Foundation	$30.00
Carolinas Golf Association	$30.00
Coastal Conservation Association	$30.00
Coastal Land Trust	$30.00
Crystal Coast	$30.00
Daniel Stowe Botanical Garden	$30.00
El Pueblo	$30.00
Farmland Preservation	$30.00
First in Forestry	$30.00
First Tee	$30.00
Girl Scouts	$30.00
Greensboro Symphony Guild	$30.00
Historical Attraction	$30.00
Home Care and Hospice	$30.00
Home of American Golf	$30.00
HOMES4NC	$30.00
Hospice Care	$30.00
In God We Trust	$30.00

Maggie Valley Trout Festival	$30.00
Morehead Planetarium	$30.00
Morgan Horse Club	$30.00
Mountains-to-Sea Trail	$30.00
Municipality Plate	$30.00
NC Civil War	$30.00
NC Coastal Federation	$30.00
NC FIRST Robotics	$30.00
NCSC	$30.00
NC Veterinary Medical Association	$30.00
National Kidney Foundation	$30.00
National Law Enforcement Officers Memorial	$30.00
Native Brook Trout	$30.00
North Carolina 4-H Development Fund	$30.00
North Carolina Bluegrass Association	$30.00
North Carolina Cattlemen's Association	$30.00
North Carolina Emergency Management Association	$30.00
North Carolina Green Industry Council	$30.00
North Carolina Libraries	$30.00
North Carolina Paddle Festival	$30.00

Operation Coming Home	$30.00
Outer Banks Preservation Association	$30.00
Pamlico-Tar River Foundation	$30.00
Pancreatic Cancer Awareness	$30.00
P.E.O. Sisterhood	$30.00
Personalized	$30.00
Red Drum	$30.00
Retired Legislator	$30.00
RiverLink	$30.00
Ronald McDonald House	$30.00
Share the Road	$30.00
S.T.A.R.	$30.00
State Attraction	$30.00
Stock Car Racing Theme	$30.00
Support NC Education	$30.00
Support Our Troops	$30.00
Sustainable Fisheries	$30.00
Toastmasters Club	$30.00
Topsail Island Shoreline Protection	$30.00
Travel and Tourism	$30.00
Turtle Rescue Team	$30.00

Volunteers in Law Enforcement	$30.00
YMCA	$30.00
AIDS Awareness	$25.00
Buffalo Soldiers	$25.00
Charlotte Checkers	$25.00
Choose Life	$25.00
Collegiate Insignia	$25.00
First in Turf	$25.00
Goodness Grows	$25.00
High School Insignia	$25.00
I.B.P.O.E.W.	$25.00
Kids First	$25.00
National Multiple Sclerosis Society	$25.00
National Wild Turkey Federation	$25.00
NC Agribusiness	$25.00
NC Children's Promise	$25.00
Nurses	$25.00
Olympic Games	$25.00
Professional Engineer	$25.00
Rocky Mountain Elk Foundation	$25.00

Special Olympics	$25.00
Support Soccer	$25.00
Surveyor Plate	$25.00
The V Foundation for Cancer Research Division	$25.00
University Health Systems of Eastern Carolina	$25.00
Alpha Phi Alpha Fraternity	$20.00
ALS Association, Jim "Catfish" Hunter Chapter	$20.00
ARC of North Carolina	$20.00
Audubon North Carolina	$20.00
Autism Society of North Carolina	$20.00
Battle of Kings Mountain	$20.00
Be Active NC	$20.00
Brain Injury Awareness	$20.00
Breast Cancer Earlier Detection	$20.00
Buddy Pelletier Surfing Foundation	$20.00
Concerned Bikers Association/ABATE of North Carolina	$20.00
Daughters of the American Revolution	$20.00
Donate Life	$20.00
Ducks Unlimited	$20.00
Fraternal Order of Police	$20.00
Greyhound Friends of North Carolina	$20.00

Guilford Battleground Company	$20.00
Harley Owners' Group	$20.00
Jaycees	$20.00
Juvenile Diabetes Research Foundation	$20.00
Kappa Alpha Order	$20.00
Litter Prevention	$20.00
March of Dimes	$20.00
Mission Foundation	$20.00
Native American	$20.00
NC Fisheries Association	$20.00
NC Horse Council	$20.00
NC Mining	$20.00
NC Tennis Foundation	$20.00
NC Trout Unlimited	$20.00
NC Victim Assistance	$20.00
NC Wildlife Federation	$20.00
NC Wildlife Habitat Foundation	$20.00
NC Youth Soccer Association	$20.00
North Carolina Master Gardener	$20.00
Omega Psi Phi Fraternity	$20.00

Order of the Long Leaf Pine	$20.00
Piedmont Airlines	$20.00
Prince Hall Mason	$20.00
Save the Sea Turtles	$20.00
Scenic Rivers	$20.00
School Technology	$20.00
SCUBA	$20.00
Soil and Water Conservation	$20.00
Special Forces Association	$20.00
Support Public Schools	$20.00
US Equine Rescue League	$20.00
USO of NC	$20.00
Wildlife Resources	$20.00
Zeta Phi Beta Sorority	$20.00
Carolina Regional Volleyball Association	$15.00
Carolina's Aviation Museum	$15.00
Leukemia & Lymphoma Society	$15.00
Lung Cancer Research	$15.00
NC Beekeepers	$15.00
Shag Dancing	$15.00
Active Member of the National Guard	None

Bronze Star Combat Recipient	None
Bronze Star Recipient	None
Combat Veteran	None
100% Disabled Veteran	None
Ex-Prisoner of War	None
Gold Star Lapel Button	None
Legion of Merit	None
Legion of Valor	None
Military Veteran	None
Military Wartime Veteran	None
Partially Disabled Veteran	None
Pearl Harbor Survivor	None
Purple Heart Recipient	None
Silver Star Recipient	None
All Other Special Plates	$10.00.

(b) Distribution of Fees. - The Special Registration Plate Account and the Collegiate and Cultural Attraction Plate Account are established within the Highway Fund. The Division must credit the additional fee imposed for the special registration plates listed in subsection (a) of this section among the Special Registration Plate Account (SRPA), the Collegiate and Cultural Attraction Plate Account (CCAPA), the Clean Water Management Trust Fund (CWMTF), which is established under G.S. 113A-253, and the Parks and Recreation Trust Fund, which is established under G.S. 113-44.15, as follows:

Special Plate	SRPA	CCAPA	NHTF	PRTF

AIDS Awareness	$10	$15	0	0
Alpha Phi Alpha Fraternity	$10	$10	0	0
ALS Association, Jim "Catfish" Hunter Chapter	$10	$10	0	0
American Red Cross	$10	$20	0	0
Animal Lovers	$10	$20	0	0
ARC of North Carolina	$10	$10	0	0
Arthritis Foundation	$10	$20	0	0
ARTS NC	$10	$20	0	0
Audubon North Carolina	$10	$10	0	0
Autism Society of North Carolina	$10	$10	0	0
Back Country Horsemen of NC	$10	$20	0	0
Battle of Kings Mountain	$10	$10	0	0
Be Active NC	$10	$10	0	0
Boy Scouts of America	$10	$20	0	0
Brain Injury Awareness	$10	$10	0	0
Breast Cancer Earlier Detection	$10	$10	0	0
Brenner Children's Hospital	$10	$20	0	0
Buddy Pelletier Surfing				

Foundation	$10	$10	0	0
Buffalo Soldiers	$10	$15	0	0
Carolina Raptor Center	$10	$20	0	0
Carolina Regional Volleyball Association	$10	$5	0	0
Carolina's Aviation Museum	$10	$5	0	0
Carolinas Credit Union Foundation	$10	$20	0	0
Carolinas Golf Association	$10	$20	0	0
Charlotte Checkers	$10	$15	0	0
Choose Life	$10	$15	0	0
Coastal Conservation Association	$10	$20	0	0
Coastal Land Trust	$10	$20	0	0
Concerned Bikers Association/ ABATE of North Carolina	$10	$10	0	0
Crystal Coast	$10	$20	0	0
Daniel Stowe Botanical Gardens	$10	$20	0	0
Daughters of the American Revolution	$10	$10	0	0
Donate Life	$10	$10	0	0

Ducks Unlimited	$10	$10	0	0
El Pueblo	$10	$20	0	0
Farmland Preservation	$10	$20	0	0
First in Forestry First in Turf	$10	$15	0	0
First Tee	$10	$20	0	0
Fraternal Order of Police	$10	$10	0	0
Girl Scouts	$10	$20	0	0
Goodness Grows	$10	$15	0	0
Greensboro Symphony Guild	$10	$20	0	0
Greyhound Friends of North Carolina	$10	$10	0	0
Guilford Battleground Company	$10	$10	0	0
Harley Owners' Group	$10	$10	0	0
High School Insignia	$10	$15	0	0
Historical Attraction	$10	$20	0	0
Home Care and Hospice	$10	$20	0	0
Home of American Golf	$10	$20	0	0
HOMES4NC	$10	$20	0	0
Hospice Care	$10	$20	0	0

I.B.P.O.E.W.	$10	$15	0	0
In God We Trust	$10	$20	0	0
In-State Collegiate Insignia	$10	$15	0	0
Jaycees	$10	$10	0	0
Juvenile Diabetes Research Foundation	$10	$10	0	0
Kappa Alpha Order	$10	$10	0	0
Kids First	$10	$15	0	0
Leukemia & Lymphoma Society	$10	$5	0	0
Litter Prevention	$10	$10	0	0
Lung Cancer Research	$10	$5	0	0
Maggie Valley Trout Festival	$10	$20	0	0
March of Dimes	$10	$10	0	0
Mission Foundation	$10	$10	0	0
Morgan Horse Club	$10	$20	0	0
Morehead Planetarium	$10	$20	0	0
Mountains-to-Sea Trail	$10	$20	0	0
Municipality Plate	$10	$20	0	0
National Kidney Foundation	$10	$20	0	0
National Law Enforcement Officers				

Memorial	$10	$20	0	0
National Multiple Sclerosis Society	$10	$15	0	0
National Wild Turkey Federation	$10	$15	0	0
Native American	$10	$10	0	0
NC Agribusiness	$10	$15	0	0
NC Beekeepers	$10	$5	0	0
NC Children's Promise	$10	$15	0	0
NC Civil War	$10	$20	0	0
NC Coastal Federation	$10	$20	0	0
NC 4-H Development Fund	$10	$20	0	0
NC FIRST Robotics	$10	$20	0	0
NC Fisheries Association	$10	$10	0	0
NC Horse Council	$10	$10	0	0
NC Mining	$10	$10	0	0
NCSC	$10	$20	0	0
NC Tennis Foundation	$10	$10	0	0
NC Trout Unlimited	$10	$10	0	0
NC Veterinary Medical				

Association	$10	$20	0	0
NC Victim Assistance	$10	$10	0	0
NC Wildlife Federation	$10	$10	0	0
NC Wildlife Habitat Foundation	$10	$10	0	0
NC Youth Soccer Association	$10	$10	0	0
North Carolina Bluegrass Association	$10	$20	0	0
North Carolina Cattlemen's Association	$10	$20	0	0
North Carolina Emergency Management Association	$10	$20	0	0
North Carolina Green Industry Council	$10	$20	0	0
North Carolina Libraries	$10	$20	0	0
North Carolina Master Gardener	$10	$10	0	0
North Carolina Paddle Festival	$10	$20	0	0
Nurses	$10	$15	0	0
Olympic Games	$10	$15	0	0
Omega Psi Phi Fraternity	$10	$10	0	0

Operation Coming Home	$10	$20	0	0
Order of the Long Leaf Pine	$10	$10	0	0
Out-of-state Collegiate Insignia	$10	0	$15	0
Outer Banks Preservation Association	$10	$20	0	0
Pamlico-Tar River Foundation	$10	$20	0	0
Pancreatic Cancer Awareness	$10	$20	0	0
P.E.O. Sisterhood	$10	$20	0	0
Personalized	$10	0	$15	$5
Piedmont Airlines	$10	$10	0	0
Prince Hall Mason	$10	$10	0	0
Professional Engineer	$10	$15	0	0
Retired Legislator	$10	$20	0	0
RiverLink	$10	$20	0	0
Rocky Mountain Elk Foundation	$10	$15	0	0
Ronald McDonald House	$10	$20	0	0
Save the Sea Turtles	$10	$10	0	0
Scenic Rivers	$10	$10	0	0
School Technology	$10	$10	0	0
SCUBA	$10	$10	0	0

Shag Dancing	$10	$5	0	0
Share the Road	$10	$20	0	0
Sneads Ferry Shrimp Festival	$10	0	0	0
Soil and Water Conservation	$10	$10	0	0
Special Forces Association	$10	$10	0	0
Special Olympics	$10	$15	0	0
S.T.A.R.	$10	$20	0	0
State Attraction	$10	$20	0	0
Stock Car Racing Theme	$10	$20	0	0
Support NC Education	$10	$20	0	0
Support Our Troops	$10	$20	0	0
Support Public Schools	$10	$10	0	0
Support Soccer	$10	$15	0	0
Surveyor Plate	$10	$15	0	0
Sustainable Fisheries	$10	$20	0	0
The V Foundation for Cancer Research	$10	$15	0	0
Toastmasters Club	$10	$20	0	0
Topsail Island Shoreline Protection	$10	$20	0	0

Travel and Tourism	$10	$20	0	0
Turtle Rescue Team	$10	$20	0	0
University Health Systems of Eastern Carolina	$10	$15	0	0
US Equine Rescue League	$10	$10	0	0
USO of NC	$10	$10	0	0
Volunteers in Law Enforcement	$10	$20	0	0
Wildlife Resources	$10	$10	0	0
YMCA	$10	$20	0	0
Zeta Phi Beta Sorority	$10	$10	0	0
All other Special Plates	$10	0	0	0.

(c) Use of Funds in Special Registration Plate Account. -

(1) The Division shall deduct the costs of special registration plates, including the costs of issuing, handling, and advertising the availability of the special plates, from the Special Registration Plate Account.

(2) From the funds remaining in the Special Registration Plate Account after the deductions in accordance with subdivision (1) of this subsection, there is annually appropriated from the Special Registration Plate Account the sum of one million three hundred thousand dollars ($1,300,000) to provide operating assistance for the Visitor Centers:

a. on U.S. Highway 17 in Camden County, ninety-two thousand eight hundred fifty-seven dollars ($92,857);

b. on U.S. Highway 17 in Brunswick County, ninety-two thousand eight hundred fifty-seven dollars ($92,857);

c. on U.S. Highway 441 in Macon County, ninety-two thousand eight hundred fifty-seven dollars ($92,857);

d. in the Town of Boone, Watauga County, ninety-two thousand eight hundred fifty-seven dollars ($92,857);

e. on U.S. Highway 29 in Caswell County, ninety-two thousand eight hundred fifty-seven dollars ($92,857);

f. on U.S. Highway 70 in Carteret County, ninety-two thousand eight hundred fifty-seven dollars ($92,857);

g. on U.S. Highway 64 in Tyrrell County, ninety-two thousand eight hundred fifty-seven dollars ($92,857);

h. at the intersection of U.S. Highway 701 and N.C. 904 in Columbus County, ninety-two thousand eight hundred fifty-seven dollars ($92,857);

i. on U.S. Highway 221 in McDowell County, ninety-two thousand eight hundred fifty-seven dollars ($92,857);

j. on Staton Road in Transylvania County, ninety-two thousand eight hundred fifty-seven dollars ($92,857);

k. in the Town of Fair Bluff, Columbus County, near the intersection of U.S. Highway 76 and N.C. 904, ninety-two thousand eight hundred fifty-seven dollars ($92,857);

l. on U.S. Highway 421 in Wilkes County, ninety-two thousand eight hundred fifty-seven dollars ($92,857); and

m. at the intersection of Interstate 73 and Interstate 74 in Randolph County, ninety-two thousand eight hundred fifty-eight dollars ($92,858) each, for two centers.

(3) The Division shall transfer the remaining revenue in the Special Registration Plate Account quarterly, and funds are hereby appropriated, as follows:

a. Thirty-three percent (33%) to the account of the Department of Commerce to aid in financing out-of-state print and other media advertising under the program for the promotion of travel and industrial development in this State.

b. Fifty percent (50%) to the Department of Transportation to be used solely for the purpose of beautification of highways. These funds shall be administered by the Department of Transportation for beautification purposes not inconsistent with good landscaping and engineering principles.

c. Seventeen percent (17%) to the account of the Department of Health and Human Services to promote travel accessibility for disabled persons in this State. These funds shall be used to collect and update site information on travel attractions designated by the Department of Commerce in its publications, to provide technical assistance to travel attractions concerning accommodation of disabled tourists, and to develop, print, and promote the publication ACCESS NORTH CAROLINA as provided in G.S. 168-2. Any funds allocated for these purposes that are neither spent nor obligated at the end of the fiscal year shall be transferred to the Department of Administration for removal of man-made barriers to disabled travelers at State-funded travel attractions. Guidelines for the removal of man-made barriers shall be developed in consultation with the Department of Health and Human Services. (1967, c. 413; 1971, c. 42; 1973, c. 507, s. 5; c. 1262, s. 86; 1975, c. 716, s. 5; 1977, c. 464, s. 3; c. 771, s. 4; 1979, c. 126, ss. 1, 2; 1981 (Reg. Sess., 1982), c. 1258, s. 6; 1983, c. 848; 1985, c. 766; 1987, c. 252; c. 738, s. 140; c. 830, ss. 113(a), 116(a)-(c); 1989, c. 751, s. 7(1); c. 774, s. 1; 1989 (Reg. Sess., 1990), c. 814, s. 31; 1991, c. 672, s. 3; c. 726, s. 23; 1991 (Reg. Sess., 1992), c. 959, s. 2; c. 1042, s. 2; c. 1044, ss. 33, 34; 1993, c. 321, s. 169.3(a); c. 543, s. 3; 1995, c. 163, s. 2; c. 324, s. 18.7(a); c. 433, ss. 2, 3; c. 507, s. 18.17(a); 1996, 2nd Ex. Sess., c. 18, s. 19.11(e); 1997-443, s. 11A.118(a); 1997-477, ss. 2, 3; 1997-484, ss. 4, 5; 1998-163, s. 1; 1999-277, ss. 2, 3; 1999-403, ss. 2, 3; 1999-450, ss. 2, 3; 2000-159, ss. 3, 4; 2001-414, s. 32; 2001-498, ss. 3(a), 3(b), 4(a), 4(b); 2002-134, ss. 5, 6; 2003-11, ss. 2, 3; 2003-68, ss. 2, 3; 2003-424, ss. 3, 4; 2004-124, s. 30.3A; 2004-131, ss. 3, 4; 2004-185, ss. 3, 4; 2004-200, ss. 2, 3; 2005-216, ss. 4, 5; 2005-276, s. 28.16; 2006-209, ss. 3, 4, 7; 2007-323, s. 27.20(b); 2007-345, s. 10.1; 2007-400, ss. 3, 4; 2007-483, ss. 4, 5, 8(a), (b); 2009-228, s. 1; 2010-31, ss. 11.4(i), (j), 28.11; 2010-132, s. 7; 2011-145, s. 28.30(b); 2011-392, ss. 4, 5, 5.1; 2012-79, s. 1.12(b); 2013-360, ss. 14.3(c), 34.22; 2013-376, ss. 3, 4, 9(c), (d); 2013-414, s. 57(b), (c).)

§ 20-79.8. Expiration of special registration plate authorization.

(a) Expiration. - A special registration plate authorized pursuant to G.S. 20-79.4 shall expire, as a matter of law, on July 1 of the second calendar year following the year in which the special plate was authorized if the number of required applications for the authorized special plate has not been received by the Division. The Division shall not accept applications for nor advertise any special registration plate that has expired pursuant to this section.

(b) Notification. - The Division shall notify the Revisor of Statutes in writing, not later than July 15 of each year, which special registration plate authorizations have expired as a matter of law pursuant to subsection (a) of this section. The Division shall publish a copy of the written notification sent to the Revisor of Statutes pursuant to this subsection on a Web site maintained by the Division or the Department of Transportation.

(c) Revisor of Statutes Responsibilities. - Upon notification of expiration of the authorization for any special registration plate by the Division pursuant to this section, the Revisor of Statutes shall verify that the authorization for each special registration plate listed has expired and shall notate such expiration in the applicable statutes. If an authorization for a special registration plate listed in G.S. 20-79.4 expires, the Revisor of Statutes shall revise the subdivision referring to the special registration plate to leave the name of the special registration plate authorized and the date the special registration plate's authorization expired. If an authorization for a special registration plate listed in G.S. 20-79.4 expires, the Revisor of Statutes shall also make corresponding changes to reflect the expiration of the special registration plate's authorization, if applicable, in G.S. 20-63(b), 20-79.7, and 20-81.12. (2011-392, s. 8.)

§§ 20-80 through 20-81.2: Repealed by Session Laws 1991, c. 672, s. 1, as amended by Session Laws 1991, c. 726, s. 23.

§ 20-81.3: Recodified as § 20-79.7 by Session Laws 1991, c. 672, s. 3, as amended by Session Laws 1991, c. 726, s. 23.

§§ 20-81.4 through 20-81.11: Repealed by Session Laws 1991, c. 672, s. 1, as amended by Session Laws 1991, c. 726, s. 23.

§ 20-81.12. Collegiate insignia plates and certain other special plates.

(a) Collegiate Insignia Plates. - The Division must receive 300 or more applications for a collegiate insignia license plate for a college or university before a collegiate license plate may be developed. The color, design, and material for the plate must be approved by both the Division and the alumni or alumnae association of the appropriate college or university. The Division must transfer quarterly the money in the Collegiate and Cultural Attraction Plate Account derived from the sale of in-State collegiate insignia plates to the Board of Governors of The University of North Carolina for in-State, public colleges and universities and to the respective board of trustees for in-State, private colleges and universities in proportion to the number of collegiate plates sold representing that institution for use for academic enhancement.

(b) Historical Attraction Plates. - The Division must receive 300 or more applications for an historical attraction plate representing a publicly owned or nonprofit historical attraction located in North Carolina and listed below before the plate may be developed. The Division must transfer quarterly the money in the Collegiate and Cultural Attraction Plate Account derived from the sale of historical attraction plates to the organizations named below in proportion to the number of historical attraction plates sold representing that organization:

(1) Historical Attraction Within Historic District. - The revenue derived from the special plate shall be transferred quarterly to the appropriate Historic Preservation Commission, or entity designated as the Historic Preservation Commission, and used to maintain property in the historic district in which the attraction is located. As used in this subdivision, the term "historic district" means a district created under G.S. 160A-400.4.

(2) Nonprofit Historical Attraction. - The revenue derived from the special plate shall be transferred quarterly to the nonprofit corporation that is responsible for maintaining the attraction for which the plate is issued and used to develop and operate the attraction.

(3) State Historic Site. - The revenue derived from the special plate shall be transferred quarterly to the Department of Cultural Resources and used to develop and operate the site for which the plate is issued. As used in this

subdivision, the term "State historic site" has the same meaning as in G.S. 121-2(11).

(b1)   Special Olympics Plates. - The Division must receive 300 or more applications for a special olympics plate before the plate may be developed. The Division must transfer quarterly the money in the Collegiate and Cultural Attraction Plate Account derived from the sale of special olympics plates to the North Carolina Special Olympics, Inc., to be used to train volunteers to assist in the statewide games and to help pay the costs of the statewide games.

(b2)   State Attraction Plates. - The Division must receive 300 or more applications for a State attraction plate before the plate may be developed. The Division must transfer quarterly the money in the Collegiate and Cultural Attraction Plate Account derived from the sale of State attraction plates to the organizations named below in proportion to the number of State attraction plates sold representing that organization:

(1)   Aurora Fossil Museum. - The revenue derived from the special plate shall be transferred quarterly to the Aurora Fossil Museum Foundation, Inc., to be used for educational programs, for enhancing collections, and for operating expenses of the Aurora Fossil Museum.

(2)   Blue Ridge Parkway Foundation. - The revenue derived from the special plate shall be transferred quarterly to Blue Ridge Parkway Foundation for use in promoting and preserving the Blue Ridge Parkway as a scenic attraction in North Carolina. A person may obtain from the Division a special registration plate under this subdivision for the registered owner of a motor vehicle or a motorcycle. The registration fees and the restrictions on the issuance of a specialized registration plate for a motorcycle are the same as for any motor vehicle. The Division must receive a minimum of 300 applications to develop a special registration plate for a motorcycle.

(3)   Friends of the Appalachian Trail. - The revenue derived from the special plate shall be transferred quarterly to The Appalachian Trail Conference to be used for educational materials, preservation programs, trail maintenance, trailway and viewshed acquisitions, trailway and viewshed easement acquisitions, capital improvements for the portions of the Appalachian Trail and connecting trails that are located in North Carolina, and related administrative and operating expenses.

(4) Friends of the Great Smoky Mountains National Park. - The revenue derived from the special plate shall be transferred quarterly to the Friends of the Great Smoky Mountains National Park, Inc., to be used for educational materials, preservation programs, capital improvements for the portion of the Great Smoky Mountains National Park that is located in North Carolina, and operating expenses of the Great Smoky Mountains National Park.

(5) The North Carolina Aquariums. - The revenue derived from the special plate shall be transferred quarterly to the North Carolina Aquarium Society, Inc., for its programs in support of the North Carolina Aquariums.

(6) The North Carolina Arboretum. - The revenue derived from the special plate shall be transferred quarterly to The North Carolina Arboretum Society and used to help the Society obtain grants for the North Carolina Arboretum and for capital improvements to the North Carolina Arboretum.

(7) The North Carolina Maritime Museum. - The revenue derived from the special plate shall be transferred quarterly to Friends of the Museum, North Carolina Maritime Museum, Inc., to be used for educational programs and conservation programs and for operating expenses of the North Carolina Maritime Museum.

(8) The North Carolina Museum of Natural Sciences. - The revenue derived from the special plate shall be transferred quarterly to the Friends of the North Carolina State Museum of Natural Sciences for its programs in support of the museum.

(9) North Carolina State Parks. - The revenue derived from the special plate shall be transferred quarterly to Friends of State Parks, Inc., for its educational, conservation, and other programs in support of the operations of the State Parks System established in Article 2C of Chapter 113 of the General Statutes.

(10) The North Carolina Transportation Museum. - The revenue derived from the special plate shall be transferred quarterly to the North Carolina Transportation Museum Foundation to be used for educational programs and conservation programs and for operating expenses of the North Carolina Transportation Museum.

(11) The North Carolina Zoological Society. - The revenue derived from the special plate shall be transferred quarterly to The North Carolina Zoological Society, Incorporated, to be used for educational programs and conservation

programs at the North Carolina Zoo at Asheboro and for operating expenses of the North Carolina Zoo at Asheboro.

(12)   "Old Baldy," Bald Head Island Lighthouse. - The revenue derived from the special plate shall be transferred quarterly to the Old Baldy Foundation, Inc., for its programs in support of the Bald Head Island Lighthouse.

(13)   U.S.S. North Carolina Battleship Commission. - The revenue derived from the special plate shall be transferred quarterly to the U.S.S. North Carolina Battleship Commission to be used for educational programs and preservation programs on the U.S.S. North Carolina (BB-55) and for operating expenses of the U.S.S. North Carolina Battleship Commission.

(b3)   Wildlife Resources Plates. - The Division must receive 300 or more applications for a wildlife resources plate with a picture representing a particular native wildlife species occurring in North Carolina before the plate may be developed. The Division must transfer quarterly the money in the Collegiate and Cultural Attraction Plate Account derived from the sale of wildlife resources plates to the Wildlife Conservation Account established by G.S. 143-247.2.

(b4)   Olympic Games. - The Division may not issue an Olympic Games special plate unless it receives 300 or more applications for the plate and the U.S. Olympic Committee licenses, without charge, the State to develop a plate bearing the Olympic Games symbol and name. The Division must transfer quarterly the money in the Collegiate and Cultural Attraction Plate Account derived from the sale of Olympic Games plates to North Carolina Amateur Sports, which will allocate the funds as follows:

(1)   Sixty-seven percent (67%) to the U.S. Olympic Committee to assist in training Olympic athletes.

(2)   Thirty-three percent (33%) to North Carolina Amateur Sports to assist with administration of the State Games of North Carolina.

(3)   Repealed by Session Laws 2013-376, s. 7, effective July 29, 2013.

(b5)   March of Dimes Plates. - The Division must receive 300 or more applications for a March of Dimes plate before the plate may be developed. The Division shall transfer quarterly the money in the Collegiate and Cultural Attraction Plate Account derived from the sale of March of Dimes plates to the Eastern Carolina Chapter of the March of Dimes Birth Defects Foundation. The

Eastern Carolina Chapter shall disperse the revenue proportionately among the Eastern Carolina Chapter, the Western Carolina Chapter, the Greater Triad Chapter, and the Greater Piedmont Chapter of the March of Dimes Birth Defects Foundation based upon the population of the area each Chapter represents. The money must be used for the prevention of birth defects through local community services and educational programs and through research and development.

(b6)   School Technology Plates. - The Division must receive 300 or more applications for a School Technology plate before the plate may be developed. The Division shall transfer quarterly the money in the Collegiate and Cultural Attraction Plate Account derived from the sale of School Technology plates to the State School Technology Fund, which is established under G.S. 115C-102.6D.

(b7)   Scenic Rivers Plates. - The Division must receive 300 or more applications for a Scenic Rivers plate before the plate may be developed. The Division shall transfer quarterly the money in the Collegiate and Cultural Attraction Plate Account derived from the sale of Scenic Rivers plates to the Clean Water Management Trust Fund established in G.S. 113A-253.

(b8)   Soil and Water Conservation Plates. - The Division must receive 300 or more applications for a soil and water conservation plate before the plate may be developed. The Division shall transfer quarterly the money in the Collegiate and Cultural Attraction Plate Account derived from the sale of the soil and water conservation plates to the Soil and Water Conservation Account established in G.S. 106-844.

(b9)   Kids First Plates. - The Division must receive 300 or more applications for a Kids First plate before the plate may be developed. The Division shall transfer quarterly the money in the Collegiate and Cultural Attraction Plate Account derived from the sale of Kids First plates to the North Carolina Children's Trust Fund established in G.S. 7B-1302.

(b10)   University Health Systems of Eastern Carolina. - The Division must receive 300 or more applications for a University Health Systems of Eastern Carolina plate before the plate may be developed. The Division shall transfer quarterly the money in the Collegiate and Cultural Attraction Plate Account derived from the sale of University Health Systems of Eastern Carolina plates to the Pitt Memorial Hospital Foundation, Inc., for use in the Children's Hospital of Eastern North Carolina.

(b11) Animal Lovers Plates. - The Division must receive 300 or more applications before an animal lovers plate may be developed. The Division shall transfer quarterly the money in the Collegiate and Cultural Attraction Plate Account derived from the sale of the animal lovers plate to the Spay/Neuter Account established in G.S. 19A-62.

(b12) Support Public Schools Plates. - The Division must receive 300 or more applications for a Support Public Schools plate before the plate may be developed. The Division shall transfer quarterly the money in the Collegiate and Cultural Attraction Plate Account derived from the sale of Support Public Schools plates to the Fund for the Reduction of Class Size in Public Schools created pursuant to G.S. 115C-472.10.

(b13) Ducks Unlimited Plates. - The Division must receive 300 or more applications for a Ducks Unlimited plate and receive any necessary licenses from Ducks Unlimited, Inc., for use of their logo before the plate may be developed. The Division shall transfer quarterly the money in the Collegiate and Cultural Attraction Plate Account derived from the sale of Ducks Unlimited plates to the Wildlife Resources Commission to be used to support the conservation programs of Ducks Unlimited, Inc., in this State.

(b14) Omega Psi Phi Fraternity Plates. - The Division must receive 300 or more applications for an Omega Psi Phi Fraternity plate and receive any necessary licenses, without charge, from Omega Psi Phi Fraternity, Incorporated, before the plate may be developed. The Division must transfer quarterly the money in the Collegiate and Cultural Attraction Plate Account derived from the sale of Omega Psi Phi Fraternity plates to the Carolina Uplift Foundation, Inc., for youth activity and scholarship programs.

(b15) Litter Prevention Plates. - The Division must receive 300 or more applications for a Litter Prevention plate before the plate may be developed. The Division shall transfer quarterly the money in the Collegiate and Cultural Attraction Plate Account derived from the sale of the litter prevention plates to the Litter Prevention Account created pursuant to G.S. 136-125.1.

(b16) Goodness Grows Plates. - The Division must receive 300 or more applications for a Goodness Grows plate before the plate may be developed. The Division shall transfer quarterly the money in the Collegiate and Cultural Attraction Plate Account derived from the sale of Goodness Grows plates to the

North Carolina Agricultural Promotions, Inc., to be used to promote the sale of North Carolina agricultural products.

(b17)   Audubon North Carolina Plates. - The Division must receive 300 or more applications for an Audubon North Carolina plate before the plate may be developed. The Division must transfer quarterly the money in the Collegiate and Cultural Attraction Plate Account derived from the sale of Audubon North Carolina plates to the National Audubon Society, Inc., a nonprofit corporation, for the account of the NC State Office to be used for bird and other wildlife conservation and educational activities in the State of North Carolina.

(b18)   Special Forces Association. - The Division must receive 300 or more applications for a Special Forces Association plate before the plate may be developed. The Division shall transfer quarterly the money in the Collegiate and Cultural Attraction Plate Account derived from the sale of Special Forces Association plates to the Airborne & Special Operations Museum in Fayetteville, North Carolina.

(b19)   The V Foundation for Cancer Research. - The Division must receive 300 or more applications for a V Foundation plate before the plate may be developed. The Division shall transfer quarterly the money in the Collegiate and Cultural Attraction Plate Account derived from the sale of V Foundation plates to The V Foundation for Cancer Research to fund cancer research grants.

(b20)   Save the Sea Turtles. - The Division must receive 300 or more applications for a Save the Sea Turtles plate before the plate may be developed. The Division must transfer quarterly the money in the Collegiate and Cultural Attraction Plate Account derived from the sale of Save the Sea Turtles plates to The Karen Beasley Sea Turtle Rescue and Rehabilitation Center.

(b21)   Harley Owners' Group. - The Division must receive 300 or more applications for a Harley Owners' Group plate before the plate may be developed. The Division shall transfer quarterly the money in the Collegiate and Cultural Attraction Plate Account derived from the sale of Harley Owners' Group plates to the State Board of Community Colleges to support the motorcycle safety instruction program established pursuant to G.S. 115D-72.

(b22)   Rocky Mountain Elk Foundation. - The Division must receive 300 or more applications for a Rocky Mountain Elk Foundation plate before the plate may be developed. The Division must transfer quarterly the money in the

Collegiate and Cultural Attraction Account derived from the sale of Rocky Mountain Elk Foundation plates to Rocky Mountain Elk Foundation, Inc.

(b23) NC Agribusiness. - The Division must receive 300 or more applications for a NC Agribusiness plate before the plate may be developed. The Division must transfer quarterly the money in the Collegiate and Cultural Attraction Plate Account derived from the sale of NC Agribusiness plates to the North Carolina Agribusiness Council, Inc., to be used to promote awareness of the importance of agribusiness in North Carolina.

(b24) Nurses. - The Division must receive 300 or more applications for a Nurses plate before the plate may be developed. The Division shall transfer quarterly the money in the Collegiate and Cultural Attraction Plate Account derived from the sale of Nurses plates to the NC Foundation for Nursing for nursing scholarships for citizens of North Carolina to be awarded annually.

(b25) NC Coastal Federation. - The Division must receive 300 or more applications for a NC Coastal Federation plate before the plate may be developed. The Division shall transfer quarterly the money in the Collegiate and Cultural Attraction Plate Account derived from the sale of NC Coastal Federation plates to the North Carolina Coastal Federation, Inc.

(b26) Be Active NC. - The Division must receive 300 or more applications for the Be Active NC plate before the plate may be developed. The Division shall transfer quarterly the money in the Collegiate and Cultural Attraction Plate Account derived from the sale of the Be Active NC plates to Be Active North Carolina, Inc., to be used to promote physical activity in North Carolina communities.

(b27) Buffalo Soldiers. - The Division must receive 300 or more applications for the Buffalo Soldiers plate before the plate may be developed. The Division shall transfer quarterly the money in the Collegiate and Cultural Attraction Plate Account derived from the sale of the Buffalo Soldiers plates to the 9th & 10th (Horse) Cavalry Association of the Buffalo Soldiers Greater North Carolina Chapter (BSGNCC) for its public outreach programs.

(b28) Crystal Coast. - The Division must receive 300 or more applications for the Crystal Coast plate before the plate may be developed. The Division shall transfer quarterly the money in the Collegiate and Cultural Attraction Plate Account derived from the sale of Crystal Coast plates to the Crystal Coast

Artificial Reef Association to be used to promote scuba diving off the Crystal Coast.

(b29) Surveyor Plate. - The Division must receive 300 or more applications for a Surveyor plate before the plate may be developed. The Division shall transfer quarterly the money in the Collegiate and Cultural Attraction Plate Account derived from the sale of Surveyor plates to The North Carolina Society of Surveyors Education Foundation, Inc., for public educational programs.

(b30) Zeta Phi Beta Sorority. - The Division must receive 300 or more applications for a Zeta Phi Beta Sorority plate before the plate may be developed. The Division shall transfer quarterly the money in the Collegiate and Cultural Attraction Plate Account derived from the sale of Zeta Phi Beta Sorority plates to the Zeta Phi Beta Sorority Education Foundation, through the Raleigh office, for the benefit of undergraduate scholarships in this State.

(b31) In God We Trust. - The Division must receive 300 or more applications for the In God We Trust plate before the plate may be developed. The Division shall transfer quarterly the money in the Collegiate and Cultural Attraction Plate Account derived from the sale of the In God We Trust plates to the Department of Public Safety to be deposited into The N.C. National Guard Soldiers and Airmen Assistance Fund of The Minuteman Partnership to help provide assistance to the families of North Carolina National Guardsmen who have been activated and deployed in federal service.

(b32) North Carolina 4-H Development Fund. - The Division must receive 300 or more applications for a North Carolina 4-H Development Fund plate before the plate may be developed. The Division shall transfer quarterly the money in the Collegiate and Cultural Attraction Plate Account derived from the sale of North Carolina 4-H Development Fund plates to The North Carolina 4-H Development Fund, to be used to support county and State 4-H programs and to provide funding for repairs and renovations at North Carolina 4-H camps and conference centers.

(b33) High School Insignia Plate. - The Division must receive 300 or more applications for a high school insignia plate for a public high school in North Carolina before a high school insignia plate may be issued for that school. The Division must transfer quarterly the money in the Collegiate and Cultural Attraction Plate Account derived from the sale of high school insignia plates to the Department of Public Instruction to be deposited into the State Aid to Local School Administrative Units account. The Division must also send the

Department of Public Instruction information as to the number of plates sold representing a particular high school. The Department of Public Instruction must annually transfer the money in the State Aid to Local School Administrative Units account that is derived from the sale of the high school insignia plates to the high schools which have a high school insignia plate in proportion to the number of high school insignia plates sold representing that school. The high school must use the money for academic enhancement.

(b34)   HOMES4NC. - The Division must receive 300 or more applications for the HOMES4NC plate before the plate may be developed. The Division shall transfer quarterly the money in the Collegiate and Cultural Attraction Plate Account derived from the sale of the HOMES4NC plates to the NCAR Housing Opportunity Foundation to promote safe, decent, and affordable housing for all in North Carolina.

(b35)   First in Forestry. - The Division must receive 300 or more applications for the First in Forestry plate before the plate may be developed. The Division shall transfer quarterly one-half of the money in the Collegiate and Cultural Attraction Plate Account derived from the sale of the First in Forestry plates to the North Carolina Forest Service of the Department of Agriculture and Consumer Services for a State forests and forestry education program and shall transfer quarterly one-half of the money in the Collegiate and Cultural Attraction Plate Account derived from the sale of the First in Forestry plates to the Forest Education and Conservation Foundation for their programs.

(b36)   El Pueblo. - The Division must receive 300 or more applications for the El Pueblo plate before the plate may be developed. The Division shall transfer quarterly the money in the Collegiate and Cultural Plate Account derived from the sale of the El Pueblo plates to El Pueblo, Inc., for its Scholarship Fund which provides scholarships for Latino students entering any community college, college, or university in North Carolina.

(b37)   Daughters of the American Revolution. - The Division must receive 300 or more applications for a Daughters of the American Revolution plate before the plate may be developed. The Division shall transfer quarterly the money in the Collegiate and Cultural Attraction Plate Account derived from the sale of Daughters of the American Revolution plates to the North Carolina Daughters of the American Revolution License Plate Trust Fund located in Wilmington, North Carolina, to be used to carry out the objectives of the National Society Daughters of the American Revolution including the protection of historical spots and the erection of monuments, the encouragement and support of historical research and educational endeavors, the preservation of historical documents and relics, and the promotion of all patriotic celebrations.

(b38) Stock Car Racing Theme. - The Division may issue any plate in this series without a minimum number of applications if the person providing the State with the license to use the words, logos, trademarks, or designs associated with the plate produces the plate for the State without a minimum order quantity.

The cost of the Stock Car Racing Theme plate shall include all costs to produce blank plates for issuance by the Division. Notwithstanding G.S. 66-58(b), the Division or the Division of Adult Correction of the Department of Public Safety may contract for the production of the blank plates in this series to be issued by the Division, provided the plates meet or exceed the State's specifications including durability and retroreflectivity, and provided the plates are manufactured using high-quality embossable aluminum. The cost of the blank plates to the State shall be substantially equivalent to the price paid to the Division of Adult Correction of the Department of Public Safety for license tags, as provided in G.S. 66-58(b)(15).

The Division shall transfer quarterly the money in the Collegiate and Cultural Attraction Plate Account derived from the sale of Stock Car Racing Theme plates to the North Carolina Motorsports Foundation, Inc.; except that the Division shall transfer quarterly the money in the Collegiate and Cultural Attraction Plate Account derived from the sale of Charlotte Motor Speedway plates to Speedway Children's Charities.

(b39) Alpha Phi Alpha Fraternity. - The Division must receive 300 or more applications for the Alpha Phi Alpha Fraternity plate before the plate may be developed. The Division shall transfer quarterly the money in the Collegiate and Cultural Attraction Plate Account derived from the sale of the Alpha Phi Alpha Fraternity plates to the Association of North Carolina Alphamen (ANCA) Educational Foundation for scholarships for the benefit of African-American males in ANCA attending accredited North Carolina colleges and universities.

(b40) ARC of North Carolina. - The Division must receive 300 or more applications for the Arc of North Carolina plate before the plate may be developed. The Division shall transfer quarterly the money in the Collegiate and Cultural Attraction Plate Account derived from the sale of the Arc of North Carolina plates to The Arc of North Carolina, Inc., for its programs in support of retarded citizens in North Carolina.

(b41) Autism Society of North Carolina. - The Division must receive 300 or more applications for an Autism Society of North Carolina plate before the plate may be developed. The Division must transfer quarterly the money in the Collegiate and Cultural Attraction Plate Account derived from the sale of Autism Society of North Carolina plates to the Autism Society of North Carolina, Inc., for support services to individuals with autism and their families.

(b42) Buddy Pelletier Surfing Foundation. - The Division must receive 300 or more applications for the Buddy Pelletier Surfing Foundation plate before the plate may be developed. The Division shall transfer quarterly the money in the Collegiate and Cultural Attraction Plate Account derived from the sale of the Buddy Pelletier Surfing Foundation to the Foundation to fund the Foundation's scholastic and humanitarian aid programs.

(b43) Coastal Conservation Association. - The Division must receive 300 or more applications for the Coastal Conservation Association plate before the plate may be developed. The Division shall transfer quarterly the money in the Collegiate and Cultural Attraction Plate Account derived from the sale of the Coastal Conservation Association plates to the Division of Marine Fisheries for its conservation programs.

(b44) Guilford Battleground Company. - The Division must receive 300 or more applications for a Guilford Battleground Company plate before the plate may be developed. The Division shall transfer quarterly the money in the Collegiate and Cultural Attraction Plate Account derived from the sale of Guilford Battleground Company plates to the Guilford Battleground Company for its programs.

(b45) National Multiple Sclerosis Society. - The Division must receive 300 or more applications for the National Multiple Sclerosis Society plate before the plate may be developed. The Division shall transfer quarterly the money in the Collegiate and Cultural Attraction Plate Account derived from the sale of the National Multiple Sclerosis Society plates to the National Multiple Sclerosis Society for its public awareness programs.

(b46) National Wild Turkey Federation. - The Division must receive 300 or more applications for the National Wild Turkey Federation plate before the plate may be developed. The Division shall transfer quarterly the money in the Collegiate and Cultural Attraction Plate Account derived from the sale of the

National Wild Turkey Federation plates to the North Carolina State Chapter of the National Wild Turkey Federation for special projects to benefit the public.

(b47) SCUBA. - The Division must receive 300 or more applications for the SCUBA plate before the plate may be developed. The Division shall transfer quarterly the money in the Collegiate and Cultural Plate Account derived for the sale of the SCUBA plates to the Division of Marine Fisheries for the purpose of developing the State's artificial reefs.

(b48) Share the Road. - The Division must receive 300 or more applications for the Share the Road plate before the plate may be developed. The Division shall transfer quarterly the money in the Collegiate and Cultural Attraction Plate Account derived from the sale of the Share the Road plates to the Department of Transportation, Division of Bicycle and Pedestrian Transportation, for its programs.

(b49) North Carolina Wildlife Habitat Foundation. - The Division must receive 300 or more applications for the North Carolina Wildlife Habitat Foundation plate before the plate may be developed. The Division shall transfer quarterly the money in the Collegiate and Cultural Attraction Plate Account derived from the sale of the North Carolina Wildlife Habitat Foundation plates to the North Carolina Wildlife Habitat Foundation for its programs.

(b50) Shag Dancing. - The Division must receive 300 or more applications for the Shag Dancing plate before the plate may be developed. The Division shall transfer quarterly the money in the Collegiate and Cultural Attraction Plate Account derived from the sale of Shag Dancing plates to the Hall of Fame Foundation.

(b51) North Carolina Libraries. - The Division must receive 300 or more applications for the North Carolina Libraries plate before the plate may be developed. The Division shall transfer quarterly the money in the Collegiate and Cultural Attraction Plate Account derived from the sale of the North Carolina Libraries plates to the North Carolina Library Association, Inc., for the Association's public programs.

(b52) NC Trout Unlimited. - The Division must receive 300 or more applications for an NC Trout Unlimited plate before the plate may be developed. The Division shall transfer quarterly the money in the Collegiate and Cultural Attraction Plate Account derived from the sale of NC Trout Unlimited plates to North Carolina Trout Unlimited for its programs.

(b53) Repealed by Session Laws 2007-483, s. 8(c), effective October 1, 2007.

(b54) Carolina's Aviation Museum. - The Division must receive 300 or more applications for a Carolina's Aviation Museum plate before the plate may be developed. The Division must transfer quarterly the money in the Collegiate and Cultural Attraction Plate Account derived from the sale of Carolina's Aviation Museum plates to the Carolina's Historic Aviation Commission, a domestic nonprofit corporation, to be used to help continue operation of the Museum.

(b55) Greyhound Friends of North Carolina. - The Division must receive 300 or more applications for a Greyhound Friends of North Carolina plate before the plate may be developed. The Division must transfer quarterly the money in the Collegiate and Cultural Attraction Plate Account derived from the sale of the Greyhound Friends of North Carolina plates to the Greyhound Friends of North Carolina, Inc., to be used for the care and upkeep of retired greyhound racers that are awaiting adoption.

(b56) Leukemia & Lymphoma Society. - The Division must receive 300 or more applications for a Leukemia & Lymphoma Society plate before the plate may be developed. The Division must transfer quarterly the money in the Collegiate and Cultural Attraction Plate Account derived from the sale of Leukemia & Lymphoma Society plates to the Eastern Chapter of the North Carolina Leukemia & Lymphoma Society, a State-chartered chapter of the national nonprofit organization known as The Leukemia & Lymphoma Society, Inc., a duly registered New York nonprofit corporation. These funds may be divided between the Eastern and Western chapters of the North Carolina Leukemia & Lymphoma Society which shall each use the funds for blood cancer research, awareness, and education.

(b57) Lung Cancer Research. - The Division must receive 300 or more applications for the Lung Cancer Research plate before the plate may be developed. The Division must transfer quarterly the money in the Collegiate and Cultural Attraction Plate Account derived from the sale of Lung Cancer Research plates to the American Lung Association of North Carolina, Inc., to be used for eliminating lung disease and fostering healthy breathing for all people through prevention, outreach, education, research, and advocacy.

(b58) NC Children's Promise. - The Division must receive 300 or more applications for a N.C. Children's Promise plate before the plate may be developed. The Division must transfer quarterly the money in the Collegiate and

Cultural Attraction Plate Account derived from the sale of NC Children's Promise plates to The Medical Foundation of North Carolina, Incorporated, to be used to support the North Carolina Children's Promise.

(b59) Prince Hall Mason. - The Division must receive 300 or more applications for a Prince Hall Mason plate before the plate may be developed. The Division must transfer quarterly the money in the Collegiate and Cultural Attraction Plate Account derived from the sale of Prince Hall Mason plates to The Most Worshipful Prince Hall Grand Lodge of Free and Accepted Masons of North Carolina and Jurisdiction, Inc., to be used for scholarships, family assistance, and other charitable causes.

(b60) Support Our Troops. - The Division must receive 300 or more applications for a Support Our Troops plate before the plate may be developed. The Division shall transfer quarterly the money in the Collegiate and Cultural Attraction Plate Account derived from the sale of Support Our Troops plates to NC Support Our Troops, Inc., to be used to provide support and assistance to the troops and their families.

(b61) US Equine Rescue League. - The Division must receive 300 or more applications for the US Equine Rescue League plate before the plate may be developed. The Division must transfer quarterly the money in the Collegiate and Cultural Attraction Plate Account derived from the sale of US Equine Rescue League plates to the United States Equine Rescue League, Inc., to be used for the care and upkeep of rescued equines.

(b62) Back Country Horsemen of North Carolina. - The Division must receive 300 or more applications for a Back Country Horsemen of North Carolina plate before the plate may be developed. The Division must transfer quarterly the money in the Collegiate and Cultural Attraction Plate Account derived from the sale of Back Country Horsemen of North Carolina plates to the Back Country Horsemen of North Carolina to promote the development and maintenance of back country trails for trail riding.

(b63) Maggie Valley Trout Festival. - The Division must receive 300 or more applications for a Maggie Valley Trout Festival plate before the plate may be developed. The Division must transfer quarterly the money in the Collegiate and Cultural Attraction Plate Account derived from the sale of Maggie Valley Trout Festival plates to the Town of Maggie Valley to promote trout fishing in Maggie Valley.

(b64) Home Care and Hospice. - The Division must receive 300 or more applications for the Home Care and Hospice plate before the plate may be developed. The Division must transfer quarterly the money in the Collegiate and Cultural Attraction Plate Account derived from the sale of Home Care and Hospice plates to The Association for Home and Hospice Care of North Carolina for its educational programs in support of home care and hospice care in North Carolina.

(b65) Hospice Care. - The Division must receive 300 or more applications for the Hospice Care plate before the plate may be developed. The Division must transfer quarterly the money in the Collegiate and Cultural Attraction Plate Account derived from the sale of Hospice Care plates to The Carolinas Center for Hospice and End of Life Care for its programs in support of hospice care in North Carolina.

(b66) Breast Cancer Earlier Detection. - The Division must receive 300 or more applications for a Breast Cancer Earlier Detection plate before the plate may be developed. The Division must transfer quarterly the money in the Collegiate and Cultural Attraction Plate Account derived from the sale of Breast Cancer Earlier Detection plates to the Friends for An Earlier Breast Cancer Test, Inc., to support services to detect breast cancer earlier.

(b67) Juvenile Diabetes Research Foundation. - The Division must receive 300 or more applications for the Juvenile Diabetes Research Foundation plate before the plate may be developed. The Division must transfer quarterly the money in the Collegiate and Cultural Attraction Plate Account derived from the sale of Juvenile Diabetes Research Foundation plates to the Triangle Eastern North Carolina Chapter of the Juvenile Diabetes Research Foundation International, Inc., to provide funding for research to cure diabetes. The Foundation must distribute the amount it receives to all Juvenile Diabetes Research Foundation, Inc., chapters located in the State in equal shares.

(b68) AIDS Awareness. - The Division must receive 300 or more applications for the AIDS Awareness plate before the plate may be developed. The Division must transfer quarterly the money in the Collegiate and Cultural Attraction Plate Account derived from the sale of AIDS Awareness plates to The Alliance of AIDS Services-Carolina for its programs in support of AIDS awareness in North Carolina.

(b69) ALS Research. - The Division must receive 300 or more applications for the ALS Research plate before the plate may be developed. The Division must transfer quarterly the money in the Collegiate and Cultural Attraction Plate Account derived from the sale of ALS Research plates to the ALS Association, Jim "Catfish" Hunter Chapter, to help provide funding for research to cure amyotrophic lateral sclerosis and provide support to families who have a loved one suffering from the disease.

(b70) Brain Injury Awareness. - The Division must receive 300 or more applications for the Brain Injury Awareness plate before the plate may be developed. The Division must transfer quarterly the money in the Collegiate and Cultural Attraction Plate Account derived from the sale of Brain Injury Awareness plates to the Brain Injury Association of North Carolina, Inc., for support services to individuals with traumatic brain injuries.

(b71) National Kidney Foundation. - The Division must receive 300 or more applications for a National Kidney Foundation plate before the plate may be developed. The Division must transfer quarterly the money in the Collegiate and Cultural Attraction Plate Account derived from the sale of National Kidney Foundation plates to the National Kidney Foundation of North Carolina, Inc., to support the Foundation's services for the detection, prevention, and treatment of diseases of the kidney and urinary tract.

(b72) NC Tennis Foundation. - The Division must receive 300 or more applications for the NC Tennis Foundation plate before the plate may be developed. The Division must transfer quarterly the money in the Collegiate and Cultural Attraction Plate Account derived from the sale of NC Tennis Foundation plates to the North Carolina Tennis Foundation, Inc., to provide funding for development and growth of tennis as a sport in North Carolina.

(b73) American Red Cross. - The Division must receive 300 or more applications for an "American Red Cross" plate before the plate may be developed. The Division must transfer quarterly the money in the Collegiate and Cultural Attraction Plate Account derived from the sale of "American Red Cross" plates to the Triangle Area Chapter of the American Red Cross to be used to fund disaster relief, health and safety services, blood services, services to military families, capital improvements on facilities located within the State, and related administrative and operating costs.

(b74) ARTS NC. - The Division must receive 300 or more applications for the ARTS NC plate before the plate may be developed. The Division must transfer quarterly the money in the Collegiate and Cultural Attraction Plate Account derived from the sale of ARTS NC plates to ARTS North Carolina, Inc., to provide funding to promote the arts in North Carolina.

(b75) Arthritis Foundation. - The Division must receive 300 or more applications for an Arthritis Foundation plate before the plate may be developed. The Division shall transfer quarterly the money in the Collegiate and Cultural Attraction Plate Account derived from the sale of Arthritis Foundation plates to The Arthritis Foundation, Inc., to fund arthritis research grants.

(b76) Battle of Kings Mountain. - The Division must receive 300 or more applications for the "Battle of Kings Mountain" plate before the plate may be developed. The Division shall transfer quarterly the money in the Collegiate and Cultural Attraction Plate Account derived from the sale of "Battle of Kings Mountain" plates by transferring fifty percent (50%) to the Kings Mountain Tourism Development Authority and fifty percent (50%) to Kings Mountain Gateway Trails, Inc., to be used to develop tourism to the area and provide safe and adequate trails for visitors to the park.

(b77) Battleship North Carolina. - The Division must receive 300 or more applications for the "Battleship North Carolina" plate before the plate may be developed. The Division must transfer quarterly the money in the Collegiate and Cultural Attraction Plate Account derived from the sale of "Battleship North Carolina" plates to the U.S.S. North Carolina Battleship Commission to provide funding for information and education about the role of the Battleship U.S.S. North Carolina in history and for administrative and operating costs of the U.S.S. North Carolina Battleship Commission.

(b78) Boy Scouts of America. - The Division must receive 300 or more applications for the "Boy Scouts of America" plate before the plate may be developed. The Division shall transfer quarterly the money in the Collegiate and Cultural Attraction Plate Account derived from the sale of "Boy Scouts of America" plates to the Old Hickory Council of the Boy Scouts of America, where the proceeds will be divided equally among the Boy Scouts of America Councils in this State to be used for educational programs, preservation programs, capital improvements on facilities located in this State, and related administrative and operating expenses.

(b79) Brenner Children's Hospital. - The Division must receive 300 or more applications for the "Brenner Children's Hospital" plate before the plate may be developed. The Division shall transfer quarterly the money in the Collegiate and Cultural Attraction Plate Account derived from the sale of "Brenner Children's

Hospital" plates to the NCBH Special Purpose-Pediatric Unit Fund to provide funding for Brenner Children's Hospital.

(b80) Carolina Raptor Center. - The Division must receive 300 or more applications for a "Carolina Raptor Center" plate before the plate may be developed. The Division must transfer quarterly the money in the Collegiate and Cultural Attraction Plate Account derived from the sale of "Carolina Raptor Center" plates to the Carolina Raptor Center to be used for educational materials, preservation programs, capital improvements for the Carolina Raptor Center, and operating expenses of the Carolina Raptor Center.

(b81) Carolina Regional Volleyball Association. - The Division must receive 300 or more applications for the "Carolina Regional Volleyball Association" plate before the plate may be developed. The Division must transfer quarterly the money in the Collegiate and Cultural Attraction Plate Account derived from the sale of the "Carolina Regional Volleyball Association" plates to the Carolina Regional Volleyball Association to promote and develop the sport of volleyball throughout North Carolina.

(b82) Carolinas Credit Union Foundation. - The Division must receive 300 or more applications for the "Carolinas Credit Union Foundation" plate before the plate may be developed. The Division shall transfer quarterly the money in the Collegiate and Cultural Attraction Plate Account derived from the sale of "Carolinas Credit Union Foundation" plates to the Carolinas Credit Union Foundation, Inc., for youth-focused programs.

(b83) Carolinas Golf Association. - The Division must receive 300 or more applications for the "Carolinas Golf Association" plate before the plate may be developed. The Division shall transfer quarterly the money in the Collegiate and Cultural Attraction Plate Account derived from the sale of "Carolinas Golf Association" plates to the Carolinas Golf Association to be used to promote amateur golf in North Carolina.

(b84) Choose Life. - The Division must receive 300 or more applications for a "Choose Life" plate before the plate may be developed. The Division shall transfer quarterly the money in the Collegiate and Cultural Attraction Plate Account derived from the sale of "Choose Life" plates to the Carolina Pregnancy Care Fellowship, which shall distribute the money annually to nongovernmental, not-for-profit agencies that provide pregnancy services that are limited to counseling and/or meeting the physical needs of pregnant women. Funds received pursuant to this section shall not be distributed to any agency, organization, business, or other entity that provides, promotes, counsels, or refers for abortion and shall not be distributed to any entity that charges women for services received.

(b85) Coastal Land Trust. - The Division must receive 300 or more applications for the "Coastal Land Trust" plate before the plate may be developed. The Division shall transfer quarterly the money in the Collegiate and Cultural Attraction Plate Account derived from the sale of the "Coastal Land Trust" plates to the North Carolina Coastal Land Trust to be used to acquire open space and natural areas, to ensure conservation education, to promote good land stewardship, to set aside lands for conservation, and for other administrative and operating costs.

(b86) Concerned Bikers Association/ABATE of North Carolina. - The Division must receive 300 or more applications for the "Concerned Bikers Association/ABATE of North Carolina" plate before the plate may be developed. The Division shall transfer quarterly the money in the Collegiate and Cultural Attraction Plate Account derived from the sale of the "Concerned Bikers Association/ABATE of North Carolina" plates to the Department of Public Instruction to support the driver training and safety education program established pursuant to G.S. 115C-215 and to support motorcycle safety and awareness training as part of the driver training program.

(b87) Daniel Stowe Botanical Garden. - The Division must receive 300 or more applications for the "Daniel Stowe Botanical Garden" plate before the plate may be developed. The Division must transfer quarterly the money in the Collegiate and Cultural Attraction Plate Account derived from the sale of "Daniel Stowe Botanical Garden" plates to the Daniel Stowe Botanical Garden Foundation, Inc., to provide funding for the Daniel Stowe Botanical Garden outreach program.

(b88) Donate Life. - The Division must receive 300 or more applications for the "Donate Life" plate before the plate may be developed. The Division must transfer quarterly the money in the Collegiate and Cultural Attraction Plate Account derived from the sale of "Donate Life" plates to Donate Life North Carolina to be divided equally among Donate Life North Carolina and each of the transplant centers in North Carolina to include Bowman Gray Medical Center, Carolinas Medical Center, Duke University, East Carolina University, and the University of North Carolina at Chapel Hill. The transplant centers shall use all of the proceeds received from this plate to provide funding for expenses incurred by needy families, recipients, and expenses related to organ donation.

(b89)   Farmland Preservation. - The Division must receive 300 or more applications for the "Farmland Preservation" plate before the plate may be developed. The Division must transfer quarterly the money in the Collegiate and Cultural Attraction Plate Account derived from the sale of "Farmland Preservation" plates to the North Carolina Agricultural Development and Farmland Preservation Trust Fund established pursuant to G.S. 106-744.

(b90)   First in Turf. - The Division must receive 300 or more applications for the "First in Turf" plate before the plate may be developed. The Division shall transfer quarterly the money in the Collegiate and Cultural Attraction Plate Account derived from the sale of "First in Turf" plates to the Center for Environmental Turfgrass Research at North Carolina State University for its programs.

(b91)   Girl Scouts. - The Division must receive 300 or more applications for the "Girl Scouts" plate before the plate may be developed. The Division shall transfer quarterly the money in the Collegiate and Cultural Attraction Plate Account derived from the sale of "Girl Scouts" plates to the Girl Scouts North Carolina Coastal Pines, where the proceeds will be divided equally among the officially chartered Girl Scout Councils in this State to be used for educational programs, preservation programs, capital improvements on facilities located in this State, and related administrative and operating expenses.

(b92)   Greensboro Symphony Guild. - The Division must receive 300 or more applications for the Greensboro Symphony Guild plate before the plate may be developed. The Division shall transfer quarterly the money in the Collegiate and Cultural Attraction Plate Account derived from the sale of Greensboro Symphony Guild plates to the Greensboro Symphony Guild, Inc., to be used to support educational programs offered by the Greensboro Symphony Orchestra.

(b93)   Home of American Golf. - The Division must receive 300 or more applications for the "Home of American Golf" plate before the plate may be developed. The Division must transfer quarterly the money in the Collegiate and Cultural Attraction Plate Account derived from the sale of "Home of American Golf" plates to the Given Memorial Library, Inc., to provide funding for the Given Memorial Library - The Tufts Archives.

(b94)   Jaycees. - The Division must receive 300 or more applications for the "Jaycees" plate before the plate may be developed. The Division shall transfer quarterly the money in the Collegiate and Cultural Attraction Plate Account derived from the sale of "Jaycees" plates to the North Carolina JCI Senate, Inc., to be used to support and underwrite Jaycee activities in North Carolina.

(b95) Kappa Alpha Order. - The Division shall transfer quarterly the money in the Collegiate and Cultural Attraction Plate Account derived from the sale of Kappa Alpha Order plates to the Kappa Alpha Order Educational Foundation to provide educational and leadership opportunities for students attending North Carolina colleges and universities.

(b96) Morgan Horse Club. - The Division must receive 300 or more applications for a Morgan Horse Club plate before the plate may be developed. The Division must transfer quarterly the money in the Collegiate and Cultural Attraction Plate Account derived from the sale of Morgan Horse Club plates to the Morgan Horse Club to support the mission of the Virginia-Carolinas Morgan Horse Club, Inc., to promote Morgan horses in North Carolina.

(b97) Mountains-to-Sea Trail. - The Division must receive 300 or more applications for the "Mountains-to-Sea Trail" plate before the plate may be developed. The Division shall transfer quarterly the money in the Collegiate and Cultural Attraction Plate Account derived from the sale of "Mountains-to-Sea Trail" plates to the Friends of the Mountains-to-Sea Trail, Inc., to be used to fund trail projects and related administrative and operating expenses.

(b98) Native American. - The Division must receive 300 or more applications for the "Native American" plate before the plate may be developed. The Division shall transfer quarterly the money in the Collegiate and Cultural Attraction Plate Account derived from the sale of "Native American" plates to the Native American College Fund for scholarships to be awarded to Native American students from North Carolina.

(b99) NC Beekeepers. - The Division must receive 300 or more applications for the "NC Beekeepers" plate before the plate may be developed. The Division shall transfer quarterly the money in the Collegiate and Cultural Attraction Plate Account derived from the sale of "NC Beekeepers" plates to North Carolina State University for research on the importance of bees to agriculture and the State's agricultural economy.

(b100) NC Civil War. - The Division must receive 300 or more applications for the "NC Civil War" plate before the plate may be developed. The Division must transfer quarterly the money in the Collegiate and Cultural Attraction Plate Account derived from the sale of "NC Civil War" plates to the North Carolina

Department of Cultural Resources, Division of Archives and History, to provide funding to acquire, interpret, and preserve North Carolina's Civil War history.

(b101) NC Fisheries Association. - The Division must receive 300 or more applications for a "NC Fisheries Association" plate before the plate may be developed. The Division must transfer quarterly the money in the Collegiate and Cultural Attraction Plate Account derived from the sale of "NC Fisheries Association" plates to the NC Fisheries Association to facilitate the promotion of North Carolina families, heritage, and seafood through accessible data about the ever-changing commercial fishing industry.

(b102) NC Horse Council. - The Division must receive 300 or more applications for the "NC Horse Council" plate before the plate may be developed. The Division shall transfer quarterly the money in the Collegiate and Cultural Attraction Plate Account derived from the sale of "NC Horse Council" plates to the North Carolina Horse Council, Inc., to promote and enhance the equine industry in North Carolina.

(b103) NC Mining. - The Division must receive 300 or more applications for the "NC Mining" plate before the plate may be developed. The Division must transfer quarterly the money in the Collegiate and Cultural Attraction Plate Account derived from the sale of "NC Mining" plates to the North Carolina Gold Foundation, Inc., to provide funding for information and education about mining in North Carolina.

(b104) NC Veterinary Medical Association. - The Division must receive 300 or more applications for the "NC Veterinary Medical Association" plate before the plate may be developed. The Division shall transfer quarterly the money in the Collegiate and Cultural Attraction Plate Account derived from the sale of "NC Veterinary Medical Association" plates to the Friends of NCVMA Foundation, Inc., to be used to provide compassionate, quality health care for all animals, to protect the health of the public, to strengthen the human-animal bond, and to provide advanced continuing education for the public.

(b105) NC Victim Assistance Network. - The Division must receive 300 or more applications for a "NC Victim Assistance Network" plate before the plate may be developed. The Division must transfer quarterly the money in the Collegiate and Cultural Attraction Plate Account derived from the sale of "NC Victim Assistance Network" plates to the NC Victim Assistance Network to support the mission of the NC Victim Assistance Network to provide support and information for crime victims across the State and to advocate for their fair treatment.

(b106) NC Wildlife Federation. - The Division must receive 300 or more applications for the "NC Wildlife Federation" plate before the plate may be developed. The Division shall transfer quarterly the money in the Collegiate and Cultural Attraction Plate Account derived from the sale of "NC Wildlife Federation" plates to the North Carolina Wildlife Federation, Inc., to provide funding for a grassroots program to involve anglers, hunters, and wildlife enthusiasts in conservation issues affecting North Carolina.

(b107) NC Youth Soccer Association. - The Division must receive 300 or more applications for the "NC Youth Soccer Association" plate before the plate may be developed. The Division shall transfer quarterly the money in the Collegiate and Cultural Attraction Plate Account derived from the sale of "NC Youth Soccer Association" plates to the North Carolina Youth Soccer Association to be used to promote the sport of soccer in North Carolina.

(b108) North Carolina Emergency Management Association. - The Division must receive 300 or more applications for the "North Carolina Emergency Management Association" plate before the plate may be developed. The Division shall transfer quarterly the money in the Collegiate and Cultural Attraction Plate Account derived from the sale of "North Carolina Emergency Management Association" plates to the North Carolina Emergency Management Association to be used for training and education purposes.

(b109) North Carolina Green Industry Council. - The Division must receive 300 or more applications for the North Carolina Green Industry Council plate before the plate may be developed. The Division shall transfer quarterly the money in the Collegiate and Cultural Attraction Plate Account derived from the sale of North Carolina Green Industry Council plates to The North Carolina Green Industry Council, Inc. to be used to provide an umbrella of advocacy for green industry issues, the promotion of the green industry, and educational activities.

(b110) North Carolina Master Gardener. - The Division must receive 300 or more applications for the "North Carolina Master Gardener" plate before the plate may be developed. The Division shall transfer quarterly the money in the Collegiate and Cultural Attraction Plate Account derived from the sale of "North Carolina Master Gardener" plates to the Master Gardener's Endowment Fund maintained by the Agricultural Foundation of North Carolina State University to be used for educational programs by trained volunteers who work in partnership with their county Cooperative Extension offices to extend information in consumer horticulture.

(b111) Outer Banks Preservation Association. - The Division must receive 300 or more applications for an "Outer Banks Preservation Association" plate before the plate may be developed. The Division must transfer quarterly the money in the Collegiate and Cultural Attraction Plate Account derived from the sale of "Outer Banks Preservation Association" plates to the Outer Banks Preservation Association to facilitate the protection of the public's right to access beaches in North Carolina.

(b112) Pamlico-Tar River Foundation. - The Division must receive 300 or more applications for the "Pamlico-Tar River Foundation" plate before the plate may be developed. The Division shall transfer quarterly the money in the Collegiate and Cultural Attraction Plate Account derived from the sale of "Pamlico-Tar River Foundation" plates to the Pamlico-Tar River Foundation, Inc., to provide funding for the cleanup, preservation, and oversight of the Pamlico and Tar Rivers, and their watersheds and basins.

(b113) P.E.O. Sisterhood. - The Division must receive 300 or more applications for the "P.E.O. Sisterhood" plate before the plate may be developed. The Division shall transfer quarterly the money in the Collegiate and Cultural Attraction Plate Account derived from the sale of "P.E.O. Sisterhood" plates to P.E.O. International to be used for scholarships for young women.

(b114) Phi Beta Sigma Fraternity. - The Division must receive 300 or more applications for the "Phi Beta Sigma Fraternity" plate before the plate may be developed. The Division shall transfer quarterly the money in the Collegiate and Cultural Attraction Plate Account derived from the sale of "Phi Beta Sigma Fraternity" plates to the Phi Beta Sigma Fraternity, Inc., to provide funding for scholarships, education, and professional development, or similar programs. None of the proceeds from this special plate may be distributed to any board member as compensation or as an honorarium.

(b115) Piedmont Airlines. - The Division must receive 300 or more applications for a "Piedmont Airlines" plate before the plate may be developed. The Division must transfer quarterly the money in the Collegiate and Cultural Attraction Plate Account derived from the sale of "Piedmont Airlines" plates to Piedmont Silver Eagles Charitable Funds, Inc., to be used for scholarships and family assistance for Piedmont Airlines employees and their families, including surviving spouses and dependents, suffering economic hardship.

(b116) Retired Legislator. - The Division shall transfer quarterly the money in the Collegiate and Cultural Attraction Plate Account derived from the sale of Retired Legislator plates to the State Capitol Foundation, Inc., to be used to provide support for the mission and goals of the foundation.

(b117) Ronald McDonald House. - The Division must receive 300 or more applications for the "Ronald McDonald House" plate before the plate may be developed. The Division shall transfer quarterly the money in the Collegiate and Cultural Attraction Plate Account derived from the sale of "Ronald McDonald House" plates to Ronald McDonald House Charities of North Carolina, Inc., to be used for Ronald McDonald Houses located within North Carolina and related administrative and operating expenses.

(b118) S.T.A.R. - The Division must receive 300 or more applications for the "S.T.A.R." plate before the plate may be developed. The Division shall transfer quarterly the money in the Collegiate and Cultural Attraction Plate Account derived from the sale of "S.T.A.R." plates to Save the Animals Rescue, Inc., to provide funding to rescue distressed horses.

(b119) Support NC Education. - The Division must receive 300 or more applications for the "Support NC Education" plate before the plate may be developed. The Division shall transfer quarterly the money in the Collegiate and Cultural Attraction Plate Account derived from the sale of "Support NC Education" plates to the Board of Governors of The University of North Carolina to be used to provide scholarship funding at the 16 constituent universities of The University of North Carolina.

(b120) Support Soccer. - The Division must receive 300 or more applications for the "Support Soccer" plate before the plate may be developed. The Division shall transfer quarterly the money in the Collegiate and Cultural Attraction Plate Account derived from the sale of "Support Soccer" plates to the North Carolina Soccer Hall of Fame, Inc., to provide funding to promote the sport of soccer in North Carolina.

(b121) Sustainable Fisheries. - The Division must receive 300 or more applications for the "Sustainable Fisheries" plate before the plate may be developed. The Division shall transfer quarterly the money in the Collegiate and Cultural Attraction Plate Account derived from the sale of "Sustainable Fisheries" plates to the Center for Marine Sciences and Technology to support research, undergraduate and graduate student training, and education outreach in support of sustainable fisheries in North Carolina.

(b122) Toastmasters Club. - The Division must receive 300 or more applications for the "Toastmasters Club" plate before the plate may be developed. The Division shall transfer quarterly the money in the Collegiate and Cultural Attraction Plate Account derived from the sale of the "Toastmasters Club" plates to Toastmasters International to be used to help North Carolinians communicate more effectively, improve presentation skills, and develop leadership potential.

(b123) Topsail Island Shoreline Protection. - The Division must receive 300 or more applications for the "Topsail Island Shoreline Protection" plate before the plate may be developed. The Division shall transfer quarterly the money in the Collegiate and Cultural Attraction Plate Account derived from the sale of "Topsail Island Shoreline Protection" plates proportionately to the Town of North Topsail Beach, the Town of Surf City, and the Town of Topsail Beach to be used for support of the Topsail Island Shoreline Protection Committee and beach nourishment programs or projects for the three towns on Topsail Island.

(b124) Travel and Tourism. - The Division must receive 300 or more applications for the "Travel and Tourism" plate before the plate may be developed. The Division shall transfer quarterly the money in the Collegiate and Cultural Attraction Plate Account derived from the sale of "Travel and Tourism" plates to the Division of Tourism, Film, and Sports Development to be used for programs in support of travel and tourism in North Carolina.

(b125) USO of NC. - The Division must receive 300 or more applications for a USO of NC plate before the plate may be developed. The Division must transfer quarterly the money in the Collegiate and Cultural Attraction Plate Account derived from the sale of USO of NC plates to the United Services Organization of North Carolina to support the mission of the United Services Organization in North Carolina to lead the way to enriching the lives of America's military in North Carolina.

(b126) Charlotte Checkers. - The Division must receive 300 or more applications for a Charlotte Checkers plate before the plate may be developed. The Division shall transfer quarterly the money in the Collegiate and Cultural Attraction Plate Account derived from the sale of Charlotte Checkers plates to the Charlotte Checkers Charitable Foundation to support school programming, athletics, and various children's related nonprofit groups that promote and encourage education, physical fitness, and development of character.

(b127) First Tee. - The Division must receive 300 or more applications for a First Tee plate before the plate may be developed. The Division shall transfer quarterly the money in the Collegiate and Cultural Attraction Plate Account derived from the sale of First Tee plates to The Carol S. Petrea Youth Golf Foundation, Inc., to support its mission of helping to shape the lives of young people from all walks of life by reinforcing values like integrity, respect, and perseverance through the game of golf.

(b128) Fraternal Order of Police. - The Division shall transfer quarterly the money in the Collegiate and Cultural Attraction Plate Account derived from the sale of Fraternal Order of Police plates to The North Carolina Fraternal Order of Police to support the State Lodge.

(b129) I.B.P.O.E.W. - The Division must receive 300 or more applications for an I.B.P.O.E.W. plate before the plate may be developed. The Division shall transfer quarterly the money in the Collegiate and Cultural Attraction Plate Account derived from the sale of I.B.P.O.E.W. plates to the North Carolina Alliance of Boys and Girls Clubs to support its mission of promoting the social welfare of boys and girls as served by various Boys and Girls Clubs in North Carolina that are affiliated with the Boys and Girls Clubs of America.

(b130) Mission Foundation. - The Division must receive 300 or more applications for a Mission Foundation plate before the plate may be developed. The Division shall transfer quarterly the money in the Collegiate and Cultural Attraction Plate Account derived from the sale of Mission Foundation plates to Mission Healthcare Foundation, Inc., to support its mission of sustaining and expanding its provision of health services to Western North Carolina.

(b131) Morehead Planetarium. - The Division must receive 300 or more applications for a Morehead Planetarium plate before the plate may be developed. The Division shall transfer quarterly the money in the Collegiate and Cultural Attraction Plate Account derived from the sale of Morehead Planetarium plates to the Morehead Planetarium and Science Center to support its mission of informing and inspiring the public about the foundations and frontiers of scientific discovery.

(b132) Municipality Plate. - The Division must receive 300 or more applications for a municipality plate for a municipality before a municipality plate may be developed. The color and design for the plate must be approved by both the Division and the municipality. The Division shall transfer quarterly the money in the Collegiate and Cultural Attraction Plate Account derived from the sale of a municipality plate to the municipality represented by the plate.

(b133) National Law Enforcement Officers Memorial. - The Division must receive 300 or more applications for a National Law Enforcement Officers Memorial plate before the plate may be developed. The Division shall transfer quarterly the money in the Collegiate and Cultural Attraction Plate Account derived from the sale of "National Law Enforcement Officers Memorial" plates to the National Law Enforcement Officers Memorial Fund to support the National Law Enforcement Officers Memorial in Washington, DC.

(b134) Native Brook Trout. - The Division must receive 300 or more applications for the Native Brook Trout plate before the plate may be developed. The Division must transfer quarterly the money in the Collegiate and Cultural Attraction Plate Account derived from the sale of Native Brook Trout plates to the North Carolina Wildlife Resources Commission to be used to fund public access to and habitat protection of brook trout waters.

(b135) NC FIRST Robotics. - The Division must receive 300 or more applications for an NC FIRST Robotics plate before the plate may be developed. The Division shall transfer quarterly the money in the Collegiate and Cultural Attraction Plate Account derived from the sale of NC FIRST Robotics plates to NC FIRST Robotics to support its mission of inspiring youths to pursue further studies and careers in science and technology and helping students acquire the knowledge and skills needed to compete in the technologically driven global economy.

(b136) NCSC. - The Division must receive 300 or more applications for an NCSC plate before the plate may be developed. The Division shall transfer quarterly the money in the Collegiate and Cultural Attraction Plate Account derived from the sale of NCSC plates to the Congressional Sportsmen's Foundation to support its mission of protecting and advancing the rights of hunters, recreational anglers, shooters, and trappers in North Carolina.

(b137) North Carolina Bluegrass Association. - The Division must receive 300 or more applications for the North Carolina Bluegrass Association plate before the plate may be developed. The Division shall transfer quarterly the money in the Collegiate and Cultural Attraction Plate Account derived from the sale of North Carolina Bluegrass Association plates to the North Carolina Bluegrass Association.

(b138) North Carolina Cattlemen's Association. - The Division must receive 300 or more applications for the North Carolina Cattlemen's Association plate before the plate may be developed. The Division shall transfer quarterly the money in the Collegiate and Cultural Attraction Plate Account derived from the sale of North Carolina Cattlemen's Association plates to the North Carolina Cattlemen's Association, Inc.

(b139) Operation Coming Home. - The Division must receive 300 or more applications for an Operation Coming Home plate before the plate may be developed. The Division shall transfer quarterly the money in the Collegiate and Cultural Attraction Plate Account derived from the sale of Operation Coming Home plates to the Operation Coming Home Foundation, Inc., to support its mission of providing free, custom-built homes to injured combat veterans.

(b140) Order of the Long Leaf Pine. - The Division must receive 300 or more applications for the Order of the Long Leaf Pine plate before the plate may be developed. The Division shall transfer quarterly the money in the Collegiate and Cultural Attraction Plate Account derived from the sale of Order of the Long Leaf Pine plates to the General Fund.

(b141) Pancreatic Cancer Awareness. - The Division must receive 300 or more applications for a Pancreatic Cancer Awareness plate before the plate may be developed. The Division shall transfer quarterly the money in the Collegiate and Cultural Attraction Plate Account derived from the sale of Pancreatic Cancer Awareness plates to the Mark Daidone Cancer Research Endowment maintained by the Levine Cancer Institute at the Carolinas HealthCare System to provide funding for research in the management of the early stages of cancer.

(b142) Professional Engineer. - The Division must receive 300 or more applications for a Professional Engineer plate before the plate may be developed. The Division shall transfer quarterly the money in the Collegiate and Cultural Attraction Plate Account derived from the sale of Professional Engineer plates to The Professional Engineers of North Carolina for educational programs.

(b143) Red Drum. - The Division must receive 300 or more applications for the Red Drum plate before the plate may be developed. The Division must transfer quarterly the money in the Collegiate and Cultural Attraction Plate Account derived from the sale of Red Drum plates to the North Carolina Marine Fisheries Commission to be used to fund public access to and habitat protection of red drum waters.

(b144) RiverLink. - The Division must receive 300 or more applications for a "RiverLink" plate before the plate may be developed. The Division shall transfer quarterly the money in the Collegiate and Cultural Attraction Plate Account derived from the sale of "RiverLink" plates to RiverLink, Inc., to support the economic and environmental revitalization of the French Broad River and its tributaries as a place to work, live, and play.

(b145) Turtle Rescue Team. - The Division must receive 300 or more applications for a Turtle Rescue Team plate before the plate may be developed. The Division shall transfer quarterly the money in the Collegiate and Cultural Attraction Plate Account derived from the sale of Turtle Rescue Team plates to the North Carolina State University College of Veterinary Medicine Turtle Rescue Team to support its mission of providing medical, surgical, and husbandry services free of charge in the hope of releasing rehabilitated turtles back into the wild.

(b146) Volunteers in Law Enforcement. - The Division must receive 300 or more applications for a Volunteers in Law Enforcement plate before the plate may be developed. The Division shall transfer quarterly the money in the Collegiate and Cultural Attraction Plate Account derived from the sale of Volunteers in Law Enforcement plates to the International Association of Chiefs of Police Incorporated to support the Volunteers in Police Service (VIPS) Program and its mission of enhancing the capacity of State and local law enforcement agencies to utilize volunteers.

(b147) YMCA. - The Division must receive 300 or more applications for a YMCA plate before the plate may be developed. The Division shall transfer quarterly the money in the Collegiate and Cultural Attraction Plate Account derived from the sale of YMCA plates to the North Carolina State Alliance of YMCAs to support its mission of fighting childhood obesity, eliminating the achievement gap, and eradicating diabetes.

(b148) [North Carolina Paddle Festival.] - The Division must receive 300 or more applications for a North Carolina Paddle Festival plate before the plate may be developed. The Division shall transfer quarterly the money in the Collegiate and Cultural Attraction Plate Account derived from the sale of North Carolina Paddle Festival plates to the Friends of the Hammocks and Bear Island, Inc.

(c) General. - An application for a special license plate named in this section may be made at any time during the year. If the application is made to replace an existing current valid plate, the special plate must be issued with the appropriate decals attached. No refund shall be made to the applicant for any unused portion remaining on the original plate. The request for a special license plate named in this section may be combined with a request that the plate be a personalized license plate.

(c1) In accordance with G.S. 143C-1-2, the transfers mandated in this section are appropriations made by law.

(d) through (g) Repealed by Session Laws 1991 (Regular Session, 1992), c. 1042, s. 3. (1991, c. 758, s. 1; 1991 (Reg. Sess., 1992), c. 1007, s. 33; c. 1042, s. 3; 1993, c. 543, s. 5; 1995, c. 433, s. 4; 1997-427, s. 2; 1997-477, s. 4; 1997-484, s. 6; 1999-277, s. 4; 1999-403, s. 4; 1999-450, s. 4; 2000-159, ss. 5, 6; 2000-163, s. 3; 2001-498, ss. 6(a), 6(b); 2002-134, s. 7; 2003-11, s. 4; 2003-68, s. 4; 2003-424, ss. 5, 6; 2004-131, s. 5; 2004-185, s. 5; 2004-200, s. 4; 2005-216, ss. 6, 7; 2005-435, s. 40; 2006-209, ss. 5, 6, 7; 2007-323, s. 27.20(a); 2007-345, s. 10.1; 2007-400, ss. 5, 6; 2007-483, ss. 6(a), 7, 8(c); 2010-31, s. 11.4(m); 2010-95, s. 35; 2011-145, ss. 19.1(g), (h), 13.25(ll); 2011-392, ss. 6, 7; 2013-155, s. 2; 2013-360, s. 14.3B; 2013-376, ss. 5-8; 2013-414, s. 57(d).)

§ 20-82: Repealed by Session Laws 1995, c. 163, s. 3.

Part 6. Vehicles of Nonresidents of State; Permanent Plates; Highway Patrol.

§ 20-83. Registration by nonresidents.

(a) When a resident carrier of this State interchanges a properly licensed trailer or semitrailer with another carrier who is a resident of another state, and adequate records are on file in his office to verify such interchanges, the North Carolina licensed carrier may use the trailer licensed in such other state the same as if it is his own during the time the nonresident carrier is using the North Carolina licensed trailer.

(b) Motor vehicles duly registered in a state or territory which are not allowed exemptions by the Commissioner, as provided for in the preceding paragraph, desiring to make occasional trips into or through the State of North Carolina, or operate in this State for a period not exceeding 30 days, may be permitted the same use and privileges of the highways of this State as provided for similar vehicles regularly licensed in this State, by procuring from the Commissioner trip licenses upon forms and under rules and regulations to be adopted by the Commissioner, good for use for a period of 30 days upon the payment of a fee in compensation for said privilege equivalent to one tenth of the annual fee which would be chargeable against said vehicle if regularly licensed in this State: Provided that only one such permit allowed by this section shall be issued for the use of the same vehicle within the same registration year. Provided, however, that nothing in this provision shall prevent the extension of the privileges of the use of the roads of this State to vehicles of other states under the reciprocity provisions provided by law: Provided further, that nothing herein contained shall prevent the owners of vehicles from other states from licensing such vehicles in the State of North Carolina under the same terms and the same fees as like vehicles are licensed by owners resident in this State.

(c) Every nonresident, including any foreign corporation carrying on business within this State and owning and operating in such business any motor vehicle, trailer or semitrailer within this State, shall be required to register each such vehicle and pay the same fees therefor as is required with reference to like vehicles owned by residents of this State. (1937, c. 407, s. 47; 1941, cc. 99, 365; 1957, c. 681, s. 1; 1961, c. 642, s. 4; 1967, c. 1090.)

§ 20-84. Permanent registration plates; State Highway Patrol.

(a) General. - The Division may issue a permanent registration plate for a motor vehicle owned by one of the entities authorized to have a permanent registration plate in this section. To obtain a permanent registration plate, an authorized representative of the entity must provide proof of ownership, provide proof of financial responsibility as required by G.S. 20-309, and pay a fee of six dollars ($6.00). A permanent plate issued under this section may be transferred as provided in G.S. 20-78 to a replacement vehicle of the same classification. A permanent registration plate issued under this section must be a distinctive color and bear the word "permanent". In addition, a permanent registration plate issued under subdivision (b)(1) of this section must have distinctive color and design that is readily distinguishable from all other permanent registration plates issued under this section. Every eligible entity that receives a permanent registration plate under this section shall ensure that the permanent registration plate is registered under a single name. That single name shall be the full legal name of the eligible entity.

(b) Permanent Registration Plates. - The Division may issue permanent plates for the following motor vehicles:

(1) A motor vehicle owned by the State or one of its agencies.

(2) A motor vehicle owned by a county, city or town.

(3) A motor vehicle owned by a board of education.

(4) Repealed by Session Laws 2012-159, s. 1, effective July 1, 2012.

(5) A motor vehicle owned by the civil air patrol.

(6) A motor vehicle owned by an incorporated emergency rescue squad.

(7) through (9) Repealed by Session Laws 2012-159, s. 1, effective July 1, 2012.

(10) A motor vehicle owned by a rural fire department, agency, or association.

(11) Repealed by Session Laws 2012-159, s. 1, effective July 1, 2012.

(12) A motor vehicle owned by a local chapter of the American National Red Cross and used for emergency or disaster work.

(13) through (16) Repealed by Session Laws 2012-159, s. 1, effective July 1, 2012.

(17) A motor vehicle owned by a community college. A community college vehicle purchased with State equipment funds shall be issued a permanent registration plate with the same distinctive color and design as a permanent registration plate issued under subdivision (1) of this subsection.

(c) State Highway Patrol. - In lieu of all other registration requirements, the Commissioner shall each year assign to the State Highway Patrol, upon payment of six dollars ($6.00) per registration plate, a sufficient number of regular registration plates of the same letter prefix and in numerical sequence beginning with number 100 to meet the requirements of the State Highway Patrol for use on Division vehicles assigned to the State Highway Patrol. The commander of the Patrol shall, when such plates are assigned, issue to each member of the State Highway Patrol a registration plate for use upon the Division vehicle assigned to the member pursuant to G.S. 20-190 and assign a registration plate to each Division service vehicle operated by the Patrol. An index of such assignments of registration plates shall be kept at each State Highway Patrol radio station and a copy of it shall be furnished to the registration division of the Division. Information as to the individual assignments of the registration plates shall be made available to the public upon request to the same extent and in the same manner as regular registration information. The commander, when necessary, may reassign registration plates provided that the reassignment shall appear upon the index required under this subsection within 20 days after the reassignment.

(d) Revocation. - The Division may revoke all permanent registration plates issued to eligible entities for vehicles that are 90 days or more past due for a vehicle inspection, as required by G.S. 20-183.4C. This subsection does not limit or restrict the authority of the Division to revoke permanent registration plates pursuant to other applicable law. (1937, c. 407, s. 48; 1939, c. 275; 1949, c. 583, s. 1; 1951, c. 388; 1953, c. 1264; 1955, cc. 368, 382; 1967, c. 284; 1969, c. 800; 1971, c. 460, s. 1; 1975, c. 548; c. 716, s. 5; 1977, c. 370, s. 1; 1979, c. 801, s. 9; 1981 (Reg. Sess., 1982), c. 1159; 1983, c. 593, ss. 1, 2; 1987 (Reg. Sess., 1988), c. 885; 1991 (Reg. Sess., 1992), c. 1030, s. 11; 1997-443, s. 11A.118(a); 1999-220, s. 3; 2000-159, s. 7; 2012-159, s. 1.)

§ 20-84.1. Repealed by Session Laws 1999-220, s. 4.

Part 6A. Rental Vehicles.

§ 20-84.2. Definition; reciprocity; Commissioner's powers.

(a) The term rental vehicle when used herein shall mean and include any motor vehicle which is rented or leased to another by its owner for a period of not more than 30 days solely for the transportation of the lessee or the private hauling of the lessee's personal property.

(b) Rental vehicles owned or operated by any nonresident person engaged in the business of leasing such vehicles for use in intrastate or interstate commerce shall be extended full reciprocity and exempted from registration fees only in instances where:

(1) Such person has validly licensed all rental vehicles owned by him in the state wherein the owner actually resides; provided, that such state affords equal recognition, either in fact or in law to such vehicles licensed in the State of North Carolina and operating similarly within the owner's state of residence; and further provided, that such person is not engaged in this State in the business of leasing rental vehicles; or where

(2) Such person operates vehicles which are a part of a common fleet of vehicles which are easily identifiable as a part of such fleet and such person has validly licensed in the State of North Carolina a percentage of the total number of vehicles in each weight classification in such fleet which represents the percentage of total miles travelled in North Carolina by all vehicles in each weight classification of such fleet to total miles travelled in all jurisdictions in which such fleet is operated by all vehicles in each weight classification of such fleet.

(c) The Commissioner of Motor Vehicles requires such person to submit under oath such information as is deemed necessary for fairly administering this section. The Commissioner's determination, after hearing, as to the number of vehicles in each weight classification to be licensed in North Carolina shall be final.

Any person who licenses vehicles under subsection (b)(2) above shall keep and preserve for three years the mileage records on which the percentage of the total fleet is determined. Upon request these records shall be submitted or made available to the Commissioner of Motor Vehicles for audit or review, or the owner or operator shall pay reasonable costs of an audit by the duly appointed representative of the Commissioner at the place where the records are kept.

If the Commissioner determines that the person licensing vehicles under subsection (b)(2) above should have licensed more vehicles in North Carolina or that such person's records are insufficient for proper determination the Commissioner may deny that person the right or any further benefits under this subsection until the correct number of vehicles have been licensed, and all taxes determined by the Commissioner to be due have been paid.

(d) Upon payment by the owner of the prescribed fee, the Division shall issue registration certificates and plates for the percentage of vehicles determined by the Commissioner. Thereafter, all rental vehicles properly identified and licensed in any state, territory, province, country or the District of Columbia, and belonging to such owner, shall be permitted to operate in this State on an interstate or intrastate basis. (1959, c. 1066; 1971, c. 808; 1973, c. 1446, s. 23; 1975, c. 716, s. 5.)

Part 7. Title and Registration Fees.

§ 20-85. Schedule of fees.

(a) The following fees are imposed concerning a certificate of title, a registration card, or a registration plate for a motor vehicle. These fees are payable to the Division and are in addition to the tax imposed by Article 5A of Chapter 105 of the General Statutes.

(1)....... Each application for certificate of title.. $40.00

(2)....... Each application for duplicate or corrected certificate of title............ 15.00

(3)....... Each application of repossessor for certificate of title...................... 15.00

(4)....... Each transfer of registration... 15.00

(5)....... Each set of replacement registration plates...................................... 15.00

(6)....... Each application for duplicate registration card................................ 15.00

(7)....... Each application for recording supplementary lien............................
15.00

(8)....... Each application for removing a lien from a certificate of title...........
15.00

(9)....... Each application for certificate of title for a motor vehicle transferred to a manufacturer, as defined in G.S. 20-286, or a motor vehicle retailer for the purpose of resale.. 15.00

(10)..... Each application for a salvage certificate of title made by an insurer or by a used motor vehicle dealer pursuant to subdivision (b)(2) or subsection (e1) of G.S. 20-109.1.. 15.00

(11)..... Each set of replacement Stock Car Racing Theme plates issued under G.S. 20-79.4...
25.00.

(a1)   (Effective until December 31, 2017) One dollar ($1.00) of the fee imposed for any transaction assessed a fee under subdivision (a)(1), (a)(2), (a)(3), (a)(7), (a)(8), or (a)(9) of this section shall be credited to the North Carolina Highway Fund. The Division shall use the fees derived from transactions with commission contract agents for the payment of compensation to commission contract agents. An additional fifty cents (50¢) of the fee imposed for any transaction assessed a fee under subdivision (a)(1) of this section shall be credited to the Mercury Switch Removal Account in the Department of Environment and Natural Resources.

(a1)   (Effective December 31, 2017) One dollar ($1.00) of the fee imposed for any transaction assessed a fee under subdivision (a)(1), (a)(2), (a)(3), (a)(7), (a)(8), or (a)(9) of this section shall be credited to the North Carolina Highway Fund. The Division shall use the fees derived from transactions with commission contract agents for the payment of compensation to commission contract agents. An additional fifty cents (50¢) of the fee imposed for any transaction assessed a fee under subdivision (a)(1) of this section shall be credited to the Mercury Pollution Prevention Account in the Department of Environment and Natural Resources.

(a2)   From the fees collected under subdivisions (a)(1) through (a)(9) of this section, the Department shall annually credit the sum of four hundred thousand dollars ($400,000) to the Reserve for Visitor Centers in the Highway Fund.

(b) Except as otherwise provided in subsections (a1) and (a2) of this section, the fees collected under subdivisions (a)(1) through (a)(9) of this section shall be credited to the North Carolina Highway Trust Fund. The fees collected under subdivision (a)(10) of this section shall be credited to the Highway Fund.

(c) The Division shall not collect a fee for a certificate of title for a motor vehicle entitled to a permanent registration plate under G.S. 20-84. (1937, c. 407, s. 49; 1943, c. 648; 1947, c. 219, s. 9; 1955, c. 554, s. 4; 1961, c. 360, s. 19; c. 835, s. 11; 1975, c. 430; c. 716, s. 5; c. 727; c. 875, s. 4; c. 879, s. 46; 1979, c. 801, s. 11; 1981, c. 690, s. 19; 1989, c. 692, s. 2.1; c. 700, s. 1; c. 770, s. 74.11; 1991, c. 193, s. 8; 1993, c. 467, s. 5; 1995, c. 50, s. 2; c. 390, s. 34; c. 509, s. 135.2(i), (j); 1999-220, s. 2; 2004-77, s. 2; 2004-185, s. 6; 2005-276, s. 44.1(k); 2005-384, s. 2; 2006-255, s. 5; 2006-264, s. 35.5; 2007-142, s. 8; 2011-145, ss. 28.30(a), 31.11; 2011-391, s. 54; 2013-183, s. 2.1; 2013-360, s. 34.16(b); 2013-400, s. 5.)

§ 20-85.1. Registration by mail; one-day title service; fees.

(a) The owner of a vehicle registered in North Carolina may renew that vehicle registration by mail.

(b) The Commissioner and the employees of the Division designated by the Commissioner may prepare and deliver upon request a certificate of title, charging a fee of seventy-five dollars ($75.00) for one-day title service, in lieu of the title fee required by G.S. 20-85(a). The fee for one-day title service must be paid by cash or by certified check. This fee shall be credited to the Highway Trust Fund.

(c) Repealed by Session Laws 2010-132, s. 8, effective December 1, 2010, and applicable to offenses committed on or after that date. (1983, c. 50, s. 1; 1989, c. 692, s. 2.2; c. 700, s. 1; 1991, c. 689, s. 324; 2005-276, s. 44.1(l); 2010-132, s. 8.)

§ 20-86. Penalty for engaging in a "for-hire" business without proper license plates.

Any person, firm or corporation engaged in the business of transporting persons or property for compensation, except as otherwise provided in this Article, shall, before engaging in such business, pay the license fees prescribed by this Article and secure the license plates provided for vehicles operated for hire. Any person, firm or corporation operating vehicles for hire without having paid the tax prescribed or using private plates on such vehicles shall be liable for an additional tax of twenty-five dollars ($25.00) for each vehicle in addition to the normal fees provided in this Article; provided, that when the vehicle subject to for-hire license has attached thereto a trailer or semitrailer, each unit in the combination, including the tractor, trailer and/or semitrailer, shall be subject to the additional tax as herein prescribed; provided, further that the additional tax herein provided shall not apply to trailers having a gross weight of 3,000 pounds or less. (1937, c. 407, s. 50; 1965, c. 659.)

§ 20-86.1. International Registration Plan.

(a) The registration fees required under this Article may be proportioned for vehicles which qualify and are licensed under the provisions of the International Registration Plan.

(b) Notwithstanding any other provisions of this Chapter, the Commissioner is hereby authorized to promulgate and enforce such rules and regulations as may be necessary to carry out the provisions of any agreement entered pursuant to the International Registration Plan. (1975, c. 767, s. 2; 1981, c. 859, s. 77; c. 1127, s. 53.)

§ 20-87. Passenger vehicle registration fees.

These fees shall be paid to the Division annually for the registration and licensing of passenger vehicles, according to the following classifications and schedules:

(1) For-Hire Passenger Vehicles. - The fee for a passenger vehicle that is operated for compensation and has a capacity of 15 passengers or less is seventy-eight dollars ($78.00). The fee for a passenger vehicle that is operated

for compensation and has a capacity of more than 15 passengers is one dollar and forty cents ($1.40) per hundred pounds of empty weight of the vehicle.

(2)   U-Drive-It Vehicles. - U-drive-it vehicles shall pay the following tax:

Motorcycles:	1-passenger capacity	$18.00
	2-passenger capacity	22.00
	3-passenger capacity	26.00
Automobiles:	15 or fewer passengers	$51.00
Buses:	16 or more passengers	$2.00 per hundred pounds of empty weight
Trucks under 7,000 pounds that do not haul products for hire:	4,000 pounds	$41.50
	5,000 pounds	$51.00
	6,000 pounds	$61.00.

(3)   Repealed by Session Laws 1981, c. 976, s. 3.

(4) Limousine Vehicles. - For-hire passenger vehicles on call or demand which do not solicit passengers indiscriminately for hire between points along streets or highways, shall be taxed at the same rate as for-hire passenger vehicles under G.S. 20-87(1) but shall be issued appropriate registration plates to distinguish such vehicles from taxicabs.

(5) Private Passenger Vehicles. - There shall be paid to the Division annually, as of the first day of January, for the registration and licensing of private passenger vehicles, fees according to the following classifications and schedules:

Private passenger vehicles of not more than fifteen passengers.. $28.00

Private passenger vehicles over fifteen passengers................................ 31.00

Provided, that a fee of only one dollar ($1.00) shall be charged for any vehicle given by the federal government to any veteran on account of any disability suffered during war so long as such vehicle is owned by the original donee or other veteran entitled to receive such gift under Title 38, section 252, United States Code Annotated.

(6) Private Motorcycles. - The base fee on private passenger motorcycles shall be fifteen dollars ($15.00); except that when a motorcycle is equipped with an additional form of device designed to transport persons or property, the base fee shall be twenty-two dollars ($22.00). An additional fee of three dollars ($3.00) is imposed on each private motorcycle registered under this subdivision in addition to the base fee. The revenue from the additional fee, in addition to any other funds appropriated for this purpose, shall be used to fund the Motorcycle Safety Instruction Program created in G.S. 115D-72.

(7) Dealer License Plates. - The fee for a dealer license plate is the regular fee for each of the first five plates issued to the same dealer and is one-half the regular fee for each additional dealer license plate issued to the same dealer. The "regular fee" is the fee set in subdivision (5) of this section for a private passenger motor vehicle of not more than 15 passengers.

(8) Driveaway Companies. - Any person engaged in the business of driving new motor vehicles from the place of manufacture to the place of sale in this State for compensation shall pay a fee of one-half of the amount that would otherwise be payable under this section for each set of plates.

(9) House Trailers. - In lieu of other registration and license fees levied on house trailers under this section or G.S. 20-88, the registration and license fee on house trailers shall be eleven dollars ($11.00) for the license year or any portion thereof.

(10) Special Mobile Equipment. - The fee for special mobile equipment for the license year or any part of the license year is two times the fee in subdivision (5) for a private passenger motor vehicle of not more than 15 passengers.

(11) Any vehicle fee determined under this section according to the weight of the vehicle shall be increased by the sum of three dollars ($3.00) to arrive at the total fee.

(12) Low-Speed Vehicles. - The fee for a low-speed vehicle is the same as the fee for private passengers vehicles of not more than 15 passengers.

(13) Additional fee for certain electric vehicles. - At the time of an initial registration or registration renewal, the owner of a plug-in electric vehicle that is not a low-speed vehicle and that does not rely on a nonelectric source of power shall pay a fee in the amount of one hundred dollars ($100.00) in addition to any other required registration fees. (1937, c. 407, s. 51; 1939, c. 275; 1943, c. 648; 1945, c. 564, s. 1; c. 576, s. 2; 1947, c. 220, s. 3; c. 1019, ss. 1-3; 1949, c. 127; 1951, c. 819, ss. 1, 2; 1953, c. 478; c. 826, s. 4; 1955, c. 1313, s. 2; 1957, c. 1340, s. 3; 1961, c. 1172, s. 1a; 1965, c. 927; 1967, c. 1136; 1969, c. 600, ss. 3-11; 1971, c. 952; 1973, c. 107; 1975, c. 716, s. 5; 1981, c. 976, ss. 1-4; 1981 (Reg. Sess., 1982), c. 1255; 1983, c. 713, s. 61; c. 761, ss. 142, 143, 145; 1985, c. 454, s. 2; 1987, c. 333; 1989, c. 755, ss. 2, 4; c. 770, ss. 74.2, 74.3; 1989 (Reg. Sess., 1990), c. 830, s. 1; 1991 (Reg. Sess., 1992), c. 1015, s. 2; 1993, c. 320, s. 5; c. 440, s. 7; 1995 (Reg. Sess., 1996), c. 756, s. 7; 1999-438, s. 27; 1999-452, s. 17; 2001-356, s. 4; 2001-414, s. 31; 2002-72, s. 8; 2004-167, s. 5; 2004-199, s. 59; 2005-276, s. 44.1(m); 2013-360, s. 34.21(a).)

§ 20-87.1. Interchange of passenger buses with nonresident common carriers of passengers.

When a resident common carrier of passengers of this State interchanges a properly licensed bus with another common carrier of passengers who is a resident of another state, and adequate records are on file in its office to verify such interchanges, the North Carolina licensed common carrier of passengers may use the bus licensed in such other state the same as if it is its own during the time the nonresident carrier is using the North Carolina licensed bus. (1971, c. 871, s. 1; 1975, c. 716, s. 5; 1981, c. 976, s. 5.)

§ 20-88. Property-hauling vehicles.

(a) Determination of Weight. - For the purpose of licensing, the weight of self-propelled property-carrying vehicles shall be the empty weight and heaviest load to be transported, as declared by the owner or operator; provided, that any determination of weight shall be made only in units of 1,000 pounds or major fraction thereof, weights of over 500 pounds counted as 1,000 and weights of 500 pounds or less disregarded. The declared gross weight of self-propelled property-carrying vehicles operated in conjunction with trailers or semitrailers shall include the empty weight of the vehicles to be operated in the combination and the heaviest load to be transported by such combination at any time during the registration period, except that the gross weight of a trailer or semitrailer is not required to be included when the operation is to be in conjunction with a self-propelled property-carrying vehicle which is licensed for 6,000 pounds or less gross weight and the gross weight of such combination does not exceed 9,000 pounds, except wreckers as defined under G.S. 20-4.01(50). Those property-hauling vehicles registered for 4,000 pounds shall be permitted a tolerance of 500 pounds above the weight permitted under the table of weights and rates appearing in subsection (b) of this section.

(b) The following fees are imposed on the annual registration of self-propelled property-hauling vehicles; the fees are based on the type of vehicle and its weight:

SCHEDULE OF WEIGHTS AND RATES

Rates Per Hundred Pound Gross Weight

Farmer Rate

Not over 4,000 pounds
$0.29

4,001 to 9,000 pounds inclusive
.40

9,001 to 13,000 pounds inclusive
.50

13,001 to 17,000 pounds inclusive
.68

Over 17,000 pounds
.77

Rates Per Hundred Pound Gross Weight

General Rate

Not over 4,000 pounds
$0.59

4,001 to 9,000 pounds inclusive
.81

9,001 to 13,000 pounds inclusive
1.00

13,001 to 17,000 pounds inclusive
1.36

Over 17,000 pounds
1.54

(1)   The minimum fee for a vehicle licensed under this subsection is twenty-four dollars ($24.00) at the farmer rate and twenty-eight dollars ($28.00) at the general rate.

(2)   The term "farmer" as used in this subsection means any person engaged in the raising and growing of farm products on a farm in North Carolina not less than 10 acres in area, and who does not engage in the business of buying products for resale.

(3)   License plates issued at the farmer rate shall be placed upon trucks and truck-tractors that are operated for the primary purpose of carrying or

transporting the applicant's farm products, raised or produced on the applicant's farm, and farm supplies. The license plates shall not be used on a vehicle operated in hauling for hire.

(4) "Farm products" means any food crop, livestock, poultry, dairy products, flower bulbs, or other nursery products and other agricultural products designed to be used for food purposes, including in the term "farm products" also cotton, tobacco, logs, bark, pulpwood, tannic acid wood and other forest products grown, produced, or processed by the farmer.

(5) The Division shall issue necessary rules and regulations providing for the recall, transfer, exchange or cancellation of "farmer" plates, when vehicle bearing such plates shall be sold or transferred.

(5a) Notwithstanding any other provision of this Chapter, license plates issued pursuant to this subsection at the farmer rate may be purchased for any three-month period at one fourth of the annual fee.

(6) There shall be paid to the Division annually the following fees for "wreckers" as defined under G.S. 20-4.01(50): a wrecker fully equipped weighing 7,000 pounds or less, seventy-five dollars ($75.00); wreckers weighing in excess of 7,000 pounds shall pay one hundred forty-eight dollars ($148.00). Fees to be prorated monthly. Provided, further, that nothing herein shall prohibit a licensed dealer from using a dealer's license plate to tow a vehicle for a customer.

(c) The fee for a semitrailer or trailer is nineteen dollars ($19.00) for each year or part of a year. The fee is payable each year. Upon the application of the owner of a semitrailer or trailer, the Division may issue a multiyear plate and registration card for the semitrailer or trailer for a fee of seventy-five dollars ($75.00). A multiyear plate and registration card for a semitrailer or trailer are valid until the owner transfers the semitrailer or trailer to another person or surrenders the plate and registration card to the Division. A multiyear plate may not be transferred to another vehicle.

The Division shall issue a multiyear semitrailer or trailer plate in a different color than an annual semitrailer or trailer plate and shall include the word "multiyear" on the plate. The Division may not issue a multiyear plate for a house trailer.

(d) Rates on trucks, trailers and semitrailers wholly or partially equipped with solid tires shall be double the above schedule.

(e) Repealed by Session Laws 1981, c. 976, s. 6.

(f) Repealed by Session Laws 1995, c. 163, s. 6.

(g) Repealed by Session Laws 1969, c. 600, s. 17.

(h) Repealed by Session Laws 1979, c. 419.

(i) Any vehicle fee determined under this section according to the weight of the vehicle shall be increased by the sum of three dollars ($3.00) to arrive at the total fee.

(j) No heavy vehicle subject to the use tax imposed by Section 4481 of the Internal Revenue Code of 1954 (26 U.S.C. 4481) may be registered or licensed pursuant to G.S. 20-88 without proof of payment of the use tax imposed by that law. The proof of payment shall be on a form prescribed by the United States Secretary of Treasury pursuant to the provisions of 23 U.S.C. 141(d).

(k) A person may not drive a vehicle on a highway if the vehicle's gross weight exceeds its declared gross weight. A vehicle driven in violation of this subsection is subject to the axle-group weight penalties set in G.S. 20-118(e). The penalties apply to the amount by which the vehicle's gross weight exceeds its declared weight.

(l) The Division shall issue permanent truck and truck-tractor plates to Class A and Class B Motor Vehicles and shall include the word "permanent" on the plate. The permanent registration plates issued pursuant to this section shall be subject to annual registration fees set in this section. The Division shall issue the necessary rules providing for the recall, transfer, exchange, or cancellation of permanent plates issued pursuant to this section.

(m) Any vehicle weighing greater than the gross weight limits found in G.S. 20-118(b)(3), as authorized by G.S. 20-118(c)(12), (c)(14), and (c)(15), must be registered for the maximum weight allowed for the vehicle configuration as listed in G.S. 20-118(b). A vehicle driven in violation of this subsection is subject to the axle group penalties set out in G.S. 20-118(e). The penalties apply to the amount by which the vehicle's maximum gross weight as listed in G.S. 20-118(b) exceeds its declared weight. (1937, c. 407, s. 52; 1939, c. 275; 1941, cc. 36, 227; 1943, c. 648; 1945, c. 569, s. 1; c. 575, s. 1; c. 576, s. 3; c. 956, ss. 1, 2; 1949, cc. 355, 361; 1951, c. 583; c. 819, ss. 1, 2; 1953, c. 568; c. 694, s. 1; c.

1122; 1955, c. 554, s. 8; 1957, c. 681, s. 2; c. 1215; 1959, c. 571; 1961, c. 685; 1963, c. 501; c. 702, ss. 2, 3; 1967, c. 1095, ss. 1, 2; 1969, c. 600, ss. 12-17; c. 1056, s. 1; 1973, c. 154, ss. 1, 2; c. 291; 1975, c. 716, s. 5; 1977, c. 638; 1979, c. 419; c. 631; 1981, c. 67; c. 690, ss. 29, 30; c. 976, s. 6; 1983, c. 43; c. 190, s. 1; c. 761, s. 144; c. 768, s. 4; 1991 (Reg. Sess., 1992), c. 947, s. 1; 1993, c. 467, s. 4; c. 543, s. 1; 1995, c. 109, s. 1; c. 163, s. 6; 1995 (Reg. Sess., 1996), c. 756, s. 8; 1997-466, s. 1; 2004-167, ss. 6, 7; 2004-199, s. 59; 2005-276, s. 44.1(n); 2008-221, s. 2; 2012-78, s. 4; 2013-92, s. 1.)

§ 20-88.01. Revocation of registration for failure to register for or comply with road tax or pay civil penalty for buying or selling non-tax-paid fuel.

(a)   Road Tax. - The Secretary of Revenue may notify the Commissioner of those motor vehicles that are registered or are required to be registered under Article 36B of Chapter 105 and whose owners or lessees, as appropriate, are not in compliance with Article 36B, 36C, or 36D of Chapter 105. When notified, the Commissioner shall withhold or revoke the registration plate for the vehicle.

(b)   Non-tax-paid Fuel. - The Secretary of Revenue may notify the Commissioner of those motor vehicles for which a civil penalty imposed under G.S. 105-449.118 has not been paid. When notified, the Commissioner shall withhold or revoke the registration plate of the vehicle. (1983, c. 713, s. 54; 1989, c. 692, s. 6.1; c. 770, s. 74.5; 1991, c. 613, s. 4; 1995, c. 390, s. 11.)

§ 20-88.02. Registration of logging vehicles.

Upon receipt of an application on a form prescribed by it, the Division shall register trucks and tractor trucks used exclusively in connection with logging operations, as provided in section 4483(e) of the Internal Revenue Code and 26 C.F.R. § 41.4483-6 for the collection of the federal heavy vehicle use tax. For the purposes of this section, "logging" shall mean the harvesting of timber and transportation from a forested site to places of sale.

Fees for the registration of vehicles under this section shall be the same as those ordinarily charged for the type of vehicle being registered. (1985, c. 458, s. 1; 2010-132, s. 9.)

§ 20-88.1. Driver education.

(a) through (b1) Repealed by Session Laws 2011-145, s. 28.37(c), effective July 1, 2011.

(c) Expenses incurred by the State in carrying out the provisions of the driver education program administered by the Department of Public Instruction in accordance with G.S. 115C-215 shall be paid out of the Highway Fund based on an annual appropriation by the General Assembly.

(d) The Division shall prepare a driver license handbook that explains the traffic laws of the State and shall periodically revise the handbook to reflect changes in these laws. At the request of the Department of Public Instruction, the Division shall provide free copies of the handbook to that Department for use in the program of driver education offered at public high schools. (1957, c. 682, s. 1; 1965, c. 410, s. 1; 1975, c. 431; c. 716, s. 5; 1977, c. 340, s. 4; c. 1002; 1983, c. 761, s. 141; 1985 (Reg. Sess., 1986), c. 982, s. 25; 1991, c. 689, s. 32(a); 1993 (Reg. Sess., 1994), c. 761, s. 7; 1997-16, s. 3; 1997-443, s. 32.20; 2011-145, s. 28.37(c).)

§ 20-89: Repealed by Sessions Laws 1981, c. 976, s. 7.

§ 20-90: Repealed by Session Laws 1981, c. 976, s. 8.

§ 20-91. Audit of vehicle registrations under the International Registration Plan.

(a) Repealed by Session Laws 1995 (Regular Session, 1996), c. 756, s. 9.

(b) The Department of Revenue may audit a person who registers or is required to register a vehicle under the International Registration Plan to determine if the person has paid the registration fees due under this Article. A person who registers a vehicle under the International Registration Plan must keep any records used to determine the information when registering the vehicle. The records must be kept for three years after the date of the registration to which the records apply. The Department of Revenue may examine these records during business hours. If the records are not located in North Carolina and an auditor must travel to the location of the records, the registrant shall reimburse North Carolina for per diem and travel expense incurred in the performance of the audit. If more than one registrant is audited on the same out-of-state trip, the per diem and travel expense may be prorated.

The Secretary of Revenue may enter into reciprocal audit agreements with other agencies of this State or agencies of another jurisdiction for the purpose of conducting joint audits of any registrant subject to audit under this section.

(c)   If an audit is conducted and it becomes necessary to assess the registrant for deficiencies in registration fees or taxes due based on the audit, the assessment will be determined based on the schedule of rates prescribed for that registration year, adding thereto and as a part thereof an amount equal to five percent (5%) of the tax to be collected. If, during an audit, it is determined that:

(1)   A registrant failed or refused to make acceptable records available for audit as provided by law; or

(2)   A registrant misrepresented, falsified or concealed records, then all plates and cab cards shall be deemed to have been issued erroneously and are subject to cancellation. The Commissioner, based on information provided by the Department of Revenue audit, may assess the registrant for an additional percentage up to one hundred percent (100%) North Carolina registration fees at the rate prescribed for that registration year, adding thereto and as a part thereof an amount equal to five percent (5%) of the tax to be collected. The Commissioner may cancel all registration and reciprocal privileges.

As a result of an audit, no assessment shall be issued and no claim for refund shall be allowed which is in an amount of less than ten dollars ($10.00).

The results of any audit conducted under this section shall be provided to the Division. The notice of any assessments shall be sent by the Division to the registrant by registered or certified mail at the address of the registrant as it appears in the records of the Division of Motor Vehicles in Raleigh. The notice, when sent in accordance with the requirements indicated above, will be sufficient regardless of whether or not it was ever received.

The failure of any registrant to pay any additional registration fees or tax within 30 days after the billing date, shall constitute cause for revocation of registration license plates, cab cards and reciprocal privileges, or shall constitute cause for the denial of registration of a vehicle registered through the International Registration Plan or a vehicle no longer registered through the International Registration Plan.

(d)   Repealed by Session Laws 1995 (Regular Session, 1996), c. 756, s. 9. (1937, c. 407, s. 55; 1939, c. 275; 1941, c. 36; 1943, c. 726; 1945, c. 575, s. 3; 1947, c. 914, s. 2; 1951, c. 190, s. 1; c. 819, s. 1; 1955, c. 1313, s. 2; 1967, c. 1079, s. 2; 1975, c. 716, s. 5; c. 767, s. 3; 1981, c. 859, s. 78; c. 976, s. 9; c. 1127, s. 53; 1995 (Reg. Sess., 1996), c. 756, s. 9; 2005-435, s. 22; 2007-164, s. 7; 2007-484, s. 41.5.)

§ 20-91.1: Repealed by Session Laws 2007-491, s. 2, effective January 1, 2008.

§ 20-91.2: Repealed by Session Laws 2007-491, s. 2, effective January 1, 2008.

§ 20-92: Repealed by Session Laws 1995 (Regular Session, 1996), c. 756, s. 10.

§ 20-93: Repealed by Session Laws 1981, c. 976, s. 10.

§ 20-94. Partial payments.

In the purchase of licenses, where the gross amount of the license fee to any one owner amounts to more than four hundred dollars ($400.00), half of such payment may, if the Commissioner is satisfied of the financial responsibility of such owner, be deferred until six months from the month of renewal in any calendar year upon the execution to the Commissioner of a draft upon any bank or trust company upon forms to be provided by the Commissioner in an amount equivalent to one half of such fee, plus a carrying charge of three percent (3%) of the deferred portion of the license fee: Provided, that any person using any tag so purchased after the first day of six months from the month of renewal in any such year without having first provided for the payment of such draft, shall be guilty of a Class 2 misdemeanor. No further license plates shall be issued to any person executing such a draft after the due date of any such draft so long as such draft or any portion thereof remains unpaid. Any such draft being dishonored and not paid shall be subject to the penalties prescribed in G.S. 20-178 and shall be immediately turned over by the Commissioner to his duly authorized agents and/or the State Highway Patrol, to the end that this provision may be enforced. When the owner of the vehicles for which a draft has been given sells or transfers ownership to all vehicles covered by the draft, such draft shall become payable immediately, and such vehicles shall not be transferred by the Division until the draft has been paid. Any one owner whose gross license fee amounts to more than two hundred dollars ($200.00) but not more than four hundred dollars ($400.00) may also be permitted to sign a draft in accordance with the foregoing provisions of this section provided such owner makes application for the draft during the month of renewal.(1937, c. 407, s. 58; 1943, c. 726; 1945, c. 49, ss. 1, 2; 1947, c. 219, s. 10; 1953, c. 192; 1967, c. 712; 1975, c. 716, s. 5; 1979, c. 801, s. 12; 1987 (Reg. Sess., 1988), c. 938; 1989, c. 661; 1993, c. 539, s. 344; 1994, Ex. Sess., c. 24, s. 14(c) 2004-167, s. 8; 2004-199, s. 59.)

§ 20-95. Prorated fee for license plate issued for other than a year.

(a) Calendar-Year Plate. - The fee for a calendar-year license plate issued on or after April 1 of a year is a percentage of the annual fee determined in accordance with the following table:

Date Plate Issued	Percentage of Annual Fee
April 1 through June 30	75%
July 1 through September 30	50
October 1 through December 31	25.

(a1) Plate With Renewal Sticker. - The fee for a license plate whose registration is renewed by means of a registration renewal sticker for a period of other than 12 months is a prorated amount of the annual fee. The prorated amount is one-twelfth of the annual fee multiplied by the number of full months in the period beginning the date the renewal sticker becomes effective until the date the renewal sticker expires, rounded to the nearest dollar.

(b) Scope. - This section does not apply to license plates issued pursuant to G.S. 20-79.1, 20-79.2, 20-84, 20-84.1, 20-87(9) or (10), and 20-88(c). (1937, c. 407, s. 59; 1947, c. 914, s. 3; 1979, c. 476; 1991, c. 672, s. 6, c. 726, s. 23; 1993, c. 440, s. 6; 1993 (Reg. Sess., 1994), c. 761, s. 8.)

§ 20-96. Detaining property-hauling vehicles or vehicles regulated by the Motor Carrier Safety Regulation Unit until fines or penalties and taxes are collected.

(a) Authority to Detain Vehicles. - A law enforcement officer may seize and detain the following property-hauling vehicles operating on the highways of the State:

(1) A property-hauling vehicle with an overload in violation of G.S. 20-88(k) and G.S. 20-118.

(2) A property-hauling vehicle that does not have a proper registration plate as required under G.S. 20-118.3.

(3) A property-hauling vehicle that is owned by a person liable for any overload penalties or assessments due and unpaid for more than 30 days.

(4) A property-hauling vehicle that is owned by a person liable for any taxes or penalties under Article 36B of Chapter 105 of the General Statutes.

(5) Any commercial vehicle operating under the authority of a motor carrier when the motor carrier has been assessed a fine pursuant to G.S. 20-17.7 and that fine has not been paid.

(6) A property-hauling vehicle operating in violation of G.S. 20-119.

The officer may detain the vehicle until the delinquent fines or penalties and taxes are paid and, in the case of a vehicle that does not have the proper registration plate, until the proper registration plate is secured.

(b) Storage; Liability. - When necessary, an officer who detains a vehicle under this section may have the vehicle stored. The motor carrier under whose authority the vehicle is being operated or the owner of a vehicle that is detained or stored under this section is responsible for the care of any property being hauled by the vehicle and for any storage charges. The State shall not be liable for damage to the vehicle or loss of the property being hauled.

(c) The authority of a law enforcement officer to seize a motor vehicle pursuant to subsection (a) of this section shall not be affected by the statutes of limitations set out in Chapter 1 of the North Carolina General Statutes. (1937, c. 407, s. 60; 1943, c. 726; 1949, c. 583, s. 8; c. 1207, s. 4½; c. 1253; 1951, c. 1013, ss. 1-3; 1953, c. 694, ss. 2, 3; 1955, c. 554, s. 9; 1957, c. 65, s. 11; 1959, c. 1264, s. 5; 1973, c. 507, s. 5; 1985, c. 116, ss. 1-3; 1993, c. 539, s. 345; 1994, Ex. Sess., c. 24, s. 14(c); 1995, c. 109, s. 2; 1999-452, s. 18; 2000-67, s. 25.11; 2005-361, s. 1; 2010-129, s. 2.)

§ 20-97. Taxes credited to Highway Fund; municipal vehicle taxes.

(a) State Taxes to Highway Fund. - All taxes levied under this Article are compensatory taxes for the use and privileges of the public highways of this State. The taxes collected shall be credited to the State Highway Fund. Except as provided in this section, no county or municipality shall levy any license or privilege tax upon any motor vehicle licensed by the State.

(b) General Municipal Vehicle Tax. - Cities and towns may levy a tax of not more than five dollars ($5.00) per year upon any vehicle resident in the city or town. The proceeds of the tax may be used for any lawful purpose.

(c) Municipal Vehicle Tax for Public Transportation. - A city or town that operates a public transportation system as defined in G.S. 105-550 may levy a tax of not more than five dollars ($5.00) per year upon any vehicle resident in the city or town. The tax authorized by this subsection is in addition to the tax authorized by subsection (b) of this section. A city or town may not levy a tax under this section, however, to the extent the rate of tax, when added to the general motor vehicle taxes levied by the city or town under subsection (b) of this section and under any local legislation, would exceed thirty dollars ($30.00) per year. The proceeds of the tax may be used only for financing, constructing, operating, and maintaining local public transportation systems. Cities and towns shall use the proceeds of the tax to supplement and not to supplant or replace existing funds or other resources for public transportation systems. This subsection does not apply to the cities and towns in Gaston County.

(d) Municipal Taxi Tax. - Cities and towns may levy a tax of not more than fifteen dollars ($15.00) per year upon each vehicle operated in the city or town as a taxicab. The proceeds of the tax may be used for any lawful purpose.

(e) No Additional Local Tax. - No county, city or town may impose a franchise tax, license tax, or other fee upon a motor carrier unless the tax is authorized by this section. (1937, c. 407, s. 61; 1941, c. 36; 1943, c. 639, ss. 3, 4; 1975, c. 716, s. 5; 1977, c. 433, s. 1; c. 880, s. 1; 1979, c. 173, s. 1; c. 216, s. 1; c. 217; c. 248, s. 1; c. 398; c. 400, s. 1; c. 458; c. 530, s. 1; c. 790; 1979, 2nd Sess., c. 1152; c. 1153, s. 1; c. 1155, s. 1; c. 1189; c. 1308, s. 1; 1981, cc. 74, 129, 210, 228, 310, 311, 312, 315, 368, 370, s. 10; c. 415, s. 10; cc. 857, 858, 991; 1981 (Reg. Sess., 1982), cc. 1202, 1250; 1983, cc. 9, 75; c. 106, s. 1; c. 188, ss. 1, 2; 1993, c. 321, s. 146, c. 479, s. 4; c. 456, s. 1; 1997-417, s. 2; 2009-166, s. 2(b).)

§ 20-98: Repealed by Session Laws 2007-491, s. 2, effective January 1, 2008.

§ 20-99: Repealed by Session Laws 2007-491, s. 2, effective January 1, 2008.

§ 20-100. Vehicles junked or destroyed by fire or collision.

Upon satisfactory proof to the Commissioner that any motor vehicle, duly licensed, has been completely destroyed by fire or collision, or has been junked and completely dismantled so that the same can no longer be operated as a motor vehicle, the owner of such vehicle may be allowed on the purchase of a new license for another vehicle a credit equivalent to the unexpired proportion of the cost of the original license, dating from the first day of the next month after the date of such destruction. (1937, c. 407, s. 64; 1939, c. 369, s. 1.)

§ 20-101. Certain business vehicles to be marked.

(a)   A motor vehicle that is subject to 49 C.F.R. Part 390, the federal motor carrier safety regulations, shall be marked as required by that Part.

(b)   A motor vehicle with a gross vehicle weight rating of more than 26,000 pounds that is used in intrastate commerce shall have (i) the name of the owner and (ii) the motor carrier's identification number preceded by the letters "USDOT" and followed by the letters "NC" printed on each side of the vehicle in letters not less than three inches in height. The provisions of this subsection shall not apply if any of the following are true:

(1)   The motor vehicle is subject to 49 C.F.R. Part 390.

(2)   The motor vehicle is of a type listed in 49 C.F.R. 390.3(f).

(c)   A motor vehicle that is subject to regulation by the North Carolina Utilities Commission shall be marked as required by that Commission and as otherwise required by this section.

(d)   A motor vehicle equipped to tow or transport another motor vehicle, hired for the purpose of towing or transporting another motor vehicle, shall have the name and address of the registered owner of the vehicle, and the name of the business or person being hired if different, printed on each side of the vehicle in letters not less than three inches in height. This subsection shall not apply to motor vehicles subject to 49 C.F.R. Part 390. (1937, c. 407, s. 65; 1951, c. 819, s. 1; 1967, c. 1132; 1985, c. 132; 1995 (Reg. Sess., 1996), c. 756, s. 12; 2000-67, s. 25.8; 2001-487, s. 50(d); 2007-404, s. 1; 2009-376, s. 3; 2012-41, s. 1.)

§ 20-101.1. Conspicuous disclosure of dealer administrative fees.

(a)   A motor vehicle dealer shall not charge an administrative, origination, documentary, procurement, or other similar administrative fee related to the sale or lease of a motor vehicle, whether or not that fee relates to costs or charges that the dealer is required to pay to third parties or is attributable to the dealer's internal overhead or profit, unless the dealer complies with all of the following requirements:

(1) The dealer shall post a conspicuous notice in the sales or finance area of the dealership measuring at least 24 inches on each side informing customers that a fee regulated by this section may or will be charged and the amount of the fee.

(2) The fact that the dealer charges a fee regulated by this section and the amount of the fee shall be disclosed whenever the dealer engages in the price advertising of vehicles.

(3) The amount of a fee regulated by this section shall be separately identified on the customer's buyer's order, purchase order, or bill of sale.

(b) Nothing contained in this section or elsewhere under the law of this State shall be deemed to prohibit a dealer from, in the dealer's discretion, deciding not to charge an administrative, origination, documentary, procurement, or other similar administrative fee or reducing the amount of the fee in certain cases, as the dealer may deem appropriate.

(c) Notwithstanding the terms of any contract, franchise, novation, or agreement, it shall be unlawful for any manufacturer, manufacturer branch, distributor, or distributor branch to prevent, attempt to prevent, prohibit, coerce, or attempt to coerce, any new motor vehicle dealer located in this State from charging any administrative, origination, documentary, procurement, or other similar administrative fee related to the sale or lease of a motor vehicle. It shall further be unlawful for any manufacturer, manufacturer branch, distributor, or distributor branch, notwithstanding the terms of any contract, franchise, novation, or agreement, to prevent or prohibit any new motor vehicle dealer in this State from participating in any program relating to the sale of motor vehicles or reduce the amount of compensation to be paid to any dealer in this State, based upon the dealer's willingness to refrain from charging or reduce the amount of any administrative, origination, documentary, procurement, or other similar administrative fee related to the sale or lease of a motor vehicle. (2001-487, s. 123.5; 2001-492, s. 1.)

§ 20-101.2. Conspicuous disclosure of dealer finance yield charges.

(a) A motor vehicle dealer shall not charge a fee or receive a commission or other compensation for providing, procuring, or arranging financing for the retail purchase or lease of a motor vehicle, unless the dealer complies with both of the following requirements:

(1) The dealer shall post a conspicuous notice in the sales or finance area of the dealership measuring at least 24 inches on each side informing customers that the dealer may receive a fee, commission, or other compensation for providing, procuring, or arranging financing for the retail purchase or lease of a motor vehicle, for which the customer may be responsible.

(2) The dealer shall disclose conspicuously on the purchase order or buyer's order, or on a separate form provided to the purchaser at or prior to the closing on the sale of the vehicle, that the dealer may receive a fee, commission, or other compensation for providing, procuring, or arranging financing for the retail purchase or lease of a motor vehicle, for which the customer may be responsible.

(b) Nothing contained in this section or elsewhere under the law of this State shall be deemed to require that a motor vehicle dealer disclose to any actual or potential purchaser the dealer's contractual arrangements with any finance company, bank, leasing company, or other lender or financial institution, or the amount of markup, profit, or compensation that the dealer will receive in any particular transaction or series of transactions from the charging of such fees. (2001-487, s. 123.5; 2001-492, s. 2.)

Part 8. Anti-Theft and Enforcement Provisions.

§ 20-102. Report of stolen and recovered motor vehicles.

Every sheriff, chief of police, or peace officer upon receiving reliable information that any vehicle registered hereunder has been stolen shall report such theft to the Division. Any said officer upon receiving information that any vehicle, which he has previously reported as stolen, has been recovered, shall report the fact of such recovery to the Division. (1937, c. 407, s. 66; 1975, c. 716, s. 5; 2005-182, s. 4.)

§ 20-102.1. False report of theft or conversion a misdemeanor.

A person who knowingly makes to a peace officer or to the Division a false report of the theft or conversion of a motor vehicle shall be guilty of a Class 2 misdemeanor. (1963, c. 1083; 1975, c. 716, s. 5; 1993, c. 539, s. 346; 1994, Ex. Sess., c. 24, s. 14(c).)

§ 20-102.2. Report of failure to return hired motor vehicles.

Every sheriff, chief of police, or peace officer, upon receiving a vehicle theft report, warrant, or other reliable information that any rental, for-hire, or leased vehicle registered pursuant to this Chapter has not been returned as set forth in G.S. 14-167, shall report the failure to the National Crime Information Center. Any officer upon receiving information concerning the recovery of a vehicle that the officer previously reported as not having been returned shall report the recovery to the National Crime Information Center. The officer shall also attempt to notify the reporting party of the location and condition of the recovered vehicle by telephone, if the telephone number of the reporting party is available or readily accessible. (2005-182, s. 5.)

§ 20-103. Reports by owners of stolen and recovered vehicles.

The owner, or person having a lien or encumbrance upon a registered vehicle which has been stolen or embezzled, may notify the Division of such theft or embezzlement, but in the event of an embezzlement may make such report only after having procured the issuance of a warrant for the arrest of the person charged with such embezzlement. Every owner or other person who has given any such notice must notify the Division of the recovery of such vehicle. (1937, c. 407, s. 67; 1975, c. 716, s. 5.)

§ 20-104. Action by Division on report of stolen or embezzled vehicles.

(a) The Division, upon receiving a report of a stolen or embezzled vehicle as hereinbefore provided, shall file and appropriately index the same and shall immediately suspend the registration of the vehicle so reported, and shall not transfer the registration of the same until such time as it is notified in writing that such vehicle has been recovered.

(b)   The Division shall at least once each month compile and maintain at its headquarters office a list of all vehicles which have been stolen or embezzled or recovered as reported to it during the preceding month, and such lists shall be open to inspection by any peace officer or other persons interested in any such vehicle. (1937, c. 407, s. 68; 1975, c. 716, s. 5.)

§ 20-105. Repealed by Session Laws 1973, c. 1330, s. 39.

§ 20-106. Receiving or transferring stolen vehicles.

Any person who, with intent to procure or pass title to a vehicle which he knows or has reason to believe has been stolen or unlawfully taken, receives or transfers possession of the same from or to another, or who has in his possession any vehicle which he knows or has reason to believe has been stolen or unlawfully taken, and who is not an officer of the law engaged at the time in the performance of his duty as such officer shall be punished as a Class H felon. (1937, c. 407, s. 70; 1979, c. 760, s. 5; 1979, 2nd Sess., c. 1316, s. 47; 1981, c. 63, s. 1, c. 179, s. 14; 1993, c. 539, s. 1252; 1994, Ex. Sess., c. 24, s. 14(c).)

§ 20-106.1. Fraud in connection with rental of motor vehicles.

Any person with the intent to defraud the owner of any motor vehicle or a person in lawful possession thereof, who obtains possession of said vehicle by agreeing in writing to pay a rental for the use of said vehicle, and further agreeing in writing that the said vehicle shall be returned to a certain place, or at a certain time, and who willfully fails and refuses to return the same to the place and at the time specified, or who secretes, converts, sells or attempts to sell the same or any part thereof shall be guilty of a Class I felony. (1961, c. 1067; 1993, c. 539, s. 1253; 1994, Ex. Sess., c. 24, s. 14(c).)

§ 20-106.2. Sublease and loan assumption arranging regulated.

(a) As used in this section:

(1) "Buyer" means a purchaser of a motor vehicle under the terms of a retail installment contract. "Buyer" shall include any co-buyer on the retail installment contract.

(2) "Lease" means an agreement between a lessor and a lessee whereby the lessee obtains the possession and use of a motor vehicle for the period of time, for the purposes, and for the consideration set forth in the agreement whether or not the agreement includes an option to purchase the motor vehicle; provided, however, "lease" shall not include a residential rental agreement of a manufactured home which is subject to Chapter 42 of the General Statutes.

(3) "Lessor" means any person who in the regular course of business or as a part of regular business activity leases motor vehicles under motor vehicle lease agreements, purchases motor vehicle lease agreements, or any sales finance company that purchases motor vehicle lease agreements.

(4) "Lessee" means a person who obtains possession and use of a motor vehicle through a motor vehicle lease agreement. "Lessee" shall include any co-lessee listed on the motor vehicle lease agreement.

(5) "Person" means an individual, partnership, corporation, association or any other group however organized.

(6) "Security interest" means an interest in personal property that secures performance of an obligation.

(7) "Secured party" means a lender, seller, or other person in whose favor there is a security interest, including a person to whom accounts or retail installment sales contracts have been sold.

(8) "Sublease" means an agreement whether written or oral:

a. To transfer to a third party possession of a motor vehicle which is and will, while in that third party's possession, remain the subject of a security interest which secures performance of a retail installment contract or consumer loan; or

b. To transfer or assign to a third party any of the buyer's rights, interests, or obligations under the retail installment contract or consumer loan; or

c. To transfer to a third party possession of a motor vehicle which is and will, while in the third party's possession, remain the subject of a motor vehicle lease agreement; or

d. To transfer or assign to a third party any of the lessee's or buyer's rights, interests, or obligations under the motor vehicle lease agreement.

(9) "Sublease arranger" means a person who engages in the business of inducing by any means buyers and lessees to enter into subleases as sublessors and inducing third parties to enter into subleases as sublessees, however such contracts may be called. "Sublease arranger" does not include the publisher, owner, agent or employee of a newspaper, periodical, radio station, television station, cable-television system or other advertising medium which disseminates any advertisement or promotion of any act governed by this section.

(10) "Third party" means a person other than the buyer or the lessee of the vehicle.

(11) "Transfer" means to transfer possession of a motor vehicle by means of a sale, loan assumption, lease, sublease, or lease assignment.

(b) A sublease arranger commits an offense if the sublease arranger arranges a sublease of a motor vehicle and:

(1) Does not first obtain written authorization for the sublease from the vehicle's secured party or lessor; or

(2) Accepts a fee without having first obtained written authorization for the sublease from the vehicle's secured party or lessor; or

(3) Does not disclose the location of the vehicle on the request of the vehicle's buyer, lessee, secured party, or lessor; or

(4) Does not provide to the third party new, accurate disclosures under the Consumer Credit Protection Act, 15 U.S.C. Section 1601, et seq.; or

(5) Does not provide oral and written notice to the buyer or lessee that he will not be released from liability; or

(6) Does not ensure that all rights under warranties and service contracts regarding the motor vehicle transfer to the third party, unless a pro rata rebate for any unexpired coverage is applied to reduce the third party's cost under the sublease; or

(7) Does not take reasonable steps to ensure that the third party is financially able to assume the payment obligations of the buyer or lessee according to the terms of the lease agreement, retail installment contract, or consumer loan.

(c) It is not a defense to prosecution under subsection (b) of this section that the motor vehicle's buyer or lessee, secured party or lessor has violated a contract creating a security interest or lease in the motor vehicle, nor may any sublease arranger shift to the lessee, buyer or third party the arranger's duty under subdivision (b)(1) or (b)(2) to obtain prior written authorization for formation of a sublease.

(d) An offense under subdivision (b)(1) or (b)(2) of this section is a Class I felony.

(e) All other offenses under subsection (b) of this section are Class 1 misdemeanors. Each failure to disclose the location of the vehicle under subdivision (b)(3) shall constitute a separate offense.

(f) Any buyer, lessee, sublessee, secured party or lessor injured or damaged by reason of any act in violation of this section, whether or not there is a conviction for the violation, may file a civil action to recover damages based on the violation with the following available remedies:

(1) Three times the amount of any actual damages or fifteen hundred dollars ($1500), whichever is greater;

(2) Equitable relief, including a temporary restraining order, a preliminary or permanent injunction, or restitution of money or property;

(3) Reasonable attorney fees and costs; and

(4) Any other relief which the court deems just.

The rights and remedies provided by this section are in addition to any other rights and remedies provided by law.

(g) This section and G.S. 14-114 and G.S. 14-115 are mutually exclusive and prosecution under those sections shall not preclude criminal prosecution or civil action under this section. (1989 (Reg. Sess., 1990), c. 1011; 1993, c. 539, ss. 347, 1254; 1994, Ex. Sess., c. 24, s. 14(c).)

§ 20-107. Injuring or tampering with vehicle.

(a) Any person who either individually or in association with one or more other persons willfully injures or tampers with any vehicles or breaks or removes any part or parts of or from a vehicle without the consent of the owner is guilty of a Class 2 misdemeanor.

(b) Any person who with intent to steal, commit any malicious mischief, injury or other crime, climbs into or upon a vehicle, whether it is in motion or at rest, or with like intent attempts to manipulate any of the levers, starting mechanism, brakes, or other mechanism or device of a vehicle while the same is at rest and unattended or with like intent sets in motion any vehicle while the same is at rest and unattended, is guilty of a Class 2 misdemeanor. (1937, c. 407, s. 71; 1965, c. 621, s. 1; 1993, c. 539, s. 348; 1994, Ex. Sess., c. 24, s. 14(c).)

§ 20-108. Vehicles or component parts of vehicles without manufacturer's numbers.

(a) Any person who knowingly buys, receives, disposes of, sells, offers for sale, conceals, or has in his possession any motor vehicle, or engine or transmission or component part which has been stolen or removed from a motor vehicle and from which the manufacturer's serial or engine number or other distinguishing number or identification mark or number placed thereon under assignment from the Division has been removed, defaced, covered, altered, or destroyed for the purpose of concealing or misrepresenting the identity of said motor vehicle or engine or transmission or component part is guilty of a Class 2 misdemeanor.

(b) The Commissioner and such officers and inspectors of the Division of Motor Vehicles as he has designated may take and possess any motor vehicle or component part if its engine number, vehicle identification number, or manufacturer's serial number has been altered, changed, or obliterated or if such officer has probable cause to believe that the driver or person in charge of the motor vehicle or component part has violated subsection (a) above. Any officer who so takes possession of a motor vehicle or component part shall immediately notify the Division of Motor Vehicles and the rightful owner, if known. The notification shall contain a description of the motor vehicle or component part and any other facts that may assist in locating or establishing the rightful ownership thereof or in prosecuting any person for a violation of the provisions of this Article.

(c) Within 15 days after seizure of a motor vehicle or component part pursuant to this section, the Division shall send notice by certified mail to the person from whom the property was seized and to all claimants to the property whose interest or title is in the registration records in the Division of Motor Vehicles that the Division has taken custody of the motor vehicle or component part. The notice shall also contain the following information:

(1) The name and address of the person or persons from whom the motor vehicle or component part was seized;

(2) A statement that the motor vehicle or component part has been seized for investigation as provided in this section and that the motor vehicle or component part will be released to the rightful owner:

a. Upon a determination that the identification number has not been altered, changed, or obliterated; or

b. Upon presentation of satisfactory evidence of the ownership of the motor vehicle or component part if no other person claims an interest in it within 30 days of the date the notice is mailed. Otherwise, a hearing regarding the disposition of the motor vehicle or component part may take place in a court having jurisdiction.

(3) The name and address of the officer to whom evidence of ownership of the motor vehicle or component part may be presented; and

(4) A copy statement of the text contained in this section.

(d) Whenever a motor vehicle or component part comes into the custody of an officer, the Division of Motor Vehicles may commence a civil action in the District Court in the county in which the motor vehicle or component part was seized to determine whether the motor vehicle or component part should be destroyed, sold, converted to the use of the Division or otherwise disposed of by an order of the court. The Division shall give notice of the commencement of such an action to the person from whom the motor vehicle or component part was seized and all claimants to the property whose interest or title is in the registration records of the Division of Motor Vehicles. Notice shall be by certified mail sent within 10 days after the filing of the action. In addition, any possessor of a motor vehicle or component part described in this section may commence a civil action under the provisions of this section, to which the Division of Motor Vehicles may be made a party, to provide for the proper disposition of the motor vehicle or component part.

(e) Nothing in this section shall preclude the Division of Motor Vehicles from returning a seized motor vehicle or component part to the owner following presentation of satisfactory evidence of ownership, and, if determined necessary, requiring the owner to obtain an assignment of an identification number for the motor vehicle or component part from the Division of Motor Vehicles.

(f) No court order providing for disposition shall be issued unless the person from whom the motor vehicle or component was seized and all claimants to the property whose interest or title is in the registration records in the Division of Motor Vehicles are provided a postseizure hearing by the court having jurisdiction. Ten days' notice of the postseizure hearing shall be given by certified mail to the person from whom the motor vehicle was seized and all claimants to the property whose interest or title is in the registration records in the Division of Motor Vehicles. If such motor vehicle or component part has been held or identified as evidence in a pending civil or criminal action or proceeding, no final disposition of such motor vehicle or component part shall be ordered without prior notice to the parties in said proceeding.

(g) At a hearing held pursuant to any action filed by the Division to determine the disposition of any motor vehicle or component part seized pursuant to this section, the court shall consider the following:

(1) If the evidence reveals either that the motor vehicle or component part identification number has not been altered, changed or obliterated or that the

identification number has been altered, changed, or obliterated but satisfactory evidence of ownership has been presented, the motor vehicle or component part shall be returned to the person entitled to it. If ownership cannot be established, nothing in this section shall preclude the return of said motor vehicle or component part to a good faith purchaser following the presentation of satisfactory evidence of ownership thereof and, if necessary, upon the good faith purchaser's obtaining an assigned number from the Division of Motor Vehicles and posting a reasonable bond for a period of three years. The amount of the bond shall be set by the court.

(2) If the evidence reveals that the motor vehicle or component part identification number has been altered, changed, or obliterated and satisfactory evidence of ownership has not been presented, the motor vehicle or component part shall be destroyed, sold, converted to the use of the Division of Motor Vehicles or otherwise disposed of, as provided for by order of the court.

(h) At the hearing, the Division shall have the burden of establishing, by a preponderance of the evidence, that the motor vehicle or component part has been stolen or that its identification number has been altered, changed, or obliterated.

(i) At the hearing any claimant to the motor vehicle or component part shall have the burden of providing satisfactory evidence of ownership.

(j) An officer taking into custody a motor vehicle or component part under the provisions of this section is authorized to obtain necessary removal and storage services, but shall incur no personal liability for such services. The person or company so employed shall be entitled to reasonable compensation as a claimant under (e), and shall not be deemed an unlawful possessor under (a). (1937, c. 407, s. 72; 1965, c. 621, s. 2; 1973, c. 1149, ss. 1, 2; 1975, c. 716, s. 5; 1983, c. 592; 1985, c. 764, s. 22; 1985 (Reg. Sess., 1986), c. 852, s. 17; 1993, c. 539, s. 349; 1994, Ex. Sess., c. 24, s. 14(c).)

§ 20-109. Altering or changing engine or other numbers.

(a) It shall be unlawful and constitute a felony for:

(1) Any person to willfully deface, destroy, remove, cover, or alter the manufacturer's serial number, transmission number, or engine number; or

(2) Any vehicle owner to knowingly permit the defacing, removal, destroying, covering, or alteration of the serial number, transmission number, or engine number; or

(3) Any person except a licensed vehicle manufacturer as authorized by law to place or stamp any serial number, transmission number, or engine number upon a vehicle, other than one assigned thereto by the Division; or

(4) Any vehicle owner to knowingly permit the placing or stamping of any serial number or motor number upon a motor vehicle, except such numbers as assigned thereto by the Division.

A violation of this subsection shall be punishable as a Class I felony.

(b) It shall be unlawful and constitute a felony for:

(1) Any person, with intent to conceal or misrepresent the true identity of the vehicle, to deface, destroy, remove, cover, alter, or use any serial or motor number assigned to a vehicle by the Division; or

(2) Any vehicle owner, with intent to conceal or misrepresent the true identity of the vehicle, to permit the defacing, destruction, removal, covering, alteration, or use of a serial or motor number assigned to a vehicle by the Division; or

(3) Any vehicle owner, with the intent to conceal or misrepresent the true identity of a vehicle, to permit the defacing, destruction, removal, covering, alteration, use, gift, or sale of any manufacturer's serial number, serial number plate, or any part or parts of a vehicle containing the serial number or portions of the serial number.

A violation of this subsection shall be punishable as a Class I felony. (1937, c. 407, s. 73; 1943, c. 726; 1953, c. 216; 1965, c. 621, s. 3; 1967, c. 449; 1973, c. 1089; 1975, c. 716, s. 5; 1979, c. 760, s. 5; 1979, 2nd Sess., c. 1316, s. 47; 1981, c. 179, s. 14; 1987, c. 512; 1993, c. 539, s. 1255; 1994, Ex. Sess., c. 24, s. 14(c).)

§ 20-109.1. Surrender of titles to salvage vehicles.

(a) Option to Keep Title. - When a vehicle is damaged to the extent that it becomes a salvage vehicle and the owner submits a claim for the damages to an insurer, the insurer must determine whether the owner wants to keep the vehicle after payment of the claim. If the owner does not want to keep the vehicle after payment of the claim, the procedures in subsection (b) of this section apply. If the owner wants to keep the vehicle after payment of the claim, the procedures in subsection (c) of this section apply.

(b) Transfer to Insurer. -

(1) If a salvage vehicle owner does not want to keep the vehicle, the owner must assign the vehicle's certificate of title to the insurer when the insurer pays the claim. The insurer must send the assigned title to the Division within 10 days after receiving it from the vehicle owner. The Division must then send the insurer a form to use to transfer title to the vehicle from the insurer to a person who buys the vehicle from the insurer. If the insurer sells the vehicle, the insurer must complete the form and give it to the buyer. If the buyer rebuilds the vehicle, the buyer may apply for a new certificate of title to the vehicle.

(2) If a salvage vehicle owner fails to assign and deliver the vehicle's certificate of title to the insurer within 30 days of the payment of the claim in accordance with subdivision (b)(1) of this section, the insurer, without surrendering the certificate of title, may, at any time thereafter, request that the Division send the insurer a form to use to transfer title to the vehicle from the insurer to a person who buys the vehicle from the insurer. The request shall be made on a form prescribed by the Division and shall be accompanied by proof of payment of the claim and proof of notice sent to the owner and any lienholder requesting the vehicle's certificate of title. If the records of the Division indicate there is an outstanding lien against the vehicle immediately before the payment of the claim and if the payment was made to a lienholder or to a lienholder and the owner jointly, the proof of payment shall include evidence that funds were paid to the first lienholder shown on the records of the Division. The notice must be sent by the insurer at least 30 days prior to requesting the Division send the insurer a form to use to transfer title and must be sent by certified mail or by another commercially available delivery service providing proof of delivery to the address on record with the Division. Upon the Division's receipt of such request, the vehicle's certificate of title is deemed to be assigned to the insurer. Notwithstanding any outstanding liens against the vehicle, the Division must send the insurer a form to use to transfer title to the vehicle from the insurer to a person who buys the vehicle from the insurer. The Division's issuance of the form extinguishes all existing liens on the motor vehicle. If the insurer sells the

vehicle, the insurer must complete the form and give it to the buyer. In such a sale by the insurer, the motor vehicle shall be transferred free and clear of any liens. If the buyer rebuilds the vehicle, the buyer may apply for a new certificate of title to the vehicle.

(c)   Owner Keeps Vehicle. - If a salvage vehicle owner wants to keep the vehicle, the insurer must give the owner an owner-retained salvage form. The owner must complete the form and give it to the insurer when the insurer pays the claim. The owner's signature on the owner-retained salvage form must be notarized. The insurer must send the completed form to the Division within 10 days after receiving it from the vehicle owner. The Division must then note in its vehicle registration records that the vehicle listed on the form is a salvage vehicle.

(d)   Theft Claim on Salvage Vehicle. - An insurer that pays a theft loss claim on a vehicle and, upon recovery of the vehicle, determines that the vehicle has been damaged to the extent that it is a salvage vehicle must send the vehicle's certificate of title to the Division within 10 days after making the determination. The Division and the insurer must then follow the procedures set in subdivision (1) of subsection (b) of this section.

(e)   Out-of-State Vehicle. - A person who acquires a salvage vehicle that is registered in a state that does not require surrender of the vehicle's certificate of title must send the title to the Division within 10 days after the vehicle enters this State. The Division and the person must then follow the procedures set in subdivision (1) of subsection (b) of this section.

(e1)   Owner or Lienholder Abandons Vehicle. - If an insurer requests a used motor vehicle dealer, the primary business of which is the sale of salvage vehicles on behalf of insurers, to take possession of a salvage vehicle that is the subject of an insurance claim and subsequently the insurer does not take ownership of the vehicle, the insurer may direct the used motor vehicle dealer to release the vehicle to the owner or lienholder. The insurer shall provide the used motor vehicle dealer a release statement authorizing the used motor vehicle dealer to release the vehicle to the vehicle's owner or lienholder.

Upon receiving a release statement from an insurer, the used motor vehicle dealer shall send notice to the owner and any lienholder of the vehicle informing the owner or lienholder that the vehicle is available for pick up. The notice shall include an invoice for any outstanding charges owed to the used motor vehicle dealer. The notice shall inform the owner and any lienholder that the owner or lienholder has 30 days from the date of the notice, and upon payment of applicable charges owed to the used motor vehicle dealer, to pick up the vehicle from the used motor vehicle dealer. Notice under this subsection must be sent by certified mail or by another commercially available delivery service providing proof of delivery to the address on record with the Division.

If the owner or any lienholder of the vehicle does not pick up the vehicle within 30 days after notice was sent to the owner and any lienholder in accordance with this subsection, the vehicle shall be considered abandoned, the vehicle's certificate of title is deemed to be assigned to the used motor vehicle dealer, and the used motor vehicle dealer, without surrendering the certificate of title, may request that the Division send the used motor vehicle dealer a form to use to transfer title to the vehicle from the used motor vehicle dealer to a person who buys the vehicle from the used motor vehicle dealer. The request shall be accompanied by a copy of the notice required by this subsection and proof of delivery of the notice required by this subsection sent to the owner and any lienholder. Notwithstanding any outstanding liens against the vehicle, the Division must send the used motor vehicle dealer a form to use to transfer title to the vehicle from the used motor vehicle dealer to a person who buys the vehicle from the used motor vehicle dealer. The Division's issuance of the form extinguishes all existing liens on the motor vehicle. If the used motor vehicle dealer sells the vehicle, the used motor vehicle dealer must complete the form and give it to the buyer. In such a sale by the used motor vehicle dealer, the motor vehicle shall be transferred free and clear of any liens. If the buyer rebuilds the vehicle, the buyer may apply for a new certificate of title.

(f) Sanctions. - Violation of this section is a Class 1 misdemeanor. In addition to this criminal sanction, a person who violates this section is subject to a civil penalty of up to one hundred dollars ($100.00), to be imposed in the discretion of the Commissioner.

(g) Fee. - G.S. 20-85 sets the fee for issuing a salvage certificate of title.

(h) Claims. - The Division shall not be subject to a claim under Article 31 of Chapter 143 of the General Statutes related to the cancellation of a title pursuant to this section if the claim is based on reliance by the Division on any proof of payment or proof of notice submitted to the Division by a third party pursuant to subdivision (b)(2) or subsection (e1) of this section. (1973, c. 1095, s. 1; 1975, c. 716, s. 5; c. 799; 1983, c. 713, s. 94; 1989, c. 455, s. 5; 1993, c. 539, s. 350; 1994, Ex. Sess., c. 24, s. 14(c); 1995, c. 50, s. 3; c. 517, s. 33.1; 2013-400, s. 1.)

§ 20-109.2. Surrender of title to manufactured home.

(a)   Surrender of Title. - If a certificate of title has been issued for a manufactured home, the owner listed on the title has the title, and the manufactured home qualifies as real property as defined in G.S. 105-273(13), the owner listed on the title shall submit an affidavit to the Division that the manufactured home meets this definition and surrender the certificate of title to the Division.

(a1)   Surrender When Title Not Available. - If a certificate of title has been issued for a manufactured home, no issued title is available, and the manufactured home qualifies as real property as defined in G.S. 105-273(13), the owner listed on the title shall be deemed to have surrendered the title to the Division if the owner of the real property on which the manufactured home is affixed (i) submits an affidavit to the Division that the manufactured home meets the definition of real property under G.S. 105-273(13) and in compliance with subsection (b) of this section and (ii) submits a tax record showing the manufactured home listed for ad valorem taxes as real property pursuant to Article 17 of Chapter 105 of the General Statutes in the name of the record owner of the real property on which the manufactured home is affixed.

(b)   Affidavit. - The affidavit must be in a form approved by the Commissioner and shall include or provide for all of the following information:

(1)   The manufacturer and, if applicable, the model name of the manufactured home affixed to real property upon which cancellation is sought.

(2)   The vehicle identification number and serial number of the manufactured home affixed to real property upon which cancellation is sought.

(3)   The legal description of the real property on which the manufactured home is affixed, stating that the owner of the manufactured home also owns the real property or that the owner of the manufactured home has entered into a lease with a primary term of at least 20 years for the real property on which the manufactured home is affixed with a copy of the lease or a memorandum thereof pursuant to G.S. 47-18 attached to the affidavit, if not previously recorded.

(4) A description of any security interests in the manufactured home affixed to real property upon which cancellation is sought.

(5) A section for the Division's notation or statement that either the procedure in subsection (a) of this section for surrendering the title has been surrendered and the title has been cancelled by the Division or the affiant submits this affidavit pursuant to subsection (a1) of this section to have the title deemed surrendered by the owner listed on the certificate of title.

(6) An affirmative statement that the affiant is (i) the record owner of the real property on which the manufactured home is affixed and the lease for the manufactured home does not include a provision allowing the owner listed on the certificate of title to dispose of the manufactured home prior to the end of the primary term of the lease or (ii) is the owner of the manufactured home and either owns the real property on which the manufactured home is affixed or has entered into a lease with a primary term of at least 20 years for the real property on which the manufactured home is affixed.

(7) The affiant affirms that he or she has sent notice of this cancellation by hand delivery or by first-class mail to the last known address of the owner listed on the certificate of title prior to filing this affidavit with the Division.

(c) Cancellation. - Upon compliance with the procedures in subsection (a) or (a1) of this section for surrender of title, the Division shall rescind and cancel the certificate of title. If a security interest has been recorded on the certificate of title and not released by the secured party, the Division may not cancel the title without written consent from all secured parties. After canceling the title, the Division shall return the original of the affidavit to the affiant, or to the secured party having the first recorded security interest, with the Division's notation or statement that the title has been surrendered and has been cancelled by the Division. The affiant or secured party shall file the affidavit returned by the Division with the office of the register of deeds of the county where the real property is located. The Division may charge five dollars ($5.00) for a cancellation of a title under this section.

(d) Application for Title After Cancellation. - If the owner of a manufactured home whose certificate of title has been cancelled under this section subsequently seeks to separate the manufactured home from the real property, the owner may apply for a new certificate of title. The owner must submit to the Division an affidavit containing the same information set out in subsection (b) of this section, verification that the manufactured home has been removed from the real property, and written consent of any affected owners of recorded mortgages, deeds of trust, or security interests in the real property where the manufactured home was placed. The Commissioner may require evidence sufficient to demonstrate that all affected owners of security interests have been notified and consent. Upon receipt of this information, together with a title application and required fee, the Division is authorized to issue a new title for the manufactured home.

(e)   Sanctions. - Any person who violates this section is subject to a civil penalty of up to one hundred dollars ($100.00), to be imposed in the discretion of the Commissioner.

(f)   No Right of Action. - A person damaged by the cancellation of a certificate of title pursuant to subsection (a1) of this section does not have a right of action against the Division. (2001-506, s. 2; 2003-400, s. 1; 2013-79, s. 1.)

§ 20-110. When registration shall be rescinded.

(a)   The Division shall rescind and cancel the registration of any vehicle which the Division shall determine is unsafe or unfit to be operated or is not equipped as required by law.

(b)   The Division shall rescind and cancel the registration of any vehicle whenever the person to whom the registration card or registration number plates therefor have been issued shall make or permit to be made any unlawful use of the said card or plates or permit the use thereof by a person not entitled thereto.

(c)   Repealed by Session Laws 1993, c. 440, s. 8.

(d)   The Division shall rescind and cancel the certificate of title to any vehicle which has been erroneously issued or fraudulently obtained or is unlawfully detained by anyone not entitled to possession.

(e)   and (f) Repealed by Session Laws 1993, c. 440, s. 8.

(g)   The Division shall rescind and cancel the registration plates issued to a carrier of passengers or property which has been secured by such carrier as provided under G.S. 20-50 when the license is being used on a vehicle other than the one for which it was issued or which is being used by the lessor-owner after the lease with such lessee has been terminated.

(h)   The Division may rescind and cancel the registration or certificate of title on any vehicle on the grounds that the application therefor contains any false or fraudulent statement or that the holder of the certificate was not entitled to the issuance of a certificate of title or registration.

(i)   The Division may rescind and cancel the registration or certificate of title of any vehicle when the Division has reasonable grounds to believe that the vehicle is a stolen or embezzled vehicle, or that the granting of registration or the issuance of certificate of title constituted a fraud against the rightful owner or person having a valid lien upon such vehicle.

(j)   The Division may rescind and cancel the registration or certificate of title of any vehicle on the grounds that the registration of the vehicle stands suspended or revoked under the motor vehicle laws of this State.

(k)   The Division shall rescind and cancel a certificate of title when the Division finds that such certificate has been used in connection with the registration or sale of a vehicle other than the vehicle for which the certificate was issued.

(l)   The Division may rescind and cancel the registration and certificate of title of a vehicle when presented with evidence, such as a sworn statement, that the vehicle has been transferred to a person who has failed to get a new certificate of title for the vehicle as required by G.S. 20-73. A person may submit evidence to the Division by mail.

(m)   The Division shall rescind and cancel the registration of vehicles of a motor carrier that is subject to an order issued by the Federal Motor Carrier Safety Administration or the Division to cease all operations based on a finding that the continued operations of the motor carrier pose an "imminent hazard" as defined in 49 C.F.R. § 386.72(b)(1). (1937, c. 407, s. 74; 1945, c. 576, s. 5; 1947, c. 220, s. 4; 1951, c. 985, s. 1; 1953, c. 831, s. 4; 1955, c. 294, s. 1; c. 554, s. 11; 1975, c. 716, s. 5; 1981, c. 976, s. 11; 1991, c. 183, s. 1; 1993, c. 440, s. 8; 2002-152, s. 2.)

§ 20-111. Violation of registration provisions.

It shall be unlawful for any person to commit any of the following acts:

(1)   To drive a vehicle on a highway, or knowingly permit a vehicle owned by that person to be driven on a highway, when the vehicle is not registered with the Division in accordance with this Article or does not display a current registration plate. Violation of this subdivision is a Class 3 misdemeanor.

(2)   To display or cause or permit to be displayed or to have in possession any registration card, certificate of title or registration number plate knowing the same to be fictitious or to have been canceled, revoked, suspended or altered, or to willfully display an expired license or registration plate on a vehicle knowing the same to be expired. Violation of this subdivision is a Class 3 misdemeanor.

(3)   The giving, lending, or borrowing of a license plate for the purpose of using same on some motor vehicle other than that for which issued shall make the giver, lender, or borrower guilty of a Class 3 misdemeanor. Where license plate is found being improperly used, such plate or plates shall be revoked or canceled, and new license plates must be purchased before further operation of the motor vehicle.

(4)   To fail or refuse to surrender to the Division, upon demand, any title certificate, registration card or registration number plate which has been suspended, canceled or revoked as in this Article provided. Service of the demand shall be in accordance with G.S. 20-48.

(5)   To use a false or fictitious name or address in any application for the registration of any vehicle or for a certificate of title or for any renewal or duplicate thereof, or knowingly to make a false statement or knowingly to conceal a material fact or otherwise commit a fraud in any such application. A violation of this subdivision shall constitute a Class 1 misdemeanor.

(6)   To give, lend, sell or obtain a certificate of title for the purpose of such certificate being used for any purpose other than the registration, sale, or other use in connection with the vehicle for which the certificate was issued. Any person violating the provisions of this subdivision shall be guilty of a Class 2 misdemeanor. (1937, c. 407, s. 75; 1943, c. 592, s. 2; 1945, c. 576, s. 6; c. 635; 1949, c. 360; 1955, c. 294, s. 2; 1961, c. 360, s. 20; 1975, c. 716, s. 5; 1981, c. 938, s. 3; 1993, c. 440, s. 9; c. 539, ss. 351-353; 1994, Ex. Sess., c. 24, s. 14(c); 2013-360, s. 18B.14(i).)

§ 20-112. Making false affidavit perjury.

Any person who shall knowingly make any false affidavit or shall knowingly swear or affirm falsely to any matter or thing required by the terms of this Article to be sworn or affirmed to shall be guilty of a Class I felony. (1937, c. 407, s. 76; 1993, c. 539, s. 1256; 1994, Ex. Sess., c. 24, s. 14(c).)

§ 20-113: Repealed by Session Laws 1995 (Regular Session, 1996), c. 756, s. 13.

§ 20-114. Duty of officers; manner of enforcement.

(a) For the purpose of enforcing the provisions of this Article, it is hereby made the duty of every police officer of any incorporated city or village, and every sheriff, deputy sheriff, and all other lawful officers of any county to arrest within the limits of their jurisdiction any person known personally to any such officer, or upon the sworn information of a creditable witness, to have violated any of the provisions of this Article, and to immediately bring such offender before any magistrate or officer having jurisdiction, and any such person so arrested shall have the right of immediate trial, and all other rights given to any person arrested for having committed a misdemeanor. Every officer herein named who shall neglect or refuse to carry out the duties imposed by this Chapter shall be liable on his official bond for such neglect or refusal as provided by law in like cases.

(b) It shall be the duty of all sheriffs, police officers, deputy sheriffs, deputy police officers, and all other officers within the State to cooperate with and render all assistance in their power to the officers herein provided for, and nothing in this Article shall be construed as relieving said sheriffs, police officers, deputy sheriffs, deputy police officers, and other officers of the duties imposed on them by this Chapter.

(c) It shall also be the duty of every law enforcement officer to make immediate report to the Commissioner of all motor vehicles reported to the officer as abandoned or that are seized by the officer for being used for illegal transportation of alcoholic beverages or other unlawful purposes, or seized and are subject to forfeiture pursuant to G.S. 20-28.2, et seq., or any other statute, and no motor vehicle shall be sold by any sheriff, police or peace officer, or by any person, firm or corporation claiming a mechanic's or storage lien, or under judicial proceedings, until notice on a form approved by the Commissioner shall have been given the Commissioner at least 20 days before the date of such sale. (1937, c. 407, s. 78; 1943, c. 726; 1967, c. 862; 1971, c. 528, s. 13; 1981, c. 412, s. 4; c. 747, s. 66; 1998-182, s. 12.)

§ 20-114.1. Willful failure to obey law-enforcement or traffic-control officer; firemen as traffic-control officers; appointment, etc., of traffic-control officers.

(a) No person shall willfully fail or refuse to comply with any lawful order or direction of any law-enforcement officer or traffic-control officer invested by law with authority to direct, control or regulate traffic, which order or direction related to the control of traffic.

(b) In addition to other law enforcement or traffic control officers, uniformed regular and volunteer firemen and uniformed regular and volunteer members of a rescue squad may direct traffic and enforce traffic laws and ordinances at the scene of or in connection with fires, accidents, or other hazards in connection with their duties as firemen or rescue squad members. Except as herein provided, firemen and members of rescue squads shall not be considered law enforcement or traffic control officers.

(b1) Any member of a rural volunteer fire department or volunteer rescue squad who receives no compensation for services shall not be liable in civil damages for any acts or omissions relating to the direction of traffic or enforcement of traffic laws or ordinances at the scene of or in connection with a fire, accident, or other hazard unless such acts or omissions amount to gross negligence, wanton conduct, or intentional wrongdoing.

(c) The chief of police of a local or county police department or the sheriff of any county is authorized to appoint traffic-control officers, who shall have attained the age of 18 years and who are hereby authorized to direct, control, or regulate traffic within their respective jurisdictions at times and places specifically designated in writing by the police chief or the sheriff. A traffic-control officer, when exercising this authority, must be attired in a distinguishing uniform or jacket indicating that he is a traffic-control officer and must possess a valid authorization card issued by the police chief or sheriff who appointed him. Unless an earlier expiration date is specified, an authorization card shall expire two years from the date of its issuance. In order to be appointed as a traffic-control officer, a person shall have received at least three hours of training in directing, controlling, or regulating traffic under the supervision of a law-enforcement officer. A traffic-control officer shall be subject to the rules and regulations of the respective local or county police department or sheriff's office as well as the lawful command of any other law-enforcement officer. The appointing police chief or sheriff shall have the right to revoke the appointment of any traffic-control officer at any time with or without cause. The appointing police chief or sheriff shall not be held liable for any act or omission of a traffic-control officer. A traffic-control officer shall not be deemed to be an agent or employee of the respective local or county police department or of the sheriff's office, nor shall he be considered a law-enforcement officer except as provided herein. A traffic-control officer shall not have nor shall he exercise the power of arrest.

(d) No police chief or sheriff who is authorized to appoint traffic-control officers under subsection (c) of this section shall appoint any person to direct, control, or regulate traffic unless there is indemnity against liability of the traffic-control officer for wrongful death, bodily injury, or property damage that is proximately caused by the negligence of the traffic-control officer while acting within the scope of his duties as a traffic-control officer. Such indemnity shall provide a minimum of twenty-five thousand dollars ($25,000) for the death of or bodily injury to one person in any one accident, fifty thousand dollars ($50,000) for the death of or bodily injury to two or more persons in any one accident, and ten thousand dollars ($10,000) for injury to or destruction of property of others in any one accident. (1961, c. 879; 1969, c. 59; 1983, c. 483, ss. 1-3; 1987, c. 146, ss. 1, 3.)

§ 20-114.3: Repealed by Session Laws 2007-433, s. 3(a), (b), effective October 1, 2007.

Part 9. The Size, Weight, Construction and Equipment of Vehicles.

§ 20-115. Scope and effect of regulations in this title.

It shall be unlawful for any person to drive or move or for the owner to cause or knowingly permit to be driven or moved on any highway any vehicle or vehicles of a size or weight exceeding the limitations stated in this title, or any vehicle or vehicles which are not so constructed or equipped as required in this title, or the rules and regulations of the Department of Transportation adopted pursuant thereto and the maximum size and weight of vehicles herein specified shall be lawful throughout this State, and local authorities shall have no power or authority to alter said limitations except as express authority may be granted in this Article. (1937, c. 407, s. 79; 1973, c. 507, s. 5; 1977, c. 464, s. 34; 1985 (Reg. Sess., 1986), c. 852, s. 8.)

§ 20-115.1. Limitations on tandem trailers and semitrailers on certain North Carolina highways.

(a) Motor vehicle combinations consisting of a truck tractor and two trailing units may be operated in North Carolina only on highways of the interstate system (except those exempted by the United States Secretary of Transportation pursuant to 49 USC 2311(i)) and on those sections of the federal-aid primary system designated by the United States Secretary of Transportation. No trailer or semitrailer operated in this combination shall exceed 28 feet in length; Provided, however, a 1982 or older year model trailer or semitrailer of up to 28 1/2 feet in length may operate in a combination permitted by this section for trailers or semitrailers which are 28 feet in length.

(b) Motor vehicle combinations consisting of a semitrailer of not more than 53 feet in length and a truck tractor may be operated on all primary highway routes of North Carolina provided the motor vehicle combination meets the requirements of this subsection. The Department may, at any time, prohibit motor vehicle combinations on portions of any route on the State highway system. If the Department prohibits a motor vehicle combination on any route, it shall submit a written report to the Joint Legislative Transportation Oversight Committee within six months of the prohibition clearly documenting through traffic engineering studies that the operation of a motor vehicle combination on that route cannot be safely accommodated and that the route does not have sufficient capacity to handle the vehicle combination. To operate on a primary highway route, a motor vehicle combination described in this subsection must meet all of the following requirements:

(1) The motor vehicle combination must comply with the weight requirements in G.S. 20-118.

(2) A semitrailer in excess of 48 feet in length must meet one or more of the following conditions:

(a) The distance between the kingpin of the trailer and the rearmost axle, or a point midway between the two rear axles, if the two rear axles are a tandem axle, does not exceed 41 feet.

(b) The semitrailer is used exclusively or primarily to transport vehicles in connection with motorsports competition events, and the distance between the kingpin of the trailer and the rearmost axle, or a point midway between the two rear axles, if the two rear axles are a tandem axle, does not exceed 46 feet.

(3) A semitrailer in excess of 48 feet must be equipped with a rear underride guard of substantial construction consisting of a continuous lateral beam extending to within four inches of the lateral extremities of the semitrailer and located not more than 30 inches from the surface as measured with the vehicle empty and on a level surface.

(c) Motor vehicles with a width not exceeding 102 inches may be operated on the interstate highways (except those exempted by the United States Secretary of Transportation pursuant to 49 USC 2316(e)) and other qualifying federal-aid highways designated by the United States Secretary of Transportation, with traffic lanes designed to be a width of 12 feet or more and any other qualifying federal-aid primary system highway designated by the United States Secretary of Transportation if the Secretary has determined that the designation is consistent with highway safety.

(d) Notwithstanding the provisions of subsections (a) and (b) of this section which limit the length of trailers which may be used in motor vehicle combinations in this State on highways of the interstate system (except those exempted by the United States Secretary of Transportation pursuant to 49 USC 2311(i)) and on those sections of the federal-aid primary system designated by the United States Secretary of Transportation, there is no limitation of the length of the truck tractor which may be used in motor vehicle combinations on these highways and therefore, in compliance with Section 411(b) of the Surface Transportation Act of 1982, there is no overall length limitation for motor vehicle combinations regulated by this section.

(e) The length and width limitations in this section are subject to exceptions and exclusions for safety devices and specialized equipment as provided for in

49 USC 2311(d)(h) and Section 416 of the Surface Transportation Act of 1982 as amended (49 USC 2316).

(f) Motor vehicle combinations operating pursuant to this section shall have reasonable access between (i) highways on the interstate system (except those exempted by the United States Secretary of Transportation pursuant to 49 USC 2311(i) and 49 USC 2316(e)) and other qualifying federal-aid highways as designated by the United States Secretary of Transportation and (ii) terminals, facilities for food, fuel, repairs, and rest and points of loading and unloading by household goods carriers and by any truck tractor-semitrailer combination in which the semitrailer has a length not to exceed 28 1/2 feet and a width not to exceed 102 inches as provided in subsection (c) of this section and which generally operates as part of a vehicle combination described in subsection (a) of this section. The North Carolina Department of Transportation may, on streets and highways on the State highway system, and any municipality may, on streets and highways on the municipal street system, impose reasonable restrictions based on safety considerations on any truck tractor-semitrailer combination in which the semitrailer has a length not to exceed 28 1/2 feet and which generally operates as part of a vehicle combination described in subsection (a) of this section. "Reasonable access" to facilities for food, fuel, repairs and rest shall be deemed to be those facilities which are located within three road miles of the interstate or designated highway. The Department of Transportation is authorized to promulgate rules and regulations providing for "reasonable access." The Department may approve reasonable access routes for one particular type of STAA (Surface Transportation Assistance Act) dimensioned vehicle when significant, substantial differences in their operating characteristics exist.

(g) Under certain conditions, and after consultation with the Joint Legislative Commission on Governmental Operations, the North Carolina Department of Transportation may designate State highway system roads in addition to those highways designated by the United States Secretary of Transportation for use by the vehicle combinations authorized in this section. Such designations by the Department shall only be made under the following conditions:

(1) A determination of the public convenience and need for such designation;

(2) A traffic engineering study which clearly shows the road proposed to be designated can safely accommodate and has sufficient capacity to handle these vehicle combinations; and

(3) A public hearing is held or the opportunity for a public hearing is provided in each county through which the designated highway passes, after two weeks notice posted at the courthouse and published in a newspaper of general circulation in each county through which the designated State highway system road passes, and consideration is given to the comments received prior to the designation.

(4) The Department may designate routes for one particular type of STAA (Surface Transportation Assistance Act) dimensioned vehicle when significant, substantial differences in their operating characteristics exist.

The Department may not designate any portion of the State highway system that has been deleted or exempted by the United States Secretary of Transportation based on safety considerations. For the purpose of this section, any highway designated by the Department shall be deemed to be the same as a federal-aid primary highway designated by the United States Secretary of Transportation pursuant to 49 USC 2311 and 49 USC 2316, and the vehicle combinations authorized in this section shall be permitted to operate on such highway.

(h) Any owner of a semitrailer less than 50 feet in length in violation of subsections (a) or (b) is responsible for an infraction and is subject to a penalty of one hundred dollars ($100.00). Any owner of a semitrailer 50 feet or greater in length in violation of subsection (b) is responsible for an infraction and subject to a penalty of two hundred dollars ($200.00).

(i) Any driver of a vehicle with a semitrailer less than 50 feet in length violating subsections (a) or (b) of this section is guilty of a Class 3 misdemeanor punishable only by a fine of one hundred dollars ($100.00). Any driver of a vehicle with a semitrailer 50 feet or more in length violating subsection (b) of this section is guilty of a Class 3 misdemeanor punishable only by a fine of two hundred dollars ($200.00).

(j) Notwithstanding any other provision of this section, a manufacturer of trailer frames, with a permit issued pursuant to G.S. 20-119, is authorized to transport the trailer frame to another location within three miles of the first place of manufacture to the location of completion on any public street or highway if the width of the trailer frame does not exceed 14 feet and oversize markings and safety flags are used during transport. Trailer frames transported pursuant to this subsection shall not exceed 7,000 pounds, and the vehicle towing the trailer frame shall have a towing capacity greater than 10,000 pounds and necessary towing equipment. The transport of trailer frames under this subsection shall only be done during daylight hours. (1983, c. 898, s. 1; 1985, c. 423, ss. 1-7; 1989, c. 790, ss. 1, 3, 3.1; 1993, c. 533, s. 10; c. 539, s. 354; 1994, Ex. Sess., c. 24, s. 14(c); 1998-149, s. 6; 2007-77, ss. 2, 3; 2008-160, s. 1; 2008-221, ss. 3, 4.)

§ 20-116. Size of vehicles and loads.

(a) The total outside width of any vehicle or the load thereon shall not exceed 102 inches, except as otherwise provided in this section. When hogsheads of tobacco are being transported, a tolerance of six inches is allowed. When sheet or bale tobacco is being transported the load must not exceed a width of 114 inches at the top of the load and the bottom of the load at the truck bed must not exceed the width of 102 inches inclusive of allowance for load shifting or settling. Vehicles (other than passenger buses) that do not exceed the overall width of 102 inches and otherwise provided in this section may be operated in accordance with G.S. 20-115.1(c), (f), and (g).

(b) No passenger-type vehicle or recreational vehicle shall be operated on any highway with any load carried thereon extending beyond the line of the fenders on the left side of such vehicle nor extending more than six inches beyond the line of the fenders on the right side thereof.

(c) No vehicle, unladen or with load, shall exceed a height of 13 feet, six inches. Provided, however, that neither the State of North Carolina nor any agency or subdivision thereof, nor any person, firm or corporation, shall be required to raise, alter, construct or reconstruct any underpass, wire, pole, trestle, or other structure to permit the passage of any vehicle having a height, unladen or with load, in excess of 12 feet, six inches. Provided further, that the operator or owner of any vehicle having an overall height, whether unladen or with load, in excess of 12 feet, six inches, shall be liable for damage to any structure caused by such vehicle having a height in excess of 12 feet, six inches.

(d) Maximum Length. - The following maximum lengths apply to vehicles. A truck-tractor and semitrailer shall be regarded as two vehicles for the purpose of determining lawful length and license taxes.

(1) Except as otherwise provided in this subsection, a single vehicle having two or more axles shall not exceed 40 feet in length overall of dimensions inclusive of front and rear bumpers.

(2) Trucks transporting unprocessed cotton from farm to gin, or unprocessed sage from farm to market shall not exceed 50 feet in length overall of dimensions inclusive of front and rear bumpers.

(3) Recreational vehicles shall not exceed 45 feet in length overall, excluding bumpers and mirrors.

(4) Vehicles owned or leased by State, local, or federal government, when used for official law enforcement or emergency management purposes, shall not exceed 45 feet in length overall, excluding bumpers and mirrors.

(e) Except as provided by G.S. 20-115.1, no combination of vehicles coupled together shall consist of more than two units and no such combination of vehicles shall exceed a total length of 60 feet inclusive of front and rear bumpers, subject to the following exceptions: Motor vehicle combinations of one semitrailer of not more than 53 feet in length and a truck tractor (power unit) may exceed the 60-foot maximum length. Said maximum overall length limitation shall not apply to vehicles operated in the daytime when transporting poles, pipe, machinery or other objects of a structural nature which cannot readily be dismembered, nor to such vehicles transporting such objects operated at nighttime by a public utility when required for emergency repair of public service facilities or properties, provided the trailer length does not exceed 53 feet in length, but in respect to such night transportation every such vehicle and the load thereon shall be equipped with a sufficient number of clearance lamps on both sides and marker lamps upon the extreme ends of said projecting load to clearly mark the dimensions of such load: Provided that vehicles designed and used exclusively for the transportation of motor vehicles shall be permitted an overhang tolerance front or rear not to exceed five feet. Provided, that wreckers may tow a truck, combination tractor and trailer, trailer, or any other disabled vehicle or combination of vehicles to a place for repair, parking, or storage within 50 miles of the point where the vehicle was disabled and may tow a truck, tractor, or other replacement vehicle to the site of the disabled vehicle. Provided further, that the said limitation that no combination of vehicles coupled together shall consist of more than two units shall not apply to trailers not exceeding three in number drawn by a motor vehicle used by municipalities for the removal of domestic and commercial refuse and street rubbish, but such combination of vehicles shall not exceed a total length of 50 feet inclusive of front and rear bumpers. Provided further, that the said limitation that no combination of vehicles coupled together shall consist of more than two units shall not apply to a combination of vehicles coupled together by a saddle mount device used to transport motor vehicles in a driveway service when no more than three saddle mounts are used and provided further, that equipment used in said combination is approved by the safety regulations of the Federal Highway Administration and the safety rules of the Department of Public Safety.

(f) The load upon any vehicle operated alone, or the load upon the front vehicle of a combination of vehicles, shall not extend more than three feet beyond the foremost part of the vehicle. Under this subsection "load" shall include the boom on a self-propelled vehicle.

A utility pole carried by a self-propelled pole carrier may extend beyond the front overhang limit set in this subsection if the pole cannot be dismembered, the pole is less than 80 feet in length and does not extend more than 10 feet beyond the front bumper of the vehicle, and either of the following circumstances apply:

(1) It is daytime and the front of the extending load of poles is marked by a flag of the type required by G.S. 20-117 for certain rear overhangs.

(2) It is nighttime, operation of the vehicle is required to make emergency repairs to utility service, and the front of the extending load of poles is marked by a light of the type required by G.S. 20-117 for certain rear overhangs.

As used in this subsection, a "self-propelled pole carrier" is a vehicle designed to carry a pole on the side of the vehicle at a height of at least five feet when measured from the bottom of the brace used to carry the pole. A self-propelled pole carrier may not tow another vehicle when carrying a pole that extends beyond the front overhang limit set in this subsection.

(g) (1) No vehicle shall be driven or moved on any highway unless the vehicle is constructed and loaded to prevent any of its load from falling, blowing, dropping, sifting, leaking, or otherwise escaping therefrom, and the vehicle shall not contain any holes, cracks, or openings through which any of its load may escape. However, sand may be dropped for the purpose of securing traction, or water or other substance may be sprinkled, dumped, or spread on a roadway in cleaning or maintaining the roadway. For purposes of this subsection, the terms "load" and "leaking" do not include water accumulated from precipitation.

(2) A truck, trailer, or other vehicle licensed for more than 7,500 pounds gross vehicle weight that is loaded with rock, gravel, stone, or any other similar substance, other than sand, that could fall, blow, leak, sift, or drop shall not be driven or moved on any highway unless:

a. The height of the load against all four walls does not extend above a horizontal line six inches below their tops when loaded at the loading point; and

b. The load is securely covered by tarpaulin or some other suitable covering to prevent any of its load from falling, dropping, sifting, leaking, blowing, or otherwise escaping therefrom.

(3) A truck, trailer, or other vehicle:

a. Licensed for any gross vehicle weight and loaded with sand; or

b. Licensed for 7,500 pounds or less gross vehicle weight and loaded with rock, gravel, stone, or any other similar substance that could fall, blow, leak, sift, or drop;

shall not be driven or moved on any highway unless:

a. The height of the load against all four walls does not extend above a horizontal line six inches below the top when loaded at the loading point;

b. The load is securely covered by tarpaulin or some other suitable covering; or

c. The vehicle is constructed to prevent any of its load from falling, dropping, sifting, leaking, blowing, or otherwise escaping therefrom.

(4) This section shall not be applicable to or in any manner restrict the transportation of seed cotton, poultry or livestock, or silage or other feed grain used in the feeding of poultry or livestock.

(h) Whenever there exist two highways of the State highway system of approximately the same distance between two or more points, the Department of Transportation may, when in the opinion of the Department of Transportation, based upon engineering and traffic investigation, safety will be promoted or the public interest will be served, designate one of the highways the "truck route" between those points, and to prohibit the use of the other highway by heavy trucks or other vehicles of a gross vehicle weight or axle load limit in excess of a designated maximum. In such instances the highways selected for heavy vehicle traffic shall be designated as "truck routes" by signs conspicuously posted, and the highways upon which heavy vehicle traffic is prohibited shall likewise be designated by signs conspicuously posted showing the maximum gross vehicle weight or axle load limits authorized for those highways. The operation of any vehicle whose gross vehicle weight or axle load exceeds the maximum limits shown on signs over the posted highway shall constitute a Class 2 misdemeanor: Provided, that nothing in this subsection shall prohibit a truck or other motor vehicle whose gross vehicle weight or axle load exceeds that prescribed for those highways from using them when its destination is located solely upon that highway, road or street: Provided, further, that nothing in this subsection shall prohibit passenger vehicles or other light vehicles from using any highways designated for heavy truck traffic.

(i)   Repealed by Session Laws 1973, c. 1330, s. 39.

(j)   Nothing in this section shall be construed to prevent the operation of self-propelled grain combines or other self-propelled farm equipment with or without implements, not exceeding 25 feet in width on any highway, unless the operation violates a provision of this subsection. Farm equipment includes a vehicle that is designed exclusively to transport compressed seed cotton from a farm to a gin and has a self-loading bed. Combines or equipment which exceed 10 feet in width may be operated only if they meet all of the conditions listed in this subsection. A violation of one or more of these conditions does not constitute negligence per se.

(1)   The equipment may only be operated during daylight hours.

(2)   The equipment must display a red flag on front and rear ends or a flashing warning light. The flags or lights shall be attached to the equipment as to be visible from both directions at all times while being operated on the public highway for not less than 300 feet.

(3)   Equipment covered by this section, which by necessity must travel more than 10 miles or where by nature of the terrain or obstacles the flags or lights referred to in subdivision (2) of this subsection are not visible from both directions for 300 feet at any point along the proposed route, must be preceded at a distance of 300 feet and followed at a distance of 300 feet by a flagman in a vehicle having mounted thereon an appropriate warning light or flag. No flagman in a vehicle shall be required pursuant to this subdivision if the equipment is

being moved under its own power or on a trailer from any field to another field, or from the normal place of storage of the vehicle to any field, for no more than ten miles and if visible from both directions for 300 feet at any point along the proposed route.

(4)   Every piece of equipment so operated shall operate to the right of the center line when meeting traffic coming from the opposite direction and at all other times when possible and practical.

(5)   Repealed by Session Laws 2008-221, s. 6, effective September 1, 2008.

(6)   When the equipment is causing a delay in traffic, the operator of the equipment shall move the equipment off the paved portion of the highway at the nearest practical location until the vehicles following the equipment have passed.

(7)   The equipment shall be operated in the designed transport position that minimizes equipment width. No removal of equipment or appurtenances is required under this subdivision.

(8)   Equipment covered by this subsection shall not be operated on a highway or section of highway that is a fully controlled access highway or is a part of the National System of Interstate and Defense Highways without authorization from the North Carolina Department of Transportation. The Department shall develop an authorization process and approve routes under the following conditions:

a.   Persons shall submit an application to the Department requesting authorization to operate equipment covered by this subsection on a particular route that is part of a highway or section of highway that is a fully controlled access highway or is a part of the National System of Interstate and Defense Highways.

b.   The Department shall have a period of 30 days from receipt of a complete application to approve or reject the application. A complete application shall be deemed approved if the Department does not take action within 30 days of receipt by the Department; such a route may then be used by the original applicant.

c.   The Department shall approve an application upon a showing that the route is necessary to accomplish one or more of the following:

1. Prevent farming operations from traveling more than five miles longer than the requested route during the normal course of business.

2. Prevent excess traffic delays on local or secondary roads.

3. Allow farm equipment access due to dimension restrictions on local or secondary roads.

d. For applications that do not meet the requirements of sub-subdivision c. of this subdivision, the Department may also approve an application upon review of relevant safety factors.

e. The Department may consult with the North Carolina State Highway Patrol, the North Carolina Department of Agriculture and Consumer Services, or other parties concerning an application.

f. Any approved route may be subject to any of the following additional conditions:

1. A requirement that the subject equipment be followed by a flag vehicle with flashing lights that shall be operated at all times on the route so as to be visible from a distance of at least 300 feet.

2. Restrictions on maximum and minimum speeds of the equipment.

3. Restrictions on the maximum dimensions of the equipment.

4. Restrictions on the time of day that the equipment may be operated on the approved route.

g. The Department shall publish all approved routes, including any conditions on the routes' use, and shall notify appropriate State and local law enforcement officers of any approved route.

h. Once approved for use and published by the Department, a route may be used by any person who adheres to the route, including any conditions on the route's use imposed by the Department.

i. The Department may revise published routes as road conditions on the routes change.

(k) Nothing in this section shall be construed to prevent the operation of passenger buses having an overall width of 102 inches, exclusive of safety equipment, upon the highways of this State which are 20 feet or wider and that are designated as the State primary system, or as municipal streets, when, and not until, the federal law and regulations thereunder permit the operation of passenger buses having a width of 102 inches or wider on the National System of Interstate and Defense Highways.

(l) Nothing in this section shall be construed to prevent the operation of passenger buses that are owned and operated by units of local government, operated as a single vehicle only and having an overall length of 45 feet or less, on public streets or highways. The Department of Transportation may prevent the operation of buses that are authorized under this subsection if the operation of such buses on a street or highway presents a hazard to passengers of the buses or to the motoring public.

(m) Notwithstanding subsection (a) of this section, a boat or boat trailer with an outside width of less than 120 inches may be towed without a permit. The towing of a boat or boat trailer 102 inches to 114 inches in width may take place on any day of the week, including weekends and holidays, and may take place at night. The towing of a boat or boat trailer 114 inches to 120 inches in width may take place on any day of the week, including weekends and holidays from sun up to sun down. A boat or boat trailer in excess of 102 inches but less than 120 inches must be equipped with a minimum of two operable amber lamps on the widest point of the boat and the boat trailer such that the dimensions of the boat and the boat trailer are clearly marked and visible.

(n) Vehicle combinations used in connection with motorsports competition events that include a cab or other motorized vehicle unit with living quarters, and an attached enclosed specialty trailer, the combination of which does not exceed 90 feet in length, may be operated on the highways of this State, provided that such operation takes place for one or more of the following purposes:

(1) Driving to or from a motorsports competition event.

(2) For trips conducted for the purpose of purchasing fuel or conducting repairs or other maintenance on the competition vehicle.

(3) For other activities related to motorsports purposes, including, but not limited to, performance testing of the competition vehicle.

The Department of Transportation may prohibit combinations authorized by this subsection from specific routes, pursuant to G.S. 20-115.1(b). (1937, c. 246; c. 407, s. 80; 1943, c. 213, s. 1; 1945, c. 242, s. 1; 1947, c. 844; 1951, c. 495, s. 1; c. 733; 1953, cc. 682, 1107; 1955, c. 296, s. 2; c. 729; 1957, c. 65, s. 11; cc. 493, 1183, 1190; 1959, c. 559; 1963, c. 356, s. 1; c. 610, ss. 1, 2; c. 702, s. 4; c. 1027, s. 1; 1965, c. 471; 1967, c. 24, s. 4; c. 710; 1969, cc. 128, 880; 1971, cc. 128, 680, 688, 1079; 1973, c. 507, s. 5; c. 546; c. 1330, s. 39; 1975, c. 148, ss. 1-5; c. 716, s. 5; 1977, c. 464, s. 34; 1979, cc. 21, 218; 1981, c. 169, s. 1; 1983, c. 724, s. 2; 1985, c. 587; 1987, c. 272; 1989, c. 277, s. 1; c. 790, s. 2; 1991, c. 112, s. 1; c. 449, ss. 1, 2.1; 1993, c. 539, s. 355; 1994, Ex. Sess., c. 24, s. 14(c); 1995 (Reg. Sess., 1996), c. 573, s. 1; c. 756, s. 14; 1998-149, s. 7; 1999-438, s. 28; 2000-185, s. 2; 2001-341, ss. 3, 4; 2001-512, s. 2; 2002-72, s. 19(c); 2002-159, s. 31.5(b); 2002-190, s. 2; 2003-383, s. 8; 2005-248, s. 2; 2007-77, s. 1; 2007-194, ss. 2, 3; 2007-484, s. 5; 2007-499, s. 1; 2008-221, ss. 5, 6; 2008-229, s. 1; 2009-7, s. 1; 2009-127, s. 1; 2009-128, s. 1; 2011-145, s. 19.1(g); 2012-33, s. 1; 2012-78, s. 5; 2013-413, s. 59.2(f).)

§ 20-117. Flag or light at end of load.

(a) General Provisions. - Whenever the load on any vehicle shall extend more than four feet beyond the rear of the bed or body thereof, there shall be displayed at the end of such load, in such position as to be clearly visible at all times from the rear of such load, a red or orange flag not less than 18 inches both in length and width, except that from sunset to sunrise there shall be displayed at the end of any such load a red or amber light plainly visible under normal atmospheric conditions at least 200 feet from the rear of such vehicle. At no time shall a load extend more than 14 feet beyond the rear of the bed or body of the vehicle, with the exception of vehicles transporting forestry products or utility poles.

(b) Commercial Motor Vehicles. - A commercial motor vehicle, or a motor vehicle with a GVWR of 10,001 pounds or more that is engaged in commerce, that is being used to tow a load or that has a load that protrudes from the rear or sides of the vehicle shall comply with the provisions of 49 C.F.R. Part 393. (1937, c. 407, s. 81; 1985, c. 455; 1997-178, s. 1; 2005-361, s. 2; 2009-376, s. 4.)

§ 20-117.1. Requirements for mirrors and fuel container.

(a) Rear-Vision Mirrors. - Every bus, truck, and truck tractor with a GVWR of 10,001 pounds or more shall be equipped with two rear-vision mirrors, one at each side, firmly attached to the outside of the motor vehicle, and located as to reflect to the driver a view of the highway to the rear and along both sides of the vehicle. Only one outside mirror shall be required, on the driver's side, on trucks which are so constructed that the driver also has a view to the rear by means of an interior mirror. In driveaway-towaway operations, a driven vehicle shall have at least one mirror furnishing a clear view to the rear, and if the interior mirror does not provide the clear view, an additional mirror shall be attached to the left side of the driven vehicle to provide the clear view to the rear.

(b) Fuel Container Not to Project. - No part of any fuel tank or container or intake pipe shall project beyond the sides of the motor vehicle. (1949, c. 1207, s. 1; 1951, c. 819, s. 1; 1955, c. 1157, ss. 1, 4; 1991, c. 113, c. 761, s. 6.)

§ 20-118. Weight of vehicles and load.

(a) For the purposes of this section, the following definitions shall apply:

(1) Single-axle weight. - The gross weight transmitted by all wheels whose centers may be included between two parallel transverse vertical planes 40 inches apart, extending across the full width of the vehicle.

(2) Tandem-axle weight. - The gross weight transmitted to the road by two or more consecutive axles whose centers may be included between parallel vertical planes spaced more than 40 inches and not more than 96 inches apart, extending across the full width of the vehicle.

(3) Axle group. - Any two or more consecutive axles on a vehicle or combination of vehicles.

(4) Gross weight. - The weight of any single axle, tandem axle, or axle group of a vehicle or combination of vehicles plus the weight of any load thereon.

(5) Light-traffic roads. - Any highway on the State Highway System, excepting routes designated I, U.S. or N.C., posted by the Department of Transportation to limit the axle weight below the statutory limits.

(b) The following weight limitations shall apply to vehicles operating on the highways of the State:

(1) The single-axle weight of a vehicle or combination of vehicles shall not exceed 20,000 pounds.

(2) The tandem-axle weight of a vehicle or combination of vehicles shall not exceed 38,000 pounds.

(3) The gross weight imposed upon the highway by any axle group of a vehicle or combination of vehicles shall not exceed the maximum weight given for the respective distance between the first and last axle of the group of axles measured longitudinally to the nearest foot as set forth in the following table:

Distance Between Consecutive Axles*	Maximum Weight in Pounds for any Group of Two or More Axles				
Axles* 7 Axles	2 Axles	3 Axles	4 Axles	5 Axles	6 Axles
4	38000				
5	38000				
6	38000				
7	38000				
8 or less	38000	38000			
more than 8	38000	42000			
9	39000	42500			

10	40000	43500			
11		44000			
12		45000	50000		
13		45500	50500		
14		46500	51500		
15		47000	52000		
16		48000	52500	58000	
17		48500	53500	58500	
18		49500	54000	59000	
19		50000	54500	60000	
20		51000	55500	60500	66000
21		51500	56000	61000	66500
22		52500	56500	61500	67000
23		53000	57500	62500	68000
24		54000	58000	63000	68500
74000					
25		54500	58500	63500	69000
74500					
26		55500	59500	64000	69500
75000					
27		56000	60000	65000	70000
75500					

28	57000	60500	65500	71000
76500				
29	57500	61500	66000	71500
77000				
30	58500	62000	66500	72000
77500				
31	59000	62500	67500	72500
78000				
32	60000	63500	68000	73000
78500				
33		64000	68500	74000
79000				
34		64500	69000	74500
80000				
35		65500	70000	75000
36		66000**	70500	75500
37		66500**	71000	76000
38		67500**	72000	77000
39		68000	72500	77500
40		68500	73000	78000
41		69500	73500	78500
42		70000	74000	79000
43		70500	75000	80000
44		71500	75500	

45	72000	76000
46	72500	76500
47	73500	77500
48	74000	78000
49	74500	78500
50	75500	79000
51	76000	80000
52	76500	
53	77500	
54	78000	
55	78500	
56	79500	
57	80000	

* Distance in Feet Between the Extremes of any Group of Two or More Consecutive Axles.

** See exception in G.S. 20-118(c)(1).

(4) The Department of Transportation may establish light-traffic roads and further restrict the axle weight limit on such light-traffic roads lower than the statutory limits. The Department of Transportation shall have authority to designate any highway on the State Highway System, excluding routes designated by I, U.S. and N.C., as a light-traffic road when in the opinion of the Department of Transportation, such road is inadequate to carry and will be injuriously affected by vehicles using the said road carrying the maximum axle weight. All such roads so designated shall be conspicuously posted as light-traffic roads and the maximum axle weight authorized shall be displayed on proper signs erected thereon.

(c) Exceptions. - The following exceptions apply to G.S. 20-118(b) and 20-118(e).

(1) Two consecutive sets of tandem axles may carry a gross weight of 34,000 pounds each without penalty provided the overall distance between the first and last axles of the consecutive sets of tandem axles is 36 feet or more.

(2) When a vehicle is operated in violation of G.S. 20-118(b)(1), 20-118(b)(2), or 20-118(b)(3), but the gross weight of the vehicle or combination of vehicles does not exceed that permitted by G.S. 20-118(b)(3), the owner of the vehicle shall be permitted to shift the load within the vehicle, without penalty, from one axle to another to comply with the weight limits in the following cases:

a. Where the single-axle load exceeds the statutory limits, but does not exceed 21,000 pounds.

b. Where the vehicle or combination of vehicles has tandem axles, but the tandem-axle weight does not exceed 40,000 pounds.

(3) When a vehicle is operated in violation of G.S. 20-118(b)(4) the owner of the vehicle shall be permitted, without penalty, to shift the load within the vehicle from one axle to another to comply with the weight limits where the single-axle weight does not exceed the posted limit by 2,500 pounds.

(4) A truck or other motor vehicle shall be exempt from such light-traffic road limitations provided for pursuant to G.S. 20-118(b)(4), when transporting supplies, material or equipment necessary to carry out a farming operation engaged in the production of meats and agricultural crops and livestock or poultry by-products or a business engaged in the harvest or processing of seafood when the destination of such vehicle and load is located solely upon said light-traffic road.

(5) The light-traffic road limitations provided for pursuant to subdivision (b)(4) of this section do not apply to a vehicle while that vehicle is transporting only the following from its point of origin on a light-traffic road to either one of the two nearest highways that is not a light-traffic road. If that vehicle's point of origin is a non-light-traffic road and that road is blocked by light-traffic roads from all directions and is not contiguous with other non-light-traffic roads, then the road at point of origin is treated as a light-traffic road for purposes of this subdivision:

a. Processed or unprocessed seafood transported from boats or any other point of origin to a processing plant or a point of further distribution.

b. Meats, live poultry, or agricultural crop products transported from a farm to a processing plant or market.

c. Forest products originating and transported from a farm or from woodlands to market without interruption or delay for further packaging or processing after initiating transport.

d. Livestock or live poultry transported from their point of origin to a processing plant or market.

e. Livestock by-products or poultry by-products transported from their point of origin to a rendering plant.

f. Recyclable material transported from its point of origin to a scrap-processing facility for processing. As used in this subpart, the terms "recyclable material" and "processing" have the same meaning as in G.S. 130A-290(a).

g. Garbage collected by the vehicle from residences or garbage dumpsters if the vehicle is fully enclosed and is designed specifically for collecting, compacting, and hauling garbage from residences or from garbage dumpsters. As used in this subpart, the term "garbage" does not include hazardous waste as defined in G.S. 130A-290(a), spent nuclear fuel regulated under G.S. 20-167.1, low-level radioactive waste as defined in G.S. 104E-5, or radioactive material as defined in G.S. 104E-5.

h. Treated sludge collected from a wastewater treatment facility.

i. Apples when transported from the orchard to the first processing or packing point.

j. Trees grown as Christmas trees from the field, farm, stand, or grove, and other forest products, including chips and bark, to a processing point.

k. Water, fertilizer, pesticides, seeds, fuel, and animal waste transported to or from a farm by a farm vehicle as defined in G.S. 20-37.16(e)(3).

(6) A truck or other motor vehicle shall be exempt from such light-traffic road limitations provided by G.S. 20-118(b)(4) when such motor vehicles are owned, operated by or under contract to a public utility, electric or telephone membership corporation or municipality and such motor vehicles are used in connection with installation, restoration or emergency maintenance of utility services.

(7) A wrecker may tow any disabled truck or other motor vehicle or combination of vehicles to a place for repairs, parking, or storage within 50 miles from the point that the vehicle was disabled and may tow a truck, tractor, or other replacement vehicle to the site of the disabled vehicle without being in violation of G.S. 20-118 provided that the wrecker and towed vehicle or combination of vehicles otherwise meet all requirements of this section.

(8) A firefighting vehicle operated by any member of a municipal or rural fire department in the performance of his duties, regardless of whether members of that fire department are paid or voluntary and any vehicle of a voluntary lifesaving organization, when operated by a member of that organization while answering an official call shall be exempt from such light-traffic road limitations provided by G.S. 20-118(b)(4).

(9) Repealed by Session Laws 1993 (Reg. Sess., 1994), c. 761, s. 12.

(10) Fully enclosed motor vehicles designed specifically for collecting, compacting and hauling garbage from residences, or from garbage dumpsters shall, when operating for those purposes, be allowed a single axle weight not to exceed 23,500 pounds on the steering axle on vehicles equipped with a boom, or on the rear axle on vehicles loaded from the rear. This exemption shall not apply to vehicles operating on interstate highways, vehicles transporting hazardous waste as defined in G.S. 130A-290(a)(8), spent nuclear fuel regulated under G.S. 20-167.1, low-level radioactive waste as defined in G.S. 104E-5(9a), or radioactive material as defined in G.S. 104E-5(14).

(11) A truck or other motor vehicle shall be exempt for light-traffic road limitations issued under subdivision (b)(4) of this section when transporting heating fuel for on-premises use at a destination located on the light-traffic road.

(12) Subsections (b) and (e) of this section do not apply to a vehicle or vehicle combination that meets all of the conditions set out below:

a. Is transporting any of the following items within 150 miles of the point of origination:

1. Agriculture crop products transported from a farm to a processing plant or market.

2. Water, fertilizer, pesticides, seeds, fuel, or animal waste transported to or from a farm by a farm vehicle as defined in G.S. 20-37.16(e)(3).

3. Meats, livestock, or live poultry transported from the farm where they were raised to a processing plant or market.

3a. Feed that is used in the feeding of poultry or livestock and transported from a storage facility, holding facility, or mill to a farm.

4. Forest products originating and transported from a farm or woodlands to market with delay interruption or delay for further packaging or processing after initiating transport.

5. Wood residuals, including wood chips, sawdust, mulch, or tree bark from any site.

6. Raw logs to market.

7. Trees grown as Christmas trees from field, farm, stand, or grove to a processing point.

b. Repealed by Session Laws 1993 (Reg. Sess., 1994), c. 761, s. 13.

b1. Does not operate on an interstate highway or exceed any posted bridge weight limits during transportation or hauling of agricultural products.

c. Meets any of the following vehicle configurations:

1. Does not exceed a single-axle weight of 22,000 pounds, a tandem-axle weight of 42,000 pounds, or a gross weight of 90,000 pounds.

2. Consists of a five or more axle combination vehicle that does not exceed a single-axle weight of 26,000 pounds, a tandem-axle weight of 44,000 pounds and a gross weight of 90,000 pounds, with a length of at least 48 feet between the center of axle one and the center of the last axle of the vehicle and a

minimum of 11 feet between the center of axle one and the center of axle two of the vehicle.

3. Consists of a two-axle vehicle that does not exceed a gross weight of 37,000 pounds and a single-axle weight of no more than 27,000 pounds, with a length of at least 14 feet between the center of axle one and the center of axle two of the vehicle.

d. Repealed by Session Laws 2012-78, s. 6, effective June 26, 2012.

(13) Vehicles specifically designed for fire fighting that are owned by a municipal or rural fire department. This exception does not apply to vehicles operating on interstate highways.

(14) Subsections (b) and (e) of this section do not apply to a vehicle that meets all of the conditions below, but all other enforcement provisions of this Article remain applicable:

a. Is hauling aggregates from a distribution yard or a State-permitted production site located within a North Carolina county contiguous to the North Carolina State border to a destination in another state adjacent to that county as verified by a weight ticket in the driver's possession and available for inspection by enforcement personnel.

b. Does not operate on an interstate highway or exceed any posted bridge weight limits.

c. Does not exceed 69,850 pounds gross vehicle weight and 53,850 pounds per axle grouping for tri-axle vehicles. For purposes of this subsection, a tri-axle vehicle is a single power unit vehicle with a three consecutive axle group on which the respective distance between any two consecutive axles of the group, measured longitudinally center to center to the nearest foot, does not exceed eight feet. For purposes of this subsection, the tolerance provisions of subsection (h) of this section do not apply, and vehicles must be licensed in accordance with G.S. 20-88.

d. Repealed by Session Laws 2001-487, s. 10, effective December 16, 2001.

e. Repealed by Session Laws 2012-78, s. 6, effective June 26, 2012.

(15) Subsections (b) and (e) of this section do not apply to a vehicle or vehicle combination that meets all of the conditions below, but all other enforcement provisions of this Article remain applicable:

a. Is transporting bulk soil, bulk rock, sand, sand rock, or asphalt millings from a site that does not have a certified scale for weighing the vehicle.

b. Does not operate on an interstate highway, a posted light-traffic road, except as provided by subdivision (c)(5) of this section, or exceed any posted bridge weight limits.

c. Does not exceed a maximum gross weight 4,000 pounds in excess of what is allowed in subsection (b) of this section.

d. Does not exceed a single-axle weight of more than 22,000 pounds and a tandem-axle weight of more than 42,000 pounds.

e. Repealed by Session Laws 2012-78, s. 6, effective June 26, 2012.

(16) Subsections (b) and (e) of this section do not apply to a vehicle or vehicle combination that meets all of the conditions below, but all other enforcement provisions of this Article remain applicable:

a. Is hauling unhardened ready-mixed concrete.

b. Does not operate on an interstate highway or a posted light-traffic road, or exceed any posted bridge weight limits.

c. Has a single steer axle weight of no more than 22,000 pounds and a tandem-axle weight of no more than 46,000 pounds.

d. Does not exceed a maximum gross weight of 66,000 pounds on a three-axle vehicle with a length of at least 21 feet between the center of axle one and the center of axle three of the vehicle.

e. Does not exceed a maximum gross weight of 72,600 pounds on a four-axle vehicle with a length of at least 36 feet between the center of axle one and the center of axle four. The four-axle vehicle shall have a maximum gross weight of 66,000 pounds on axles one, two, and three with a length of at least 21 feet between the center of axle one and the center of axle three.

For purposes of this subdivision, no additional weight allowances as found in this section shall apply for the gross weight, single-axle weight, and tandem-axle weight, and the tolerance allowed by subsection (h) of this section shall not apply.

(17) Subsections (b) and (e) of this section do not apply to a truck owned, operated by, or under contract to a public utility, electric or telephone membership corporation, or municipality that meets all of the conditions listed below, but all other enforcement provisions of this Article remain applicable:

a. Is being used in connection with the installation, restoration, or maintenance of utility services within a North Carolina county located in whole or in part west of Interstate 77, and the terrain, road widths, and other naturally occurring conditions prevent the safe navigation and operation of a truck having more than a single axle or using a trailer.

b. Does not operate on an interstate highway.

c. Does not exceed a single-axle weight of more than 28,000 pounds.

d. Does not exceed a maximum gross weight in excess of 48,000 pounds.

(d) The Department of Transportation is authorized to abrogate certain exceptions. The exceptions provided for in G.S. 20-118(c)(4) and 20-118(c)(5) as applied to any light-traffic road may be abrogated by the Department of Transportation upon a determination of the Department of Transportation that undue damage to such light-traffic road is resulting from such vehicles exempted by G.S. 20-118(c)(4) and 20-118(c)(5). In those cases where the exemption to the light-traffic roads are abrogated by the Department of Transportation, the Department shall post the road to indicate no exemptions.

(e) Penalties. -

(1) Except as provided in subdivision (2) of this subsection, for each violation of the single-axle or tandem-axle weight limits set in subdivision (b)(1), (b)(2), or (b)(4) of this section or axle weights authorized by special permit according to G.S. 20-119(a), the Department of Public Safety shall assess a civil penalty against the owner or registrant of the vehicle in accordance with the following schedule: for the first 1,000 pounds or any part thereof, four cents (4¢) per pound; for the next 1,000 pounds or any part thereof, six cents (6¢) per pound; and for each additional pound, ten cents (10¢) per pound. These

penalties apply separately to each weight limit violated. In all cases of violation of the weight limitation, the penalty shall be computed and assessed on each pound of weight in excess of the maximum permitted.

(2) The penalty for a violation of the single-axle or tandem-axle weight limits by a vehicle that is transporting an item listed in subdivision (c)(5) of this section is one-half of the amount it would otherwise be under subdivision (1) of this subsection.

(3) If an axle-group weight of a vehicle exceeds the weight limit set in subdivision (b)(3) of this section plus any tolerance allowed in subsection (h) of this section or axle-group weights or gross weights authorized by special permit under G.S. 20-119(a), the Department of Public Safety shall assess a civil penalty against the owner or registrant of the motor vehicle. The penalty shall be assessed on the number of pounds by which the axle-group weight exceeds the limit set in subdivision (b)(3) of this section, or by a special permit issued pursuant to G.S. 20-119, as follows: for the first 2,000 pounds or any part thereof, two cents (2¢) per pound; for the next 3,000 pounds or any part thereof, four cents (4¢) per pound; for each pound in excess of 5,000 pounds, ten cents (10¢) per pound. Tolerance pounds in excess of the limit set in subdivision (b)(3) are subject to the penalty if the vehicle exceeds the tolerance allowed in subsection (h) of this section. These penalties apply separately to each axle-group weight limit violated. Notwithstanding any provision to the contrary, a vehicle with a special permit that is subject to additional penalties under this subsection based on a violation of any of the permit restrictions set out in G.S. 20-119(d1) shall be assessed a civil penalty, not to exceed ten thousand dollars ($10,000), based on the number of pounds by which the axle-group weight exceeds the limit set in subdivision (b)(3) of this section.

(4) The penalty for a violation of an axle-group weight limit by a vehicle that is transporting an item listed in subdivision (c)(5) of this section is one-half of the amount it would otherwise be under subdivision (3) of this subsection.

(5) A violation of a weight limit in this section or of a permitted weight under G.S. 20-119 is not punishable under G.S. 20-176.

(6) The penalty for violating the gross weight or axle-group weight by a dump truck or dump trailer vehicle transporting bulk soil, bulk rock, sand, sand rock, or asphalt millings intrastate from a site that does not have a certified scale for weighing the vehicle is one-half of the amount it otherwise would be under subdivisions (1) and (3) of this subsection.

(7) The clear proceeds of all civil penalties, civil forfeitures, and civil fines that are collected by the Department of Transportation pursuant to this section shall be remitted to the Civil Penalty and Forfeiture Fund in accordance with G.S. 115C-457.2.

(f) Repealed by Session Laws 1993 (Reg. Sess., 1994), c. 761, s. 15.

(g) General Statutes 20-118 shall not be construed to permit the gross weight of any vehicle or combination in excess of the safe load carrying capacity established by the Department of Transportation on any bridge pursuant to G.S. 136-72.

(h) Tolerance. - A vehicle may exceed maximum and the inner axle-group weight limitations set forth in subdivision (b)(3) of this section by a tolerance of ten percent (10%). This exception does not authorize a vehicle to exceed either the single-axle or tandem-axle weight limitations set forth in subdivisions (b)(1) and (b)(2) of this section, or the maximum gross weight limit of 80,000 pounds. This exception does not apply to a vehicle exceeding posted bridge weight limitations as posted under G.S. 136-72 or to vehicles operating on interstate highways. The tolerance allowed under this subsection does not authorize the weight of a vehicle to exceed the weight for which that vehicle is licensed under G.S. 20-88. No tolerance on the single-axle weight or the tandem-axle weight provided for in subdivisions (b)(1) and (b)(2) of this section shall be granted administratively or otherwise. The Department of Transportation shall report back to the Transportation Oversight Committee and to the General Assembly on the effects of the tolerance granted under this section, any abuses of this tolerance, and any suggested revisions to this section by that Department on or before May 1, 1998.

(i) Repealed by Session Laws 1993 (Reg. Sess., 1994), c. 761, s. 16.

(j) Repealed by Session Laws 1987, c. 392.

(k) A vehicle which is equipped with a self-loading bed and which is designed and used exclusively to transport compressed seed cotton from the farm to a cotton gin, or sage to market, may operate on the highways of the State, except interstate highways, with a tandem-axle weight not exceeding 50,000 pounds. Such vehicles shall be exempt from light-traffic road limitations only from point of origin on the light-traffic road to the nearest State-maintained road which is not posted to prohibit the transportation of statutory load limits.

This exemption does not apply to restricted, posted bridge structures. (1937, c. 407, s. 82; 1943, c. 213, s. 2; cc. 726, 784; 1945, c. 242, s. 2; c. 569, s. 2; c. 576, s. 7; 1947, c. 1079; 1949, c. 1207, s. 2; 1951, c. 495, s. 2; c. 942, s. 1; c. 1013, ss. 5, 6, 8; 1953, cc. 214, 1092; 1959, c. 872; c. 1264, s. 6; 1963, c. 159; c. 610, ss. 3-5; c. 702, s. 5; 1965, cc. 483, 1044; 1969, c. 537; 1973, c. 507, s. 5; c. 1449, ss. 1, 2; 1975, c. 325; c. 373, s. 2; c. 716, s. 5; c. 735; c. 736, ss. 1-3; 1977, c. 461; c. 464, s. 34; 1977, 2nd Sess., c. 1178; 1981, c. 690, ss. 27, 28; c. 726; c. 1127, s. 53.1; 1983, c. 407; c. 724, s. 1; 1983 (Reg. Sess., 1984), c. 1116, ss. 105-109; 1985, c. 54; c. 274; 1987, c. 392; c. 707, ss. 1-4; 1991, c. 202, s. 1; 1991 (Reg. Sess., 1992), c. 905, s. 1; 1993, c. 426, ss. 1, 2; c. 470, s. 1; c. 533, s. 11; 1993 (Reg. Sess., 1994), c. 761, ss. 10-16; 1995, c. 109, s. 3; c. 163, s. 4; c. 332, ss. 1-3 ; c. 509, s. 135.1(b); 1995 (Reg. Sess., 1996), c. 756, s. 29; 1997-354, s. 1; 1997-373, s. 1; 1997-466, s. 2; 1998-149, ss. 8, 9, 9.1; 1998-177, s. 1; 1999-452, s. 23; 2000-57, s. 1; 2001-487, ss. 10, 50(e); 2002-126, s. 26.16(a); 2004-145, ss. 1, 2; 2005-248, s. 1; 2005-276, s. 6.37(o); 2005-361, s. 3; 2006-135, s. 1; 2006-264, s. 37; 2008-221, ss. 7, 8, 9; 2009-127, s. 2; 2009-376, ss. 6, 16(a), 16(b); 2009-531, s. 1; 2010-129, s. 3; 2010-132, s. 10; 2011-71, s. 1; 2011-145, s. 19.1(g); 2011-200, s. 1; 2012-78, ss. 6, 13; 2013-120, s. 1; 2013-134, s. 1.)

§ 20-118.1. Officers may weigh vehicles and require overloads to be removed.

A law enforcement officer may stop and weigh a vehicle to determine if the vehicle's weight is in compliance with the vehicle's declared gross weight and the weight limits set in this Part. The officer may require the driver of the vehicle to drive to a scale located within five miles of where the officer stopped the vehicle.

Any person operating a vehicle or a combination of vehicles having a GVWR of 10,001 pounds or more or any vehicle transporting hazardous materials that is required to be placarded under 49 C.F.R. § 171-180 must enter a permanent weigh station or temporary inspection or weigh site as directed by duly erected signs or an electronic transponder for the purpose of being electronically screened for compliance, or weighed, or inspected.

If the vehicle's weight exceeds the amount allowable, the officer may detain the vehicle until the overload has been removed. Any property removed from a vehicle because the vehicle was overloaded is the responsibility of the owner or operator of the vehicle. The State is not liable for damage to or loss of the removed property.

Failure to permit a vehicle to be weighed or to remove an overload is a misdemeanor of the Class set in G.S. 20-176. An officer must weigh a vehicle with a scale that has been approved by the Department of Agriculture and Consumer Services.

A privately owned noncommercial horse trailer constructed to transport four or fewer horses shall not be required to stop at any permanent weigh station in the State while transporting horses, unless the driver of the vehicle hauling the trailer is directed to stop by a law enforcement officer. A "privately owned noncommercial horse trailer" means a trailer used solely for the occasional transportation of horses and not for compensation or in furtherance of a commercial enterprise. (1927, c. 148, s. 37; 1949, c. 1207, s. 3; 1951, c. 1013, s. 4; 1979, c. 436, ss. 1, 2; 1981 (Reg. Sess., 1982), c. 1259, s. 2; 1993, c. 539, s. 356; 1994, Ex. Sess., c. 24, s. 14(c); 1995, c. 109, s. 4; 1997-261, s. 109; 2001-487, s. 50(f); 2003-338, s. 1.)

§ 20-118.2. Authority to fix higher weight limitations at reduced speeds for certain vehicles.

The Department of Transportation is hereby authorized and empowered to fix higher weight limitations at reduced speeds for vehicles used in transporting property when the point of origin or destination of the motor vehicles is located upon any light traffic highway, county road, farm-to-market road, or any other roads of the secondary system only and/or to the extent only that the motor vehicle is necessarily using said highway in transporting the property from the bona fide point of origin of the property being transported or to the bona fide point of destination of said property and such weights may be different from the weight of those vehicles otherwise using such roads. (1951, c. 1013, s. 7A; 1957, c. 65, s. 11; 1973, c. 507, s. 5; 1977, c. 464, s. 34.)

§ 20-118.3. Vehicle or combination of vehicles operated without registration plate subject to civil penalty.

Any vehicle or combination of vehicles being operated upon the highway of this State either by a resident or nonresident without having been issued therefor a registration plate by the appropriate jurisdiction shall be subject to a civil penalty equal to the North Carolina annual fee for the gross weight of the vehicle and in addition thereto the license fee applicable for the remainder of the current registration year, provided a nonresident shall pay the North Carolina license fee or furnish satisfactory proof of payment of required registration fee to its base jurisdiction. The civil penalties provided for in this section shall not be enforceable through criminal sanctions and the provisions of G.S. 20-176 shall not apply to this section. (1981 Reg. Sess., 1982), c. 1259, s. 1.)

§ 20-118.4. Firefighting equipment exempt from size and weight restrictions while transporting or moving heavy equipment for emergency response and preparedness and fire prevention; permits.

(a) Exemption From Weight and Size Restrictions. - Any overweight or oversize vehicle owned and operated by a State or local government or cooperating federal agency is exempt from the weight and size restrictions of this Chapter and implementing rules while it is actively engaged in (i) a response to a fire under the authority of a forest ranger pursuant to G.S. 106-899(a); (ii) a county request for forest protection assistance pursuant to G.S. 106-906; (iii) a request for assistance under a state of emergency declared pursuant to G.S. 166A-19.20 or G.S. 166A-19.22, and any other applicable statutes and provisions of common law; (iv) a request for assistance under a disaster declared pursuant to G.S. 166A-19.21; or (v) performance of other required duties for emergency preparedness and fire prevention, when the vehicle meets the following conditions:

(1) The vehicle weight does not exceed the manufacturer's GVWR or 90,000 pounds gross weight, whichever is less.

(2) The tri-axle grouping weight does not exceed 50,000 pounds, tandem axle weight does not exceed 42,000 pounds, and the single axle weight does not exceed 22,000 pounds.

(3) A vehicle/vehicle combination does not exceed 12 feet in width and a total overall vehicle combination length of 75 feet from bumper to bumper.

(b) Marking, Lighting, and Bridge Requirements. - Vehicle/vehicle combinations subject to an exemption or permit under this section shall not be exempt from the requirement of a yellow banner on the front and rear measuring a total length of seven feet by 18 inches bearing the legend "Oversize Load" in 10 inch black letters 1.5 inches wide, and red or orange flags measuring 18 inches square to be displayed on all sides at the widest point of load. In addition, when operating between sunset and sunrise, flashing amber lights shall be displayed on each side of the load at the widest point. Vehicle/vehicle combinations subject to an exemption or permit under this section shall not exceed posted bridge limits without prior approval from the Department of Transportation.

(c) Definition of "Response." - A response lasts from the time an overweight or oversize vehicle is requested until the vehicle is returned to its base location and restored to a state of readiness for another response.

(c1) Definition of "Preparedness and Fire Prevention." - Movement of equipment for the purpose of hazardous fuel reduction, training, equipment maintenance, pre-suppression fire line installation, fire prevention programs, and equipment staging. In order to qualify for the exception in subsection (a) of this section, equipment must remain configured during movement for one or more of these purposes.

(d) Discretionary Annual or Single Trip Permit for Emergency Response by a Commercial Vehicle. - The Department of Transportation may, in its discretion, issue an annual or single trip special use permit waiving the weight and size restrictions of this Chapter and implementing rules for a commercial overweight or oversize vehicle actively engaged in a response to a fire or a request for assistance from a person authorized to direct emergency operations. The Department of Transportation may condition the permit with safety measures that do not unreasonably delay a response. The Department of Transportation may issue the single trip special use permit upon verbal communication, provided the requestor submits appropriate documentation and fees on the next business day.

(e) No Liability for Issuance of Permit Under This Section. - The action of issuing a permit by the Department of Transportation under this section is a governmental function and does not subject the Department of Transportation to liability for injury to a person or damage to property as a result of the activity. (2007-290, s. 1; 2012-12, s. 2(g); 2012-78, s. 7.)

§ 20-119. Special permits for vehicles of excessive size or weight; fees.

(a)   The Department of Transportation may, in its discretion, upon application, for good cause being shown therefor, issue a special permit in writing authorizing the applicant to operate or move a vehicle of a size or weight exceeding a maximum specified in this Article upon any highway under the jurisdiction and for the maintenance of which the body granting the permit is responsible. However, the Department is not authorized to issue any permit to operate or move over the State highways twin trailers, commonly referred to as double bottom trailers. Every such permit shall be carried in the vehicle to which it refers and shall be open to inspection by any peace officer. The authorities in any incorporated city or town may grant permits in writing and for good cause shown, authorizing the applicant to move a vehicle over the streets of such city or town, the size or weight exceeding the maximum expressed in this Article. The Department of Transportation shall issue rules to implement this section.

(a1)   Where permitted by the posted road and bridge limits, the Department may issue a single trip permit for a vehicle or vehicle combination responding to an emergency event that could result in severe damage, injury, or loss of life or property resulting from any natural or man-made emergency as determined by either the Secretary of Public Safety or the Secretary of Transportation or their designees. A permit issued under this subsection may allow for travel from a specific origin to destination and return 24 hours a day, seven days a week, including holidays. Permits issued under this subsection shall include a requirement for banners, flags, and other safety devices, as determined by the Department, and a requirement for a law enforcement escort or a vehicle being operated by a certified escort vehicle operator if traveling between sunset and sunrise. To obtain authorization to travel during restricted times, application shall be made with any required documentation to the proper officials as designated by the Department. If an emergency permit is issued under this subsection, the requestor shall contact the Department of Transportation's central permit office on the next business day to complete any further documentation and pay the applicable fees.

(b)   Upon the issuance of a special permit for an oversize or overweight vehicle by the Department of Transportation in accordance with this section, the applicant shall pay to the Department for a single trip permit a fee of twelve dollars ($12.00) for each dimension over lawful dimensions, including height, length, width, and weight up to 132,000 pounds. For overweight vehicles, the applicant shall pay to the Department for a single trip permit in addition to the fee imposed by the previous sentence a fee of three dollars ($3.00) per 1,000 pounds over 132,000 pounds.

Upon the issuance of an annual permit for a single vehicle, the applicant shall pay a fee in accordance with the following schedule:

Commodity: Annual Fee:

Annual Permit to Move House Trailers or Trailer Frames
$200.00

Annual Permit to Move Other Commodities
$100.00

In addition to the fees set out in this subsection, applications for permits that require an engineering study for pavement or structures or other special conditions or considerations shall be accompanied by a nonrefundable application fee of one hundred dollars ($100.00).

This subsection does not apply to farm equipment or machinery being used at the time for agricultural purposes, nor to the moving of a house as provided for by the license and permit requirements of Article 16 of this Chapter. Fees will not be assessed for permits for oversize and overweight vehicles issued to any agency of the United States Government or the State of North Carolina, its agencies, institutions, subdivisions, or municipalities if the vehicle is registered in the name of the agency.

(b1)   Neither the Department nor the Board may require review or renewal of annual permits, with or without fee, more than once per calendar year.

(b2)   The Department shall issue single trip permits for the transport and delivery of a manufactured or modular home with a maximum width of 16 feet and a gutter edge that does not exceed three inches from the manufacturer to an authorized dealership within this State, for delivery of a manufactured or modular home by a manufacturer and authorized dealer or their transporters to a location within this State, and for transport and delivery of a manufactured or modular home by a homeowner from one location to another within this State. The Department shall promulgate rules that set the days allowed for transport and delivery, times of day transport or delivery may occur, the display and use of banners and escort vehicles for public safety purposes, and any other reasonable rules as are necessary to promote public safety and commerce. For the purposes of this subsection, manufactured home and modular home shall have the same meanings as those terms are defined in G.S. 105-164.3.

(c)   Nothing in this section shall require the Department of Transportation to issue any permit for any load.

(d)   For each violation of any of the terms or conditions of a special permit issued or where a permit is required but not obtained under this section the Department of Public Safety shall assess a civil penalty for each violation against the registered owner of the vehicle as follows:

(1)   A fine of one thousand five hundred dollars ($1,500) for operating without the proper number of certified escorts as determined by the actual loaded weight or size of the vehicle combination.

(1a)   A fine of five hundred dollars ($500.00) for any of the following: operating without the issuance of a permit, moving a load off the route specified in the permit, falsifying information to obtain a permit, or failing to comply with dimension restrictions of a permit.

(2)   A fine of two hundred fifty dollars ($250.00) for moving loads beyond the distance allowances of an annual permit covering the movement of house trailers from the retailer's premises or for operating in violation of time of travel restrictions.

(3)   A fine of one hundred dollars ($100.00) for any other violation of the permit conditions or requirements imposed by applicable regulations.

The Department of Transportation may refuse to issue additional permits or suspend existing permits if there are repeated violations of subdivision (1), (1a), or (2) of this subsection.

(d1)   In addition to the penalties assessed under subsection (d) of this section, the Department of Public Safety shall assess a civil penalty, not to exceed ten thousand dollars ($10,000), in accordance with G.S. 20-118(e)(1) and (e)(3) against the registered owner of the vehicle for any of the following:

(1)   Operating without the issuance of a required permit.

(2)　　Operating off permitted route of travel.

(3)　　Failing to comply with travel restrictions of the permit.

(4)　　Operating without the proper vehicle registration or license for the class of vehicle being operated.

A violation of this subsection constitutes operating a vehicle without a special permit.

(e)　　It is the intent of the General Assembly that the permit fees provided in G.S. 20-119 shall be adjusted periodically to assure that the revenue generated by the fees is equal to the cost to the Department of administering the Oversize/Overweight Permit Unit Program within the Division of Highways. At least every two years, the Department shall review and compare the revenue generated by the permit fees and the cost of administering the program, and shall report to the Joint Legislative Transportation Oversight Committee created in G.S. 120-70.50 its recommendations for adjustments to the permit fees to bring the revenues and the costs into alignment.

(f)　　The Department of Transportation shall issue rules to establish an escort driver training and certification program for escort vehicles accompanying oversize/overweight loads. Any driver operating a vehicle escorting an oversize/overweight load shall meet any training requirements and obtain certification under the rules issued pursuant to this subsection. These rules may provide for reciprocity with other states having similar escort certification programs. Certification credentials for the driver of an escort vehicle shall be carried in the vehicle and be readily available for inspection by law enforcement personnel. The escort and training certification requirements of this subsection shall not apply to the transportation of agricultural machinery until October 1, 2004. The Department of Transportation shall develop and implement an in-house training program for agricultural machinery escorts by September 1, 2004.

(g)　　The Department of Transportation shall issue annual overwidth permits for the following:

(1)　　A vehicle carrying agricultural equipment or machinery from the dealer to the farm or from the farm to the dealer that does not exceed 14 feet in width. A permit issued under this subdivision is valid for unlimited movement without escorts on all State highways where the overwidth vehicle does not exceed posted bridge and load limits.

(2) A boat or boat trailer whose outside width equals or exceeds 120 inches. A permit issued under this subdivision must restrict a vehicle's towing of the boat or boat trailer to daylight hours only.

(h) No law enforcement officer shall issue a citation to a person for a violation of this section if the officer is able to determine by electronic means that the person has a permit valid at the time of the violation but does not have the permit in his or her possession. Any person issued a citation pursuant to this section who does not have the permit in his or her possession at the time of the issuance of the citation shall not be responsible for a violation, and the Department of Public Safety may not impose any fines under this section if the person submits evidence to the Department of the existence of a permit valid at the time of the violation within 30 days of the date of the violation. (1937, c. 407, s. 83; 1957, c. 65, s. 11; 1959, c. 1129; 1973, c. 507, s. 5; 1977, c. 464, s. 34; 1981, c. 690, ss. 31, 32; c. 736, ss. 1, 2; 1989, c. 54; 1991, c. 604, ss. 1, 2; c. 689, s. 334; 1993, c. 539, s. 357; 1994, Ex. Sess., c. 24, s. 14(c); 2000-109, ss. 7(a), 7(f), 7(g); 2001-424, s. 27.10; 2003-383, s. 7; 2004-124, s. 30.3E(a), (b); 2004-145, s. 3; 2005-361, s. 4; 2007-290, s. 2; 2008-160, s. 2; 2008-229, s. 2; 2009-376, ss. 7, 8; 2011-145, s. 19.1(g); 2011-358, s. 1.)

§ 20-119.1. Use of excess overweight and oversize fees.

Funds generated by overweight and oversize permit fees in excess of the cost of administering the program, as determined pursuant to G.S. 20-119(e), shall be used for highway and bridge maintenance required as a result of damages caused from overweight or oversize loads. (2005-276, s. 28.5.)

§ 20-120. Operation of flat trucks on State highways regulated; trucks hauling leaf tobacco in barrels or hogsheads.

It shall be unlawful for any person, firm or corporation to operate, or have operated on any public highway in the State any open, flat truck loaded with logs, cotton bales, boxes or other load piled on said truck, without having the said load securely fastened on said truck.

It shall be unlawful for any firm, person or corporation to operate or permit to be operated on any highway of this State a truck or trucks on which leaf tobacco in barrels or hogsheads is carried unless each section or tier of such barrels or hogsheads are reasonably securely fastened to such truck or trucks by metal chains or wire cables, or manila or hemp ropes of not less than five-eighths inch in diameter, to hold said barrels or hogsheads in place under any ordinary traffic or road condition: Provided that the provisions of this paragraph shall not apply to any truck or trucks on which the hogsheads or barrels of tobacco are arranged in a single layer, tier, or plane, it being the intent of this paragraph to require the use of metal chains or wire cables only when barrels or hogsheads of tobacco are stacked or piled one upon the other on a truck or trucks. Nothing in this paragraph shall apply to trucks engaged in transporting hogsheads or barrels of tobacco between factories and storage houses of the same company unless such hogsheads or barrels are placed upon the truck in tiers. In the event the hogsheads or barrels of tobacco are placed upon the truck in tiers same shall be securely fastened to the said truck as hereinbefore provided in this paragraph.

Any person violating the provisions of this section shall be guilty of a Class 2 misdemeanor. (1939, c. 114; 1947, c. 1094; 1953, c. 240; 1993, c. 539, s. 358; 1994, Ex. Sess., c. 24, s. 14(c).)

§ 20-121. When authorities may restrict right to use highways.

The Department of Transportation or local authorities may prohibit the operation of vehicles upon or impose restrictions as to the weight thereof, for a total period not to exceed 90 days in any one calendar year, when operated upon any highway under the jurisdiction of and for the maintenance of which the body adopting the ordinance is responsible, whenever any said highway by reason of deterioration, rain, snow or other climatic conditions will be damaged unless the use of vehicles thereon is prohibited or the permissible weights thereof reduced. The local authority enacting any such ordinance shall erect, or cause to be erected and maintained, signs designating the provisions of the ordinance at each end of that portion of any highway to which the ordinance is applicable, and the ordinance shall not be effective until or unless such signs are erected and maintained. (1937, c. 407, s. 84; 1957, c. 65, s. 11; 1973, c. 507, s. 5; 1977, c. 464, s. 34.)

§ 20-121.1. Operation of a low-speed vehicle on certain roadways.

The operation of a low-speed vehicle is authorized with the following restrictions:

(1)   A low-speed vehicle may be operated only on streets and highways where the posted speed limit is 35 miles per hour or less. This does not prohibit a low-speed vehicle from crossing a road or street at an intersection where the road or street being crossed has a posted speed limit of more than 35 miles per hour.

(2)   A low-speed vehicle shall be equipped with headlamps, stop lamps, turn signal lamps, tail lamps, reflex reflectors, parking brakes, rearview mirrors, windshields, windshield wipers, speedometer, seat belts, and a vehicle identification number.

(3)   A low-speed vehicle shall be registered and insured in accordance with G.S. 20-50 and G.S. 20-309.

(4)   The Department of Transportation may prohibit the operation of low-speed vehicles on any road or highway if it determines that the prohibition is necessary in the interest of safety.

(5)   Low-speed vehicles must comply with the safety standards in 49 C.F.R. § 571.500. (2001-356, s. 5.)

§ 20-122. Restrictions as to tire equipment.

(a)   No vehicle will be allowed to move on any public highway unless equipped with tires of rubber or other resilient material which depend upon compressed air, for support of a load, except by special permission of the Department of Transportation which may grant such special permits upon a showing of necessity. This subsection shall have no application to the movement of farm vehicles on highways.

(b)   No tire on a vehicle moved on a highway shall have on its periphery any block, stud, flange, cleat or spike or any other protuberance of any material other than rubber which projects beyond the tread of the traction surface of the tire, except that it shall be permissible to use farm machinery with tires having protuberances which will not injure the highway and except, also, that it shall be permissible to use tire chains of reasonable proportions upon any vehicle when required for safety because of snow, ice or other conditions tending to cause a vehicle to slide or skid. It shall be permissible to use upon any vehicle for increased safety, regular and snow tires with studs which project beyond the tread of the traction surface of the tire not more than one sixteenth of an inch when compressed.

(c) The Department of Transportation or local authorities in their respective jurisdictions may, in their discretion, issue special permits authorizing the operation upon a highway of traction engines or tractors having movable tracks with transverse corrugation upon the periphery of such movable tracks or farm tractors or other farm machinery.

(d) It shall not be unlawful to drive farm tractors on dirt roads from farm to farm: Provided, in doing so they do not damage said dirt roads or interfere with traffic. (1937, c. 407, s. 85; 1939, c. 266; 1957, c. 65, s. 11; 1965, c. 435; 1973, c. 507, s. 5; 1977, c. 464, s. 34; 1979, c. 515.)

§ 20-122.1. Motor vehicles to be equipped with safe tires.

(a) Every motor vehicle subject to safety equipment inspection in this State and operated on the streets and highways of this State shall be equipped with tires which are safe for the operation of the motor vehicle and which do not expose the public to needless hazard. Tires shall be considered unsafe if cut so as to expose tire cord, cracked so as to expose tire cord, or worn so as to expose tire cord or there is a visible tread separation or chunking or the tire has less than two thirty-seconds inch tread depth at two or more locations around the circumference of the tire in two adjacent major tread grooves, or if the tread wear indicators are in contact with the roadway at two or more locations around the circumference of the tire in two adjacent major tread grooves: Provided, the two thirty-seconds tread depth requirements of this section shall not apply to dual wheel trailers. For the purpose of this section, the following definitions shall apply:

(1) "Chunking" - separation of the tread from the carcass in particles which may range from very small size to several square inches in area.

(2) "Cord" - strands forming a ply in a tire.

(3) "Tread" - portion of tire which comes in contact with road.

(4) "Tread depth" - the distance from the base of the tread design to the top of the tread.

(a1) Any motor vehicle that has a GVWR of at least 10,001 pounds or more and is operated on the streets or highways of this State shall be equipped with tires that are safe for the operation of the vehicle and do not expose the public to needless hazard. A tire is unsafe if any of the following applies:

(1) It is cut, cracked, or worn so as to expose tire cord.

(2) There is a visible tread separation or chunking.

(3) The steering axle tire has less than four thirty-seconds inch tread depth at any location around the circumference of the tire on any major tread groove.

(4) Any nonsteering axle tire has less than two thirty-seconds inch tread depth around the circumference of the tire in any major tread groove.

(5) The tread wear indicators are in contact with the roadway at any location around the circumference of the tire on any major tread groove.

(b) The driver of any vehicle who is charged with a violation of this section shall be allowed 15 calendar days within which to bring the tires of such vehicle in conformance with the requirements of this section. It shall be a defense to any such charge that the person arrested produce in court, or submit to the prosecuting attorney prior to trial, a certificate from an official safety inspection equipment station showing that within 15 calendar days after such arrest, the tires on such vehicle had been made to conform with the requirements of this section or that such vehicle had been sold, destroyed, or permanently removed from the highways. Violation of this section shall not constitute negligence per se. (1969, c. 378, s. 1; c. 1256; 1985, c. 93, ss. 1, 2; 2009-376, s. 5.)

§ 20-123. Trailers and towed vehicles.

(a) The limitations in G.S. 20-116 on combination vehicles do not prohibit the towing of farm trailers not exceeding three in number nor exceeding a total length of 50 feet during the period from one-half hour before sunrise until one-half hour after sunset when a red flag of at least 12 inches square is prominently displayed on the last vehicle. The towing of farm trailers and equipment allowed by this subsection does not apply to interstate or federal numbered highways.

(b) No trailer or semitrailer or other towed vehicle shall be operated over the highways of the State unless such trailer or semitrailer or other towed vehicle be firmly attached to the rear of the towing unit, and unless so equipped that it will not snake, but will travel in the path of the vehicle drawing such trailer or semitrailer or other towed vehicle, which equipment shall at all times be kept in good condition.

(c) In addition to the requirements of subsections (a) and (b) of this section, the towed vehicle shall be attached to the towing unit by means of safety chains or cables which shall be of sufficient strength to hold the gross weight of the towed vehicle in the event the primary towing device fails or becomes disconnected while being operated on the highways of this State if the primary towing attachment is a ball hitch. Trailers and semitrailers having locking pins or bolts in the towing attachment to prevent disconnection, and the locking pins or bolts are of sufficient strength and condition to hold the gross weight of the towed vehicle, need not be equipped with safety chains or cables unless their operation is subject to the requirements of the Federal Motor Carrier Safety Regulations. Semitrailers in combinations of vehicles that are equipped with fifth wheel assemblies that include locking devices need not be equipped with safety chains or cables. (1937, c. 407, s. 86; 1955, c. 296, s. 3; 1963, c. 356, s. 2; c. 1027, s. 2; 1965, c. 966; 1971, c. 639; 1973, c. 507, s. 5; 1975, c. 716, s. 5; 1977, c. 464, s. 34; 1981 (Reg. Sess., 1982), c. 1195; 1993, c. 71, s. 1; 1995 (Reg. Sess., 1996), c. 756, s. 15; 1997-148, s. 8.)

§ 20-123.1. Steering mechanism.

The steering mechanism of every self-propelled motor vehicle operated on the highway shall be maintained in good working order, sufficient to enable the operator to control the vehicle's movements and to maneuver it safely. (1957, c. 1038, s. 3.)

§ 20-123.2 Speedometer.

(a)   Every self-propelled motor vehicle when operated on the highway shall be equipped with a speedometer which shall be maintained in good working order.

(b)   Any person violating this section shall have committed an infraction and may be ordered to pay a penalty of not more than twenty-five dollars ($25.00). No drivers license points, insurance points or premium surcharge shall be assessed on or imputed to any party on account of a violation of this section. (1989 (Reg. Sess., 1990), c. 822, s. 2.)

§ 20-124. Brakes.

(a)   Every motor vehicle when operated upon a highway shall be equipped with brakes adequate to control the movement of and to stop such vehicle or vehicles, and such brakes shall be maintained in good working order and shall conform to regulations provided in this section.

(b)   Repealed by Session Laws 1973, c. 1330, s. 39.

(c)   Every motor vehicle when operated on a highway shall be equipped with brakes adequate to control the movement of and to stop and hold such vehicle, and shall have all originally equipped brakes in good working order, including two separate means of applying the brakes. If these two separate means of applying the brakes are connected in any way, they shall be so constructed that failure of any one part of the operating mechanism shall not leave the motor vehicle without brakes.

(d)   Every motorcycle and every motor-driven cycle when operated upon a highway shall be equipped with at least one brake which may be operated by hand or foot.

(e)   Motor trucks and tractor-trucks with semitrailers attached shall be capable of stopping on a dry, hard, approximately level highway free from loose material at a speed of 20 miles per hour within the following distances: Thirty feet with both hand and service brake applied simultaneously and 50 feet when either is applied separately, except that vehicles maintained and operated permanently for the transportation of property and which were registered in this or any other state or district prior to August, 1929, shall be capable of stopping on a dry, hard, approximately level highway free from loose material at a speed of 20 miles per hour within a distance of 50 feet with both hand and service brake applied simultaneously, and within a distance of 75 feet when either applied separately.

(e1)   Every motor truck and truck-tractor with semitrailer attached, shall be equipped with brakes acting on all wheels, except trucks and truck-tractors having three or more axles need not have brakes on the front wheels if manufactured prior to July 25, 1980. However, such trucks and truck-tractors must be capable of complying with the performance requirements of G.S. 20-124(e).

(f)   Every semitrailer, or trailer, or separate vehicle, attached by a drawbar or coupling to a towing vehicle, and having a gross weight of two tons, and all house trailers of 1,000 pounds gross weight or more, shall be equipped with brakes controlled or operated by the driver of the towing vehicle, which shall conform to the specifications set forth in subsection (e) of this section and shall be of a type approved by the Commissioner.

It shall be unlawful for any person or corporation engaged in the business of selling house trailers at wholesale or retail to sell or offer for sale any house trailer which is not equipped with the brakes required by this subsection.

This subsection shall not apply to house trailers being used as dwellings, or to house trailers not intended to be used or towed on public highways and roads. This subsection shall not apply to house trailers with a manufacturer's certificate of origin dated prior to December 31, 1974.

(g)   The provisions of this section shall not apply to a trailer when used by a farmer, a farmer's tenant, agent, or employee if the trailer is exempt from registration by the provisions of G.S. 20-51. This exemption does not apply to trailers that are equipped with brakes from the manufacturer and that are manufactured after October 1, 2009.

(h)   From and after July 1, 1955, no person shall sell or offer for sale for use in motor vehicle brake systems in this State any hydraulic brake fluid of a type and brand other than those approved by the Commissioner of Motor Vehicles. From and after January 1, 1970, no person shall sell or offer for sale in motor vehicle brake systems any brake lining of a type or brand other than those approved by the Commissioner of Motor Vehicles. Violation of the provisions of this subsection shall constitute a Class 2 misdemeanor. (1937, c. 407, s. 87; 1953, c. 1316, s. 2; 1955, c. 1275; 1959, c. 990; 1965, c. 1031; 1967, c. 1188; 1969, cc. 787, 866; 1973, c. 1203; c. 1330, s. 39; 1993, c. 539, s. 359; 1994, Ex. Sess., c. 24, s. 14(c); 2009-376, ss. 10, 11.)

§ 20-125. Horns and warning devices.

(a) Every motor vehicle when operated upon a highway shall be equipped with a horn in good working order capable of emitting sound audible under normal conditions from a distance of not less than 200 feet, and it shall be unlawful, except as otherwise provided in this section, for any vehicle to be equipped with or for any person to use upon a vehicle any siren, compression or spark plug whistle or for any person at any time to use a horn otherwise than as a reasonable warning or to make any unnecessary or unreasonable loud or harsh sound by means of a horn or other warning device. All such horns and warning devices shall be maintained in good working order and shall conform to regulation not inconsistent with this section to be promulgated by the Commissioner.

(b) Every vehicle owned or operated by a police department or by the Department of Public Safety including the State Highway Patrol or by the Wildlife Resources Commission or the Division of Marine Fisheries, or by the Division of Parks and Recreation of the Department of Environment and Natural Resources, or by the North Carolina Forest Service of the Department of Agriculture and Consumer Services, and used exclusively for law enforcement, firefighting, or other emergency response purposes, or by the Division of Emergency Management, or by a fire department, either municipal or rural, or by a fire patrol, whether such fire department or patrol be a paid organization or a voluntary association, vehicles used by an organ procurement organization or agency for the recovery and transportation of human tissues and organs for transplantation, and every ambulance or emergency medical service emergency support vehicle used for answering emergency calls, shall be equipped with special lights, bells, sirens, horns or exhaust whistles of a type approved by the Commissioner of Motor Vehicles.

The operators of all such vehicles so equipped are hereby authorized to use such equipment at all times while engaged in the performance of their duties and services, both within their respective corporate limits and beyond.

In addition to the use of special equipment authorized and required by this subsection, the chief and assistant chiefs of any police department or of any fire department, whether the same be municipal or rural, paid or voluntary, county fire marshals, assistant fire marshals, transplant coordinators, and emergency management coordinators, are hereby authorized to use such special equipment on privately owned vehicles operated by them while actually engaged in the performance of their official or semiofficial duties or services either within or beyond their respective corporate limits.

And vehicles driven by law enforcement officers of the North Carolina Division of Motor Vehicles shall be equipped with a bell, siren, or exhaust whistle of a type approved by the Commissioner, and all vehicles owned and operated by the State Bureau of Investigation for the use of its agents and officers in the performance of their official duties may be equipped with special lights, bells, sirens, horns or exhaust whistles of a type approved by the Commissioner of Motor Vehicles.

Every vehicle used or operated for law enforcement purposes by the sheriff or any salaried deputy sheriff or salaried rural policeman of any county, whether owned by the county or not, may be, but is not required to be, equipped with special lights, bells, sirens, horns or exhaust whistles of a type approved by the Commissioner of Motor Vehicles. Such special equipment shall not be operated or activated by any person except by a law enforcement officer while actively engaged in performing law enforcement duties.

In addition to the use of special equipment authorized and required by this subsection, the chief and assistant chiefs of each emergency rescue squad which is recognized or sponsored by any municipality or civil preparedness agency, are hereby authorized to use such special equipment on privately owned vehicles operated by them while actually engaged in their official or semiofficial duties or services either within or beyond the corporate limits of the municipality which recognizes or sponsors such organization.

(c) Repealed by Session Laws 1979, c. 653, s. 2. (1937, c. 407, s. 88; 1951, cc. 392, 1161; 1955, c. 1224; 1959, c. 166, s. 1; c. 494; c. 1170, s. 1; c. 1209; 1965, c. 257; 1975, c. 588; c. 734, s. 15; 1977, c. 52, s. 1; c. 438, s. 1; 1979, c. 653, s. 2; 1981, c. 964, s. 19; 1983, c. 32, s. 2; c. 768, s. 5; 1987, c. 266; 1989, c. 537; 1989 (Reg. Sess., 1990), c. 1020, s. 1; 1993 (Reg. Sess., 1994), c. 719, s. 2; 2011-145, s. 19.1(g); 2013-415, s. 1(a).)

§ 20-125.1. Directional signals.

(a)   It shall be unlawful for the owner of any motor vehicle of a changed model or series designation indicating that it was manufactured or assembled after July 1, 1953, to register such vehicle or cause it to be registered in this State, or to obtain, or cause to be obtained in this State registration plates therefor, unless such vehicle is equipped with a mechanical or electrical signal device by which the operator of the vehicle may indicate to the operator of another vehicle, approaching from either the front or rear and within a distance of 200 feet, his intention to turn from a direct line. Such signal device must be of a type approved by the Commissioner of Motor Vehicles.

(b)   It shall be unlawful for any dealer to sell or deliver in this State any motor vehicle of a changed model or series designation indicating that it was manufactured or assembled after July 1, 1953, if he knows or has reasonable cause to believe that the purchaser of such vehicle intends to register it or cause it to be registered in this State or to resell it to any other person for registration in and use upon the highways of this State, unless such motor vehicle is equipped with a mechanical or electrical signal device by which the operator of the vehicle may indicate to the operator of another vehicle, approaching from either of the front or rear or within a distance of 200 feet, his intention to turn from a direct line. Such signal device must be of a type approved by the Commissioner of Motor Vehicles: Provided that in the case of any motor vehicle manufactured or assembled after July 1, 1953, the signal device with which such motor vehicle is equipped shall be presumed prima facie to have been approved by the Commissioner of Motor Vehicles. Irrespective of the date of manufacture of any motor vehicle a certificate from the Commissioner of Motor Vehicles to the effect that a particular type of signal device has been approved by his Division shall be admissible in evidence in all the courts of this State.

(c)   Trailers satisfying the following conditions are not required to be equipped with a directional signal device:

(1)   The trailer and load does not obscure the directional signals of the towing vehicle from the view of a driver approaching from the rear and within a distance of 200 feet;

(2)   The gross weight of the trailer and load does not exceed 4,000 pounds.

(d)   Nothing in this section shall apply to motorcycles. (1953, c. 481; 1957, c. 488, s. 1; 1963, c. 524; 1969, c. 622; 1975, c. 716, s. 5.)

§ 20-126. Mirrors.

(a)   No person shall drive a motor vehicle on the streets or highways of this State unless equipped with an inside rearview mirror of a type approved by the Commissioner, which provides the driver with a clear, undistorted, and reasonably unobstructed view of the highway to the rear of such vehicle; provided, a vehicle so constructed or loaded as to make such inside rearview mirror ineffective may be operated if equipped with a mirror of a type to be approved by the Commissioner located so as to reflect to the driver a view of the highway to the rear of such vehicle. A violation of this subsection shall not constitute negligence per se in civil actions. Farm tractors, self-propelled implements of husbandry and construction equipment and all self-propelled vehicles not subject to registration under this Chapter are exempt from the provisions of this section. Provided that pickup trucks equipped with an outside rearview mirror approved by the Commissioner shall be exempt from the inside rearview mirror provision of this section. Any inside mirror installed in any motor vehicle by its manufacturer shall be deemed to comply with the provisions of this subsection.

(b)   It shall be unlawful for any person to operate upon the highways of this State any vehicle manufactured, assembled or first sold on or after January 1, 1966 and registered in this State unless such vehicle is equipped with at least one outside mirror mounted on the driver's side of the vehicle. Mirrors herein required shall be of a type approved by the Commissioner.

(c)   No person shall operate a motorcycle upon the streets or highways of this State unless such motorcycle is equipped with a rearview mirror so mounted as to provide the operator with a clear, undistorted and unobstructed view of at least 200 feet to the rear of the motorcycle. No motorcycle shall be registered in this State after January 1, 1968, unless such motorcycle is equipped with a rearview mirror as described in this section. Violation of the provisions of this subsection shall not be considered negligence per se or contributory negligence per se in any civil action. (1937, c. 407, s. 89; 1965, c. 368; 1967, c. 282, s. 1; c. 674, s. 2; c. 1139; 2002-159, ss. 22(a), 22(b).)

§ 20-127. Windows and windshield wipers.

(a) Windshield Wipers. - A vehicle that is operated on a highway and has a windshield shall have a windshield wiper to clear rain or other substances from the windshield in front of the driver of the vehicle and the windshield wiper shall be in good working order. If a vehicle has more than one windshield wiper to clear substances from the windshield, all the windshield wipers shall be in good working order.

(b) Window Tinting Restrictions. - A window of a vehicle that is operated on a highway or a public vehicular area shall comply with this subsection. The windshield of the vehicle may be tinted only along the top of the windshield and the tinting may not extend more than five inches below the top of the windshield or below the AS1 line of the windshield, whichever measurement is longer. Provided, however, an untinted clear film which does not obstruct vision but which reduces or eliminates ultraviolet radiation from entering a vehicle may be applied to the windshield. Any other window of the vehicle may be tinted in accordance with the following restrictions:

(1) The total light transmission of the tinted window shall be at least thirty-five percent (35%). A vehicle window that, by use of a light meter approved by the Commissioner, measures a total light transmission of more than thirty-two percent (32%) is conclusively presumed to meet this restriction.

(2) The light reflectance of the tinted window shall be twenty percent (20%) or less.

(3) Tinted film or another material used to tint the window shall be nonreflective and shall not be red, yellow, or amber.

(b1) Notwithstanding subsection (b) of this section, a window of a vehicle that is operated on a public street or highway and which is subject to the provisions of Part 393 of Title 49 of the Code of Federal Regulations shall comply with the provisions of that Part.

(c) Tinting Exceptions. - The window tinting restrictions in subsection (b) of this section apply without exception to the windshield of a vehicle. The window tinting restrictions in subdivisions (b)(1) and (b)(2) of this section do not apply to any of the following vehicle windows:

(1) A window of an excursion passenger vehicle, as defined in G.S. 20-4.01(27)a.

(2), (3) Repealed by Session Laws 2012-78, s. 8, effective December 1, 2012. For applicability, see Editor's notes.

(4) A window of a motor home, as defined in G.S. 20-4.01(27)d2.

(5) A window of an ambulance, as defined in G.S. 20-4.01(27)f.

(6) The rear window of a property-hauling vehicle, as defined in G.S. 20-4.01(31).

(7) A window of a limousine.

(8) A window of a law enforcement vehicle.

(9) A window of a multipurpose vehicle that is behind the driver of the vehicle. A multipurpose vehicle is a passenger vehicle that is designed to carry 10 or fewer passengers and either is constructed on a truck chassis or has special features designed for occasional off-road operation. A minivan and a pickup truck are multipurpose vehicles.

(10) A window of a vehicle that is registered in another state and meets the requirements of the state in which it is registered.

(11) A window of a vehicle for which the Division has issued a medical exception permit under subsection (f) of this section.

(d) Violations. - A person who does any of the following commits a Class 3 misdemeanor:

(1) Applies tinting to the window of a vehicle that is subject to a safety inspection in this State and the resulting tinted window does not meet the window tinting restrictions set in this section.

(2) Drives on a highway or a public vehicular area a vehicle that has a window that does not meet the window tinting restrictions set in this section.

(e) Defense. - It is a defense to a charge of driving a vehicle with an unlawfully tinted window that the tinting was removed within 15 days after the charge and the window now meets the window tinting restrictions. To assert this defense, the person charged shall produce in court, or submit to the prosecuting attorney before trial, a certificate from the Division of Motor Vehicles or the Highway Patrol showing that the window complies with the restrictions.

(f) Medical Exception. - A person who suffers from a medical condition that causes the person to be photosensitive to visible light may obtain a medical exception permit. To obtain a permit, an applicant shall apply in writing to the Drivers Medical Evaluation Program and have his or her doctor complete the required medical evaluation form provided by the Division. The permit shall be valid for five years from the date of issue, unless a shorter time is directed by the Drivers Medical Evaluation Program. The renewal shall require a medical recertification that the person continues to suffer from a medical condition requiring tinting.

A person may receive no more than two medical exception permits that are valid at any one time. A permit issued under this subsection shall specify the vehicle to which it applies, the windows that may be tinted, and the permitted levels of tinting. The permit shall be carried in the vehicle to which it applies when the vehicle is driven on a highway.

The Division shall give a person who receives a medical exception permit a sticker to place on the lower left-hand corner of the rear window of the vehicle to which it applies. The sticker shall be designed to give prospective purchasers of the vehicle notice that the windows of the vehicle do not meet the requirements of G.S. 20-127(b), and shall be placed between the window and the tinting when the tinting is installed. The Division shall adopt rules regarding the specifications of the medical exception sticker. Failure to display the sticker is an infraction punishable by a two hundred dollar ($200.00) fine. (1937, c. 407, s. 90; 1953, c. 1254; 1955, c. 1157, s. 2; 1959, c. 1264, s. 7; 1967, c. 1077; 1985, c. 789; 1985 (Reg. Sess., 1986), c. 997; 1987, c. 567; 1987 (Reg. Sess., 1988), c. 1082, ss. 7-8.1; 1989, c. 770, s. 66; 1991 (Reg. Sess., 1992), c. 1007, s. 34; 1993, c. 539, s. 360; 1994, Ex. Sess., c. 24, s. 14(c); 1993 (Reg. Sess., 1994), c. 683, s. 1; c. 754, s. 4; 1995, c. 14, s. 1; c. 473, s. 1; 2000-75, s. 1; 2012-78, s. 8; 2013-360, s. 18B.14(j).)

§ 20-128. Exhaust system and emissions control devices.

(a)   No person shall drive a motor vehicle on a highway unless such motor vehicle is equipped with a muffler, or other exhaust system of the type installed at the time of manufacture, in good working order and in constant operation to prevent excessive or unusual noise, annoying smoke and smoke screens.

(b)   It shall be unlawful to use a "muffler cut-out" on any motor vehicle upon a highway.

(c)   No motor vehicle registered in this State that was manufactured after model year 1967 shall be operated in this State unless it is equipped with emissions control devices that were installed on the vehicle at the time the vehicle was manufactured and these devices are properly connected.

(d)   The requirements of subsection (c) of this section shall not apply if the emissions control devices have been removed for the purpose of converting the motor vehicle to operate on natural or liquefied petroleum gas or other modifications have been made in order to reduce air pollution and these modifications are approved by the Department of Environment and Natural Resources. (1937, c. 407, s. 91; 1971, c. 455, s. 1; 1983, c. 132; 1989, c. 727, s. 9; 1997-443, s. 11A.119(a); 2000-134, s. 6.)

§ 20-128.1. Control of visible emissions.

(a)   It shall be a violation of this Article:

(1)   For any gasoline-powered motor vehicle registered and operated in this State to emit visible air contaminants under any mode of operation for longer than five consecutive seconds.

(2)   For any diesel-powered motor vehicle registered and operated in this State to emit for longer than five consecutive seconds under any mode of operation visible air contaminants which are equal to or darker than the shade or density designated as No. 1 on the Ringelmann Chart or are equal to or darker than a shade or density of twenty percent (20%) opacity.

(b)   Any person charged with a violation of this section shall be allowed 30 days within which to make the necessary repairs or modification to bring the motor vehicle into conformity with the standards of this section and to have the motor vehicle inspected and approved by the agency issuing the notice of violation. Any person who, within 30 days of receipt of a notice of violation, and prior to inspection and approval by the agency issuing the notice, receives additional notice or notices of violation, may exhibit a certificate of inspection and approval from the agency issuing the first notice in lieu of inspection and approval by the agencies issuing the subsequent notices.

(c) The provisions of this section shall be enforceable by all persons designated in G.S. 20-49; by all law-enforcement officers of this State within their respective jurisdictions; by the personnel of local air pollution control agencies within their respective jurisdictions; and by personnel of State air pollution control agencies throughout the State.

(d) Any person who fails to comply with the provisions of this section shall be subject to the penalties provided in G.S. 20-176. (1971, c. 1167, s. 10.)

§ 20-128.2. Motor vehicle emission standards.

(a) The rules and regulations promulgated pursuant to G.S. 143-215.107(a)(6) shall be implemented when the Environmental Management Commission certifies to the Commissioner of Motor Vehicles that the ambient air quality in an area will be improved by the implementation of a motor vehicle inspection/maintenance program within a specified county or group of counties, as necessary to effect attainment or preclude violations of the National Ambient Air Quality Standards for carbon monoxide or ozone; provided the Environmental Management Commission may prescribe different vehicle emission limits for different areas as may be necessary and appropriate to meet the stated purposes of this section.

(b) Repealed by Session Laws 1993 (Reg. Sess., 1994), c. 754, s. 5. (1979, 2nd Sess., c. 1180, s. 2; 1989, c. 391, s. 1; 1993 (Reg. Sess., 1994), c. 754, s. 5.)

§ 20-129. Required lighting equipment of vehicles.

(a) When Vehicles Must Be Equipped. - Every vehicle upon a highway within this State shall be equipped with lighted headlamps and rear lamps as required for different classes of vehicles, and subject to exemption with reference to lights on parked vehicles as declared in G.S. 20-134:

(1)   During the period from sunset to sunrise,

(2)   When there is not sufficient light to render clearly discernible any person on the highway at a distance of 400 feet ahead, or

(3)   Repealed by Session Laws 1989 (Reg. Sess., 1990), c. 822, s. 1.

(4)   At any other time when windshield wipers are in use as a result of smoke, fog, rain, sleet, or snow, or when inclement weather or environmental factors severely reduce the ability to clearly discern persons and vehicles on the street and highway at a distance of 500 feet ahead, provided, however, the provisions of this subdivision shall not apply to instances when windshield wipers are used intermittently in misting rain, sleet, or snow. Any person violating this subdivision during the period from October 1, 1990, through December 31, 1991, shall be given a warning of the violation only. Thereafter, any person violating this subdivision shall have committed an infraction and shall pay a fine of five dollars ($5.00) and shall not be assessed court costs. No drivers license points, insurance points or premium surcharge shall be assessed on account of violation of this subdivision and no negligence or liability shall be assessed on or imputed to any party on account of a violation of this subdivision. The Commissioner of Motor Vehicles and the Superintendent of Public Instruction shall incorporate into driver education programs and driver licensing programs instruction designed to encourage compliance with this subdivision as an important means of reducing accidents by making vehicles more discernible during periods of limited visibility.

(b)   Headlamps on Motor Vehicles. - Every self-propelled motor vehicle other than motorcycles, road machinery, and farm tractors shall be equipped with at least two headlamps, all in good operating condition with at least one on each side of the front of the motor vehicle. Headlamps shall comply with the requirements and limitations set forth in G.S. 20-131 or 20-132.

(c)   Headlamps on Motorcycles. - Every motorcycle shall be equipped with at least one and not more than two headlamps which shall comply with the requirements and limitations set forth in G.S. 20-131 or 20-132. The headlamps on a motorcycle shall be lighted at all times while the motorcycle is in operation on highways or public vehicular areas.

(d) Rear Lamps. - Every motor vehicle, and every trailer or semitrailer attached to a motor vehicle and every vehicle which is being drawn at the end of a combination of vehicles, shall have all originally equipped rear lamps or the equivalent in good working order, which lamps shall exhibit a red light plainly visible under normal atmospheric conditions from a distance of 500 feet to the rear of such vehicle. One rear lamp or a separate lamp shall be so constructed and placed that the number plate carried on the rear of such vehicle shall under like conditions be illuminated by a white light as to be read from a distance of 50 feet to the rear of such vehicle. Every trailer or semitrailer shall carry at the rear, in addition to the originally equipped lamps, a red reflector of the type which has been approved by the Commissioner and which is so located as to height and is so maintained as to be visible for at least 500 feet when opposed by a motor vehicle displaying lawful undimmed lights at night on an unlighted highway.

Notwithstanding the provisions of the first paragraph of this subsection, it shall not be necessary for a trailer weighing less than 4,000 pounds, or a trailer described in G.S. 20-51(6) weighing less than 6,500 pounds, to carry or be equipped with a rear lamp, provided such vehicle is equipped with and carries at the rear two red reflectors of a diameter of not less than three inches, such reflectors to be approved by the Commissioner, and which are so designed and located as to height and are maintained so that each reflector is visible for at least 500 feet when approached by a motor vehicle displaying lawful undimmed headlights at night on an unlighted highway.

The rear lamps of a motorcycle shall be lighted at all times while the motorcycle is in operation on highways or public vehicular areas.

(e) Lamps on Bicycles. - Every bicycle shall be equipped with a lighted lamp on the front thereof, visible under normal atmospheric conditions from a distance of at least 300 feet in front of such bicycle, and shall also be equipped with a reflex mirror or lamp on the rear, exhibiting a red light visible under like conditions from a distance of at least 200 feet to the rear of such bicycle, when used at night.

(f) Lights on Other Vehicles. - All vehicles not heretofore in this section required to be equipped with specified lighted lamps shall carry on the left side one or more lighted lamps or lanterns projecting a white light, visible under normal atmospheric conditions from a distance of not less than 500 feet to the front of such vehicle and visible under like conditions from a distance of not less than 500 feet to the rear of such vehicle, or in lieu of said lights shall be equipped with reflectors of a type which is approved by the Commissioner. Farm tractors operated on a highway at night must be equipped with at least one white lamp visible at a distance of 500 feet from the front of the tractor and with at least one red lamp visible at a distance of 500 feet to the rear of the tractor. Two red reflectors each having a diameter of at least four inches may be used on the rear of the tractor in lieu of the red lamp.

(g) No person shall sell or operate on the highways of the State any motor vehicle, motorcycle or motor-driven cycle, manufactured after December 31, 1955, unless it shall be equipped with a stop lamp on the rear of the vehicle. The stop lamp shall display a red or amber light visible from a distance of not less than 100 feet to the rear in normal sunlight, and shall be actuated upon application of the service (foot) brake. The stop lamp may be incorporated into a unit with one or more other rear lamps. (1937, c. 407, s. 92; 1939, c. 275; 1947, c. 526; 1955, c. 1157, ss. 3-5, 8; 1957, c. 1038, s. 1; 1967, cc. 1076, 1213; 1969, c. 389; 1973, c. 531, ss. 1, 2; 1979, c. 175; 1981, c. 549, s. 1; 1985, c. 66; 1987, c. 611; 1989 (Reg. Sess., 1990), c. 822, s. 1; 1991, c. 18, s. 1; 1999-281, s. 1.)

§ 20-129.1. Additional lighting equipment required on certain vehicles.

In addition to other equipment required by this Chapter, the following vehicles shall be equipped as follows:

(1) On every bus or truck, whatever its size, there shall be the following:

On the rear, two reflectors, one at each side, and one stoplight.

(2) On every bus or truck 80 inches or more in overall width, in addition to the requirements in subdivision (1):

On the front, two clearance lamps, one at each side.

On the rear, two clearance lamps, one at each side.

On each side, two side marker lamps, one at or near the front and one at or near the rear.

On each side, two reflectors, one at or near the front and one at or near the rear.

(3) On every truck tractor:

On the front, two clearance lamps, one at each side.

On the rear, one stoplight.

(4) On every trailer or semitrailer having a gross weight of 4,000 pounds or more:

On the front, two clearance lamps, one at each side.

On each side, two side marker lamps, one at or near the front and one at or near the rear.

On each side, two reflectors, one at or near the front and one at or near the rear.

On the rear, two clearance lamps, one at each side, also two reflectors, one at each side, and one stoplight.

(5) On every pole trailer having a gross weight of 4,000 pounds or more:

On each side, one side marker lamp and one clearance lamp which may be in combination, to show to the front, side and rear.

On the rear of the pole trailer or load, two reflectors, one at each side.

(6) On every trailer, semitrailer or pole trailer having a gross weight of less than 4,000 pounds:

On the rear, two reflectors, one on each side. If any trailer or semitrailer is so loaded or is of such dimensions as to obscure the stoplight on the towing vehicle, then such vehicle shall also be equipped with one stoplight.

(7) Front clearance lamps and those marker lamps and reflectors mounted on the front or on the side near the front of a vehicle shall display or reflect an amber color.

(8) Rear clearance lamps and those marker lamps and reflectors mounted on the rear or on the sides near the rear of a vehicle shall display or reflect a red color.

(9) Brake lights (and/or brake reflectors) on the rear of a motor vehicle shall have red lenses so that the light displayed is red. The light illuminating the license plate shall be white. All other lights shall be white, amber, yellow, clear or red.

(10) On every trailer and semitrailer which is 30 feet or more in length and has a gross weight of 4,000 pounds or more, one combination marker lamp showing amber and mounted on the bottom side rail at or near the center of each side of the trailer. (1955, c. 1157, s. 4; 1969, c. 387; 1983, c. 245; 1987, c. 363, s. 1; 2000-159, s. 10.)

§ 20-129.2. Lighting equipment for mobile homes.

Notwithstanding the provisions of G.S. 20-129 and 20-129.1, the lighting equipment required to be provided and equipped on a house trailer, mobile home, modular home, or structural component thereof shall be as designated by the Commissioner of Motor Vehicles and from time to time promulgated by regulation of the Division. (1975, c. 716, s. 5; c. 833, s. 1.)

§ 20-130. Additional permissible light on vehicle.

(a) Spot Lamps. - Any motor vehicle may be equipped with not to exceed two spot lamps, except that a motorcycle shall not be equipped with more than one spot lamp, and every lighted spot lamp shall be so aimed and used upon approaching another vehicle that no part of the beam will be directed to the left of the center of the highway nor more than 100 feet ahead of the vehicle. No spot lamps shall be used on the rear of any vehicle.

(b) Auxiliary Driving Lamps. - Any motor vehicle may be equipped with not to exceed two auxiliary driving lamps mounted on the front, and every such auxiliary driving lamp or lamps shall meet the requirements and limitations set forth in G.S. 20-131, subsection (c).

(c) Restrictions on Lamps. - Any device, other than headlamps, spot lamps, or auxiliary driving lamps, which projects a beam of light of an intensity greater than 25 candlepower, shall be so directed that no part of the beam will strike the level of the surface on which the vehicle stands at a distance of more than 50 feet from the vehicle.

(d) Electronically Modulated Headlamps. - Nothing contained in this Chapter shall prohibit the use of electronically modulated headlamps on motorcycles, law-enforcement and fire department vehicles, county fire marshals and Emergency Management coordinators, public and private ambulances, and rescue squad emergency service vehicles, provided such headlamps and light modulator are of a type or kind which have been approved by the Commissioner of Motor Vehicles.

(e) High Mounted Flashing Deceleration Lamps. - Public transit vehicles may be equipped with amber, high mounted, flashing deceleration lamps on the rear of the vehicle. (1937, c. 407, s. 93; 1977, c. 104; 1989, c. 770, s. 7; 2004-82, s. 1.)

§ 20-130.1. Use of red or blue lights on vehicles prohibited; exceptions.

(a) It is unlawful for any person to install or activate or operate a red light in or on any vehicle in this State. As used in this subsection, unless the context requires otherwise, "red light" means an operable red light not sealed in the manufacturer's original package which: (i) is designed for use by an emergency vehicle or is similar in appearance to a red light designed for use by an emergency vehicle; and (ii) can be operated by use of the vehicle's battery, vehicle's electrical system, or a dry cell battery. As used in this subsection, the term "red light" shall also mean any forward facing red light installed on a vehicle after initial manufacture of the vehicle.

(b) The provisions of subsection (a) of this section do not apply to the following:

(1) A police vehicle.

(2) A highway patrol vehicle.

(3) A vehicle owned by the Wildlife Resources Commission and operated exclusively for law enforcement, firefighting, or other emergency response purposes.

(4) An ambulance.

(5) A vehicle used by an organ procurement organization or agency for the recovery and transportation of blood, human tissues, or organs for transplantation.

(6) A fire-fighting vehicle.

(7) A school bus.

(8) A vehicle operated by any member of a municipal or rural fire department in the performance of his duties, regardless of whether members of that fire department are paid or voluntary.

(9) A vehicle of a voluntary lifesaving organization (including the private vehicles of the members of such an organization) that has been officially approved by the local police authorities and which is manned or operated by members of that organization while answering an official call.

(10) A vehicle operated by medical doctors or anesthetists in emergencies.

(11) A motor vehicle used in law enforcement by the sheriff, or any salaried rural policeman in any county, regardless of whether or not the county owns the vehicle.

(11a) A vehicle operated by the State Fire Marshal or his representatives in the performance of their duties, whether or not the State owns the vehicle.

(12) A vehicle operated by any county fire marshal, assistant fire marshal, or emergency management coordinator in the performance of his duties, regardless of whether or not the county owns the vehicle.

(13) A light required by the Federal Highway Administration.

(14) A vehicle operated by a transplant coordinator who is an employee of an organ procurement organization or agency when the transplant coordinator is responding to a call to recover or transport human tissues or organs for transplantation.

(15) A vehicle operated by an emergency medical service as an emergency support vehicle.

(16) A State emergency management vehicle.

(17) An Incident Management Assistance Patrol vehicle operated by the Department of Transportation, when using rear-facing red lights while stopped for the purpose of providing assistance or incident management.

(18) A vehicle operated by the Division of Marine Fisheries or the Division of Parks and Recreation of the Department of Environment and Natural Resources that is used for law enforcement, firefighting, or other emergency response purpose.

(19) A vehicle operated by the North Carolina Forest Service of the Department of Agriculture and Consumer Services that is used for law enforcement, firefighting, or other emergency response purpose.

(20) A vehicle operated by official members or Teams of REACT International, Inc., that is used to provide additional manpower authorized by law enforcement, firefighting, or other emergency response entities.

(c) It is unlawful for any person to possess a blue light or to install, activate, or operate a blue light in or on any vehicle in this State, except for a publicly owned vehicle used for law enforcement purposes or any other vehicle when used by law enforcement officers in the performance of their official duties. As used in this subsection, unless the context requires otherwise, "blue light" means any forward facing blue light installed on a vehicle after initial manufacture of the vehicle; or an operable blue light which:

(1) Is not (i) being installed on, held in inventory for the purpose of being installed on, or held in inventory for the purpose of sale for installation on a vehicle on which it may be lawfully operated or (ii) installed on a vehicle which is used solely for the purpose of demonstrating the blue light for sale to law enforcement personnel;

(1a) Is designed for use by an emergency vehicle, or is similar in appearance to a blue light designed for use by an emergency vehicle; and

(2) Can be operated by use of the vehicle's battery, the vehicle's electrical system, or a dry cell battery.

(c1) The provisions of subsection (c) of this section do not apply to the possession and installation of an inoperable blue light on a vehicle that is inspected by and registered with the Department of Motor Vehicles as a specially constructed vehicle and that is used primarily for participation in shows, exhibitions, parades, or holiday/weekend activities, and not for general daily transportation. For purposes of this subsection, "inoperable blue light" means a blue-colored lamp housing or cover that does not contain a lamp or other mechanism having the ability to produce or emit illumination.

(d) Repealed by Session Laws 1999-249, s. 1.

(e) Violation of subsection (a) or (c) of this section is a Class 1 misdemeanor. (1943, c. 726; 1947, c. 1032; 1953, c. 354; 1955, c. 528; 1957, c. 65, s. 11; 1959, c. 166, s. 2; c. 1170, s. 2; 1967, c. 651, s. 1; 1971, c. 1214; 1977, c. 52, s. 2; c. 438, s. 2; 1979, c. 653, s. 1; c. 887; 1983, c. 32, s. 1; c. 768, s. 6; 1985 (Reg. Sess., 1986), c. 1027, s. 50; 1989, c. 537, s. 2; 1989 (Reg. Sess., 1990), c. 1020, s. 2; 1991, c. 263, s. 1; 1993, c. 539, s. 361; 1994, Ex. Sess., c. 24, s. 14(c); 1993 (Reg. Sess., 1994), c. 719, s. 1; 1995, c. 168, s. 1; 1995 (Reg. Sess., 1996), c. 756, s. 16; 1999-249, s. 1; 2005-152, s. 1; 2009-526, s. 1; 2009-550, s. 3; 2010-132, s. 11; 2013-415, s. 1(b).)

§ 20-130.2. Use of amber lights on certain vehicles.

All wreckers operated on the highways of the State shall be equipped with an amber-colored flashing light which shall be so mounted and located as to be clearly visible in all directions from a distance of 500 feet, which light shall be activated when at the scene of an accident or recovery operation and when towing a vehicle which has a total outside width exceeding 96 inches or which exceeds the width of the towing vehicle. It shall be lawful to equip any other vehicle with a similar warning light including, but not by way of limitation, maintenance or construction vehicles or equipment of the Department of Transportation engaged in performing maintenance or construction work on the roads, maintenance or construction vehicles of any person, firm or corporation, Radio Emergency Associated Citizens Team (REACT) vehicles, and any other vehicles required to contain a warning light. (1967, c. 651, s. 2; 1973, c. 507, s. 5; 1977, c. 464, s. 34; 1979, c. 1; c. 765; 1981, c. 390; 1991, c. 44, s. 1.)

§ 20-130.3. Use of white or clear lights on rear of vehicles prohibited; exceptions.

It shall be unlawful for any person to willfully drive a motor vehicle in forward motion upon the highways of this State displaying white or clear lights on the rear of said vehicle. The provisions of this section shall not apply to the white light required by G.S. 20-129(d) or so-called backup lights lighted only when said vehicle is in reverse gear or backing. Violation of this section does not constitute negligence per se in any civil action. (1973, c. 1071.)

§ 20-131. Requirements as to headlamps and auxiliary driving lamps.

(a) The headlamps of motor vehicles shall be so constructed, arranged, and adjusted that, except as provided in subsection (c) of this section, they will at all times mentioned in G.S. 20-129, and under normal atmospheric conditions and on a level road, produce a driving light sufficient to render clearly discernible a person 200 feet ahead, but any person operating a motor vehicle upon the highways, when meeting another vehicle, shall so control the lights of the vehicle operated by him by shifting, depressing, deflecting, tilting, or dimming the headlight beams in such manner as shall not project a glaring or dazzling light to persons within a distance of 500 feet in front of such headlamp. Every new motor vehicle, other than a motorcycle or motor-driven cycle, registered in this State after January 1, 1956, which has multiple-beam road-lighting equipment shall be equipped with a beam indicator, which shall be lighted whenever the uppermost distribution of light from the headlamps is in use, and shall not otherwise be lighted. Said indicator shall be so designed and located that when lighted it will be readily visible without glare to the driver of the vehicle so equipped.

(b) Headlamps shall be deemed to comply with the foregoing provisions prohibiting glaring and dazzling lights if none of the main bright portion of the headlamp beams rises above a horizontal plane passing through the lamp centers parallel to the level road upon which the loaded vehicle stands, and in no case higher than 42 inches, 75 feet ahead of the vehicle.

(c) Whenever a motor vehicle is being operated upon a highway, or portion thereof, which is sufficiently lighted to reveal a person on the highway at a distance of 200 feet ahead of the vehicle, it shall be permissible to dim the headlamps or to tilt the beams downward or to substitute therefor the light from an auxiliary driving lamp or pair of such lamps, subject to the restrictions as to tilted beams and auxiliary driving lamps set forth in this section.

(d) Whenever a motor vehicle meets another vehicle on any highway it shall be permissible to tilt the beams of the headlamps downward or to substitute therefor the light from an auxiliary driving lamp or pair of such lamps subject to the requirement that the tilted headlamps or auxiliary lamp or lamps shall give sufficient illumination under normal atmospheric conditions and on a level road to render clearly discernible a person 75 feet ahead, but shall not project a glaring or dazzling light to persons in front of the vehicle: Provided, that at all times required in G.S. 20-129 at least two lights shall be displayed on the front of and on opposite sides of every motor vehicle other than a motorcycle, road roller, road machinery, or farm tractor.

(e) No city or town shall enact an ordinance in conflict with this section. (1937, c. 407, s. 94; 1939, c. 351, s. 1; 1955, c. 1157, ss. 6, 7.)

§ 20-132. Acetylene lights.

Motor vehicles eligible for a Historic Vehicle Owner special registration plate under G.S. 20-79.4 may be equipped with two acetylene headlamps of approximately equal candlepower when equipped with clear plane-glass fronts, bright six-inch spherical mirrors, and standard acetylene five-eighths foot burners not more and not less and which do not project a glaring or dazzling light into the eyes of approaching drivers. (1937, c. 407, s. 95; 1995, c. 379, s. 18.1.)

§ 20-133. Enforcement of provisions.

(a) The Commissioner is authorized to designate, furnish instructions to and to supervise official stations for adjusting headlamps and auxiliary driving lamps to conform with the provisions of G.S. 20-129. When headlamps and auxiliary driving lamps have been adjusted in conformity with the instructions issued by the Commissioner, a certificate of adjustment shall be issued to the driver of the motor vehicle on forms issued in duplicate by the Commissioner and showing date of issue, registration number of the motor vehicle, owner's name, make of vehicle and official designation of the adjusting station.

(b) The driver of any motor vehicle equipped with approved headlamps, auxiliary driving lamps, rear lamps or signal lamps, who is arrested upon a charge that such lamps are improperly adjusted or are equipped with bulbs of a candlepower not approved for use therewith, shall be allowed 48 hours within which to bring such lamps into conformance with the requirements of this Article. It shall be a defense to any such charge that the person arrested produce in court or submit to the prosecuting attorney a certificate from an official adjusting station showing that within 48 hours after such arrest such lamps have been made to conform with the requirements of this Article. (1937, c. 407, s. 96.)

§ 20-134. Lights on parked vehicles.

(a) Whenever a vehicle is parked or stopped upon a highway, whether attended or unattended during the times mentioned in G.S. 20-129, there shall be displayed upon such vehicle one or more lamps projecting a white or amber light visible under normal atmospheric conditions from a distance of 500 feet to the front of such vehicle, and projecting a red light visible under like conditions from a distance of 500 feet to the rear, except that local authorities may provide by ordinance that no lights need be displayed upon any such vehicle when parked in accordance with local ordinances upon a highway where there is sufficient light to reveal any person within a distance of 200 feet upon such highway.

(b) A motor vehicle operated on a highway by a rural letter carrier or by a newspaper delivery person shall be equipped and operated with flashing amber lights at any time the vehicle is being used in the delivery of mail or newspapers, regardless of whether the vehicle is attended or unattended. (1937, c. 407, s. 97; 1959, c. 1264, s. 9; 1995 (Reg. Sess., 1996), c. 715, s. 1.)

§ 20-135. Safety glass.

(a) It shall be unlawful to operate knowingly, on any public highway or street in this State, any motor vehicle which is registered in the State of North Carolina and which shall have been manufactured or assembled on or after January 1, 1936, unless such motor vehicle be equipped with safety glass wherever glass is used in doors, windows, windshields, wings or partitions; or for a dealer to sell a motor vehicle manufactured or assembled on or after January 1, 1936, for operation upon the said highways or streets unless it be so equipped. The provisions of this Article shall not apply to any motor vehicle if such motor vehicle shall have been registered previously in another state by the owner while the owner was a bona fide resident of said other state.

(b)   The term "safety glass" as used in this Article shall be construed as meaning glass so treated or combined with other materials as to reduce, in comparison with ordinary sheet glass or plate glass, the likelihood of injury to persons by glass when the glass is cracked or broken.

(c)   The Division of Motor Vehicles shall approve and maintain a list of the approved types of glass, conforming to the specifications and requirements for safety glass as set forth in this Article, and in accordance with standards recognized by the United States Bureau of Standards, and shall not issue a license for or relicense any motor vehicle subject to the provisions of this Article unless such motor vehicle be equipped as herein provided with such approved type of glass.

(d)   Repealed by Session Laws 1985, c. 764, s. 26. (1937, c. 407, s. 98; 1941, c. 36; 1975, c. 716, s. 5; 1985, c. 764, s. 26; 1985 (Reg. Sess., 1986), c. 852, s. 17.)

§ 20-135.1: Repealed by Session Laws 1995 (Regular Session, 1996), c. 756, s. 30.

§ 20-135.2. Safety belts and anchorages.

(a)   Every new motor vehicle registered in this State and manufactured, assembled, or sold after January 1, 1964, shall, at the time of registration, be equipped with at least two sets of seat safety belts for the front seat of the motor vehicle. Such seat safety belts shall be of such construction, design, and strength to support a loop load strength of not less than 5,000 pounds for each belt, and must be of a type approved by the Commissioner.

This subsection shall not apply to passenger motor vehicles having a seating capacity in the front seat of less than two passengers.

(b) After July 1, 1962, no seat safety belt shall be sold for use in connection with the operation of a motor vehicle on any highway of this State unless it shall be constructed and installed as to have a loop strength through the complete attachment of not less than 5,000 pounds and the buckle or closing device shall be of such construction and design that after it has received the aforesaid loop belt load it can be released with one hand with a pull of less than 45 pounds.

(c) The provisions of this section shall apply only to passenger vehicles of nine-passenger capacity or less, except motorcycles. (1961, c. 1076; 1963, c. 288.)

§ 20-135.2A. (See Editor's note) Seat belt use mandatory.

(a) Except as otherwise provided in G.S. 20-137.1, each occupant of a motor vehicle manufactured with seat belts shall have a seatbelt properly fastened about his or her body at all times when the vehicle is in forward motion on a street or highway in this State.

(b) Repealed by Session Laws 2006-140, s. 1, effective December 1, 2006.

(c) This section shall not apply to any of the following:

(1) A driver or occupant of a noncommercial motor vehicle with a medical or physical condition that prevents appropriate restraint by a safety belt or with a professionally certified mental phobia against the wearing of vehicle restraints.

(2) A motor vehicle operated by a rural letter carrier of the United States Postal Service while performing duties as a rural letter carrier and a motor vehicle operated by a newspaper delivery person while actually engaged in delivery of newspapers along the person's specified route.

(3) A driver or passenger frequently stopping and leaving the vehicle or delivering property from the vehicle if the speed of the vehicle between stops does not exceed 20 miles per hour.

(4) Any vehicle registered and licensed as a property-carrying vehicle in accordance with G.S. 20-88, while being used for agricultural purposes in intrastate commerce.

(5) A motor vehicle not required to be equipped with seat safety belts under federal law.

(6) Any occupant of a motor home, as defined in G.S. 20-4.01(27)d2, other than the driver and front seat passengers.

(7) Any occupant, while in the custody of a law enforcement officer, being transported in the backseat of a law enforcement vehicle.

(8) A passenger of a residential garbage or recycling truck while the truck is operating during collection rounds.

(d) Evidence of failure to wear a seat belt shall not be admissible in any criminal or civil trial, action, or proceeding except in an action based on a violation of this section or as justification for the stop of a vehicle or detention of a vehicle operator and passengers.

(d1) Failure of a rear seat occupant of a vehicle to wear a seat belt shall not be justification for the stop of a vehicle.

(e) Any driver or front seat passenger who fails to wear a seat belt as required by this section shall have committed an infraction and shall pay a penalty of twenty-five dollars and fifty cents ($25.50) plus the following court costs: the General Court of Justice fee provided for in G.S. 7A-304(a)(4), the telephone facilities fee provided for in G.S. 7A-304(a)(2a), and the law enforcement training and certification fee provided for in G.S. 7A-304(a)(3b). Any rear seat occupant of a vehicle who fails to wear a seat belt as required by this section shall have committed an infraction and shall pay a penalty of ten dollars ($10.00) and no court costs. Court costs assessed under this section are for the support of the General Court of Justice and shall be remitted to the State Treasurer. Conviction of an infraction under this section has no other consequence.

(f) No drivers license points or insurance surcharge shall be assessed on account of violation of this section.

(g)   The Commissioner of Motor Vehicles and the Department of Public Instruction shall incorporate in driver education programs and driver licensing programs instructions designed to encourage compliance with this section as an important means of reducing the severity of injury to the users of restraint devices and on the requirements and penalties specified in this law.

(h)   Repealed by Session Laws 1999-183, s. 3, effective October 1, 1999. (1985, c. 222, s. 1; 1987, c. 623; 1991, c. 448, s. 1; 1994, Ex. Sess., c. 5, s. 1; 1997-16, s. 2; 1997-443, s. 32.20; 1999-183, ss. 1-3; 2002-126, s. 29A.3(a); 2005-276, s. 43.1(g); 2006-66, s. 21.11; 2006-140, s. 1; 2006-221, s. 21(a); 2007-289, s. 1; 2007-404, s. 2; 2009-376, s. 12; 2009-451, s. 15.20(j).)

§ 20-135.2B. Transporting children under 16 years of age in open bed or open cargo area of a vehicle prohibited; exceptions.

(a)   The operator of a vehicle having an open bed or open cargo area shall ensure that no child under 16 years of age is transported in the bed or cargo area of that vehicle. An open bed or open cargo area is a bed or cargo area without permanent overhead restraining construction.

(b)   Subsection (a) of this section does not apply in any of the following circumstances:

(1)   An adult is present in the bed or cargo area of the vehicle and is supervising the child.

(2)   The child is secured or restrained by a seat belt manufactured in compliance with Federal Motor Vehicle Safety Standard No. 208, installed to support a load strength of not less than 5,000 pounds for each belt, and of a type approved by the Commissioner.

(3)   An emergency situation exists.

(4)   The vehicle is being operated in a parade.

(5)   The vehicle is being operated in an agricultural enterprise, including providing transportation to and from the principal place of the agricultural enterprise.

(6) Repealed by Session Laws 2008-216, s. 1, effective October 1, 2008.

(c) Any person violating this section shall have committed an infraction and shall pay a penalty of not more than twenty-five dollars ($25.00), even if more than one child less than 16 years of age is riding in the open bed or open cargo area of a vehicle. A person found responsible for a violation of this section may not be assessed court costs.

(d) No drivers license points or insurance surcharge shall be assessed on account of violation of this section. A violation of this section shall not constitute negligence per se. (1993 (Reg. Sess., 1994), c. 672, s. 1; 1995, c. 163, s. 7; 1999-183, s. 4; 2008-216, s. 1.)

§ 20-135.3. Seat belt anchorages for rear seats of motor vehicles.

Every new motor vehicle registered in this State and manufactured, assembled or sold after July 1, 1966, shall be equipped with sufficient anchorage units at the attachment points for attaching at least two sets of seat safety belts for the rear seat of the motor vehicle. Such anchorage units at the attachment points shall be of such construction, design and strength to support a loop load strength of not less than 5,000 pounds for each belt.

The provisions of this section shall apply to passenger vehicles of nine-passenger capacity or less, except motorcycles. (1965, c. 372.)

§ 20-135.4. Certain automobile safety standards.

(a) Definitions. - For the purposes of this section, the term "private passenger automobile" shall mean a four-wheeled motor vehicle designed principally for carrying passengers, for use on public roads and highways, except a multipurpose passenger vehicle which is constructed either on a truck chassis or with special features for occasional off-road operation.

(b), (c) Repealed by Session Laws 1975, c. 856.

(d) The manufacturer's specified height of any passenger motor vehicle shall not be elevated or lowered, either in front or back, more than six inches by modification, alteration, or change of the physical structure of said vehicle without prior written approval of the Commissioner of Motor Vehicles.

On or after January 1, 1975, no self-propelled passenger vehicle that has been so altered, modified or changed shall be operated upon any highway or public vehicular area without the prior written approval of the Commissioner. (1971, c. 485; 1973, cc. 58, 1082; 1975, c. 856.)

§ 20-136. Smoke screens.

(a) It shall be unlawful for any person or persons to drive, operate, equip or be in the possession of any automobile or other motor vehicle containing, or in any manner provided with, a mechanical machine or device designed, used or capable of being used for the purpose of discharging, creating or causing, in any manner, to be discharged or emitted, either from itself or from the automobile or other motor vehicle to which attached, any unusual amount of smoke, gas or other substance not necessary to the actual propulsion, care and keep of said vehicle, and the possession by any person or persons of any such device, whether the same is attached to any such motor vehicle, or detached therefrom, shall be prima facie evidence of the guilt of such person or persons of a violation of this section.

(b) Any person or persons violating the provisions of this section shall be guilty of a Class I felony. (1937, c. 407, s. 99; 1993, c. 539, s. 1257; 1994, Ex. Sess., c. 24, s. 14(c).)

§ 20-136.1. Location of television, computer, or video players, monitors, and screens.

No person shall drive any motor vehicle upon a public street or highway or public vehicular area while viewing any television, computer, or video player which is located in the motor vehicle at any point forward of the back of the driver's seat, and which is visible to the driver while operating the motor vehicle. This section does not apply to the use of global positioning systems; turn-by-turn navigation displays or similar navigation devices; factory-installed or aftermarket global positioning systems or wireless communications devices used to transmit or receive data as part of a digital dispatch system; equipment that displays audio system information, functions, or controls, or weather, traffic, and safety information; vehicle safety or equipment information; or image displays that enhance the driver's view in any direction, inside or outside of the vehicle. The provisions of this section shall not apply to law enforcement or emergency personnel while in the performance of their official duties, or to the operator of a vehicle that is lawfully parked or stopped. (1949, c. 583, s. 4; 2009-376, s. 13.)

§ 20-136.2. Air bag installation.

It shall be unlawful for any person, firm, or corporation to knowingly install or reinstall any object in lieu of an air bag, other than an air bag that was designed in accordance with federal safety regulations for the make, model, and year of vehicle, as part of a vehicle inflation restraint system. Any person, firm, or corporation violating this section shall be guilty of a Class 1 misdemeanor. (2003-258, s. 3.)

§ 20-137: Repealed by Session Laws 1995, c. 379, s. 18.2.

§ 20-137.1. Child restraint systems required.

(a) Every driver who is transporting one or more passengers of less than 16 years of age shall have all such passengers properly secured in a child passenger restraint system or seat belt which meets federal standards applicable at the time of its manufacture.

(a1) A child less than eight years of age and less than 80 pounds in weight shall be properly secured in a weight-appropriate child passenger restraint system. In vehicles equipped with an active passenger-side front air bag, if the vehicle has a rear seat, a child less than five years of age and less than 40 pounds in weight shall be properly secured in a rear seat, unless the child restraint system is designed for use with air bags. If no seating position equipped with a lap and shoulder belt to properly secure the weight-appropriate child passenger restraint system is available, a child less than eight years of age and between 40 and 80 pounds may be restrained by a properly fitted lap belt only.

(b)   The provisions of this section shall not apply: (i) to ambulances or other emergency vehicles; (ii) if all seating positions equipped with child passenger restraint systems or seat belts are occupied; or (iii) to vehicles which are not required by federal law or regulation to be equipped with seat belts.

(c)   Any driver found responsible for a violation of this section may be punished by a penalty not to exceed twenty-five dollars ($25.00), even when more than one child less than 16 years of age was not properly secured in a restraint system. No driver charged under this section for failure to have a child under eight years of age properly secured in a restraint system shall be convicted if he produces at the time of his trial proof satisfactory to the court that he has subsequently acquired an approved child passenger restraint system for a vehicle in which the child is normally transported.

(d)   A violation of this section shall have all of the following consequences:

(1)   Two drivers license points shall be assessed pursuant to G.S. 20-16.

(2)   No insurance points shall be assessed.

(3)   The violation shall not constitute negligence per se or contributory negligence per se.

(4)   The violation shall not be evidence of negligence or contributory negligence. (1981, c. 804, ss. 1, 4, 5; 1985, c. 218; 1993 (Reg. Sess., 1994), c. 748, s. 1; 1999-183, ss. 6, 7; 2000-117, s. 1; 2004-191, ss. 1, 2; 2007-6, s. 1.)

§ 20-137.2. Operation of vehicles resembling law-enforcement vehicles unlawful; punishment.

(a)   It is unlawful for any person other than a law-enforcement officer of the State or of any county, municipality, or other political subdivision thereof, with the intent to impersonate a law-enforcement officer, to operate any vehicle, which by its coloration, insignia, lettering, and blue or red light resembles a vehicle owned, possessed, or operated by any law-enforcement agency.

(b) Violation of subsection (a) of this section is a Class 1 misdemeanor. (1979, c. 567, s. 1; 1993, c. 539, s. 362; 1994, Ex. Sess., c. 24, s. 14(c).)

§ 20-137.3. Unlawful use of a mobile phone by persons under 18 years of age.

(a) Definitions. - The following definitions apply in this section:

(1) Additional technology. - Any technology that provides access to digital media including, but not limited to, a camera, music, the Internet, or games. The term does not include electronic mail or text messaging.

(2) Mobile telephone. - A device used by subscribers and other users of wireless telephone service to access the service. The term includes: (i) a device with which a user engages in a call using at least one hand, and (ii) a device that has an internal feature or function, or that is equipped with an attachment or addition, whether or not permanently part of the mobile telephone, by which a user engages in a call without the use of either hand, whether or not the use of either hand is necessary to activate, deactivate, or initiate a function of such telephone.

(3) Wireless telephone service. - A service that is a two-way real-time voice telecommunications service that is interconnected to a public switched telephone network and is provided by a commercial mobile radio service, as such term is defined by 47 C.F.R. § 20.3.

(b) Offense. - Except as otherwise provided in this section, no person under the age of 18 years shall operate a motor vehicle on a public street or highway or public vehicular area while using a mobile telephone or any additional technology associated with a mobile telephone while the vehicle is in motion. This prohibition shall not apply to the use of a mobile telephone or additional technology in a stationary vehicle.

(c) Seizure. - The provisions of this section shall not be construed as authorizing the seizure or forfeiture of a mobile telephone, unless otherwise provided by law.

(d) Exceptions. - The provisions of subsection (b) of this section shall not apply if the use of a mobile telephone is for the sole purpose of communicating with:

(1) Any of the following regarding an emergency situation: an emergency response operator; a hospital, physician's office, or health clinic; a public or privately owned ambulance company or service; a fire department; or a law enforcement agency.

(2) The motor vehicle operator's parent, legal guardian or spouse.

(e) Penalty. - Any person violating this section shall have committed an infraction and shall pay a fine of twenty-five dollars ($25.00). This offense is an offense for which a defendant may waive the right to a hearing or trial and admit responsibility for the infraction pursuant to G.S. 7A-148. No drivers license points, insurance surcharge, or court costs shall be assessed as a result of a violation of this section. (2006-177, s. 1; 2009-135, s. 1.)

§ 20-137.4. Unlawful use of a mobile phone.

(a) Definitions. - For purposes of this section, the following terms shall mean:

(1) Additional technology. - As defined in G.S. 20-137.3(a)(1).

(2) Emergency situation. - Circumstances such as medical concerns, unsafe road conditions, matters of public safety, or mechanical problems that create a risk of harm for the operator or passengers of a school bus.

(3) Mobile telephone. - As defined in G.S. 20-137.3(a)(2).

(4) School bus. - As defined in G.S. 20-4.01(27)d4. The term also includes any school activity bus as defined in G.S. 20-4.01(27)d3. and any vehicle transporting public, private, or parochial school students for compensation.

(b) Offense. - Except as otherwise provided in this section, no person shall operate a school bus on a public street or highway or public vehicular area while using a mobile telephone or any additional technology associated with a mobile telephone while the school bus is in motion. This prohibition shall not apply to the use of a mobile telephone or additional technology associated with a mobile telephone in a stationary school bus.

(c) Seizure. - The provisions of this section shall not be construed as authorizing the seizure or forfeiture of a mobile telephone or additional technology, unless otherwise provided by law.

(d) Exceptions. - The provisions of subsection (b) of this section shall not apply to the use of a mobile telephone or additional technology associated with a mobile telephone for the sole purpose of communicating in an emergency situation.

(e) Local Ordinances. - No local government may pass any ordinance regulating the use of mobile telephones or additional technology associated with a mobile telephone by operators of school buses.

(f) Penalty. - A violation of this section shall be a Class 2 misdemeanor and shall be punishable by a fine of not less than one hundred dollars ($100.00). No drivers license points or insurance surcharge shall be assessed as a result of a violation of this section. Failure to comply with the provisions of this section shall not constitute negligence per se or contributory negligence by the operator in any action for the recovery of damages arising out of the operation, ownership, or maintenance of a school bus. (2007-261, s. 1.)

§ 20-137.4A. Unlawful use of mobile telephone for text messaging or electronic mail.

(a) Offense. - It shall be unlawful for any person to operate a vehicle on a public street or highway or public vehicular area while using a mobile telephone to:

(1) Manually enter multiple letters or text in the device as a means of communicating with another person; or

(2) Read any electronic mail or text message transmitted to the device or stored within the device, provided that this prohibition shall not apply to any name or number stored in the device nor to any caller identification information.

(a1) Motor Carrier Offense. - It shall be unlawful for any person to operate a commercial motor vehicle subject to Part 390 or 392 of Title 49 of the Code of Federal Regulations on a public street or highway or public vehicular area while using a mobile telephone or other electronic device in violation of those Parts.

Nothing in this subsection shall be construed to prohibit the use of hands-free technology.

(b) Exceptions. - The provisions of this section shall not apply to:

(1) The operator of a vehicle that is lawfully parked or stopped.

(2) Any of the following while in the performance of their official duties: a law enforcement officer; a member of a fire department; or the operator of a public or private ambulance.

(3) The use of factory-installed or aftermarket global positioning systems (GPS) or wireless communications devices used to transmit or receive data as part of a digital dispatch system.

(4) The use of voice operated technology.

(c) Penalty. - A violation of this section while operating a school bus, as defined in G.S. 20-137.4(a)(4), shall be a Class 2 misdemeanor and shall be punishable by a fine of not less than one hundred dollars ($100.00). Any other violation of this section shall be an infraction and shall be punishable by a fine of one hundred dollars ($100.00) and the costs of court.

No drivers license points or insurance surcharge shall be assessed as a result of a violation of this section. Failure to comply with the provisions of this section shall not constitute negligence per se or contributory negligence per se by the operator in any action for the recovery of damages arising out of the operation, ownership, or maintenance of a vehicle. (2009-135, s. 2; 2012-78, s. 9.)

§ 20-137.5. Child passenger safety technician; limitation of liability.

(a) The following definitions apply in this section:

(1) Certified child passenger safety technician. - A certified child passenger safety technician is an individual who has successfully completed the U.S. Department of Transportation National Highway Traffic Safety Administration's (NHTSA) National Standardized Child Passenger Safety Certification Training Program and who maintains a current child passenger safety technician or technician instructor certification through the current certifying body for the National Child Passenger Safety Training Program as designated by the National Highway Traffic Safety Administration.

(2) Sponsoring organization. - A sponsoring organization is a person or organization other than a manufacturer of or employee or agent of a manufacturer of child safety seats that:

a. Offers or arranges for the public a nonprofit child safety seat educational program, checkup event, or checking station program utilizing certified child passenger safety technicians; or

b. Owns property upon which a nonprofit child safety seat educational program, checkup event, or checking station program for the public occurs utilizing certified child passenger safety technicians.

(b) Limitation of Liability. - Except as provided in subsection (c) of this section, a certified child passenger safety technician or sponsoring organization shall not be liable to any person as a result of any act or omission that occurs solely in the inspection, installation, or adjustment of a child safety seat or in providing education regarding the installation or adjustment of a child safety seat if:

(1) The service is provided without fee or charge other than reimbursement for expenses, and

(2) The child passenger safety technician or sponsoring organization acts in good faith and within the scope of training for which the technician is currently certified.

(c) Exceptions. - The limitation on liability shall not apply under any of the following conditions:

(1) The act or omission of the certified child passenger safety technician or sponsoring organization constitutes willful or wanton misconduct or gross negligence.

(2) The inspection, installation, or adjustment of a child safety seat or education provided regarding the installation or adjustment of a child safety seat is in conjunction with the for-profit sale of a child safety seat. (2008-178, s. 1.)

Part 9A. Abandoned and Derelict Motor Vehicles.

§ 20-137.6. Declaration of purpose.

Abandoned and derelict motor vehicles constitute a hazard to the health and welfare of the people of the State in that such vehicles can harbor noxious diseases, furnish shelter and breeding places for vermin, and present physical dangers to the safety and well-being of children and other citizens. It is therefore in the public interest that the present accumulation of abandoned and derelict motor vehicles be eliminated and that the future abandonment of such vehicles be prevented. (1973, c. 720, s. 1.)

§ 20-137.7. Definitions of words and phrases.

The following words and phrases when used in this Part shall for the purpose of this Part have the meaning respectively prescribed to them in this Part, except in those instances where the context clearly indicates a different meaning:

(1) "Abandoned vehicle" means a motor vehicle that has remained illegally on private or public property for a period of more than 10 days without the consent of the owner or person in control of the property.

(2) "Demolisher" means any person, firm or corporation whose business is to convert a motor vehicle into processed scrap or scrap metal or otherwise to wreck, or dismantle, such a vehicle.

(3) "Department" means the North Carolina Department of Transportation.

(4) "Derelict vehicle" means a motor vehicle:

a. Whose certificate of registration has expired and the registered and legal owner no longer resides at the address listed on the last certificate of registration on record with the North Carolina Department of Transportation; or

b. Whose major parts have been removed so as to render the vehicle inoperable and incapable of passing inspection as required under existing standards; or

c. Whose manufacturer's serial plates, vehicle identification numbers, license number plates and any other means of identification have been removed so as to nullify efforts to locate or identify the registered and legal owner; or

d. Whose registered and legal owner of record disclaims ownership or releases his rights thereto; or

e. Which is more than 12 years old and does not bear a current license as required by the Department.

(5) "Officer" means any law-enforcement officer of the State, of any county or of any municipality including county sanitation officers.

(6) "Salvage yard" means a business or a person who possesses five or more derelict vehicles, regularly engages in buying and selling used vehicle parts.

(7) "Secretary" means the Secretary of the North Carolina Department of Transportation.

(8) "Tag" means any type of notice affixed to an abandoned or derelict motor vehicle advising the owner or the person in possession that the same has been declared an abandoned or derelict vehicle and will be treated as such, which tag shall be of sufficient size as to be easily discernible and contain such information as the Secretary deems necessary to enforce this Part.

(9) "Vehicle" means every device in, upon, or by which any person or property is or may be transported or drawn upon a highway by mechanical means.

(10) "Vehicle recycling" means the process whereby discarded vehicles (abandoned, derelict or wrecked) are collected and then processed by shredding, bailing or shearing to produce processed scrap iron and steel which is then remelted by steel mills and foundries to make raw materials which are subsequently used to manufacture new metal-based products for the consumer. (1973, c. 720, s. 1.)

§ 20-137.8. Secretary may adopt rules and regulations.

The Secretary is hereby vested with the power and is charged with the duties of administering the provisions of this Part and is authorized to adopt such rules and regulations as may be necessary to carry out the provisions thereof. (1973, c. 720, s. 1.)

§ 20-137.9. Removal from private property.

Any abandoned or any derelict vehicle in this State shall be subject to be removed from public or private property provided not objected to by the owner of the private property after notice as hereinafter provided and disposed of in accordance with the provisions of this Part, provided, that all abandoned motor vehicles left on any right-of-way of any road or highway in this State may be removed in accordance with G.S. 20-161. (1973, c. 720, s. 1.)

§ 20-137.10. Abandoned and derelict vehicles to be tagged; determination of value.

(a)   When any vehicle is derelict or abandoned in this State, the Secretary shall cause a tag to be placed on the vehicle which shall be notice to the owner, the person in possession of the vehicle, or any lienholder that the same is considered to have been derelict or abandoned and is subject to forfeiture to the State.

(b)   Repealed by Session Laws 1975, c. 438, s. 3.

(c)   The tag shall serve as the only notice that if the vehicle is not removed within five days from the date reflected on the tag, it will be removed to a designated place to be sold. After the vehicle is removed, the Secretary shall give notice in writing to the person in whose name the vehicle was last registered at the last address reflected in the Department's records and to any lienholder of record that the vehicle is being held, designating the place where the vehicle is being held and that if it is not redeemed within 10 days from the date of the notice by paying all costs of removal and storage the same shall be sold for recycling purposes. The proceeds of the sale shall be deposited in the highway fund established for the purpose of administering the provisions of this Part.

(d) If the value of the vehicle is determined to be more than one hundred dollars ($100.00), and if the identity of the last registered owner cannot be determined or if the registration contains no address for the owner, or if it is impossible to determine with reasonable certainty the identification and addresses of any lienholders, notice by one publication in a newspaper of general circulation in the area where the vehicle was located shall be sufficient to meet all requirements of notice pursuant to this Part. The notice of publication may contain multiple listings of vehicles. Five days after date of publication the advertised vehicles may be sold. The proceeds of such sale shall be deposited in the highway fund established for the purpose of administering the provisions of this Part.

(d1) If the value of the vehicle is determined to be less than one hundred dollars ($100.00), and if the identity of the last registered owner cannot be determined or if the registration contains no address for the owner, or if it is impossible to determine with reasonable certainty the identification and addresses of any lienholders, no notice in addition to that required by subsection (a) hereof shall be required prior to sale.

(e) All officers, as defined in this Part, are given the authority to appraise or determine the value of derelict or abandoned vehicles as defined in this Part. (1973, c. 720, s. 1; 1975, c. 438, s. 3.)

§ 20-137.11. Title to vest in State.

Title to all vehicles sold or disposed of in accordance with this Part shall vest in the State. All manufacturers' serial number plates and any other identification numbers for all vehicles sold to any person other than a demolisher shall at the time of the sale be turned in to the Department for destruction. Any demolisher purchasing or acquiring any vehicle hereunder shall, under oath, state to the Department that the vehicles purchased or acquired by it have been shredded or recycled.

The Secretary shall remove and destroy all departmental records relating to such vehicles in such method and manner as he may prescribe. (1973, c. 720, s. 1.)

§ 20-137.12. Secretary may contract for disposal.

The Secretary is hereby authorized to contract with any federal, other state, county or municipal authority or private enterprise for tagging, collection, storage, transportation or any other services necessary to prepare derelict or abandoned vehicles for recycling or other methods of disposal. Publicly owned properties, when available, shall be provided as temporary collecting areas for the vehicles defined herein. The Secretary shall have full authority to sell such derelict or abandoned vehicles. If the Secretary deems it more advisable and practical, in addition, he is authorized to contract with private enterprise for the purchase of such vehicles for recycling. (1973, c. 720, s. 1.)

§ 20-137.13. No liability for removal.

No agent or employee of any federal, State, county or municipal government, no person or occupant of the premises from which any derelict or abandoned vehicle shall be removed, nor any person or firm contracting for the removal of or disposition of any such vehicle shall be held criminally or civilly liable in any way arising out of or caused by carrying out or enforcing any provisions of this Part. (1973, c. 720, s. 1.)

§ 20-137.14. Enclosed, antique, registered and certain other vehicles exempt.

The provisions of this Part shall not apply to vehicles located on used car lots, in private garages, enclosed parking lots, or on any other parking area on private property which is not visible from any public street or highway, nor to motor vehicles classified as antiques and registered under the laws of the State of North Carolina, those not required by law to be registered, or those in possession of a salvage yard as defined in G.S. 20-137.7, unless that vehicle presents some safety or health hazard or constitutes a nuisance. (1973, c. 720, s. 1.)

Part 10. Operation of Vehicles and Rules of the Road.

§ 20-138: Repealed by Session Laws 1983, c. 435, s. 23.

§ 20-138.1. Impaired driving.

(a) Offense. - A person commits the offense of impaired driving if he drives any vehicle upon any highway, any street, or any public vehicular area within this State:

(1) While under the influence of an impairing substance; or

(2) After having consumed sufficient alcohol that he has, at any relevant time after the driving, an alcohol concentration of 0.08 or more. The results of a chemical analysis shall be deemed sufficient evidence to prove a person's alcohol concentration; or

(3) With any amount of a Schedule I controlled substance, as listed in G.S. 90-89, or its metabolites in his blood or urine.

(a1) A person who has submitted to a chemical analysis of a blood sample, pursuant to G.S. 20-139.1(d), may use the result in rebuttal as evidence that the person did not have, at a relevant time after driving, an alcohol concentration of 0.08 or more.

(b) Defense Precluded. - The fact that a person charged with violating this section is or has been legally entitled to use alcohol or a drug is not a defense to a charge under this section.

(b1) Defense Allowed. - Nothing in this section shall preclude a person from asserting that a chemical analysis result is inadmissible pursuant to G.S. 20-139.1(b2).

(c) Pleading. - In any prosecution for impaired driving, the pleading is sufficient if it states the time and place of the alleged offense in the usual form and charges that the defendant drove a vehicle on a highway or public vehicular area while subject to an impairing substance.

(d) Sentencing Hearing and Punishment. - Impaired driving as defined in this section is a misdemeanor. Upon conviction of a defendant of impaired driving, the presiding judge shall hold a sentencing hearing and impose punishment in accordance with G.S. 20-179.

(e) Exception. - Notwithstanding the definition of "vehicle" pursuant to G.S. 20-4.01(49), for purposes of this section the word "vehicle" does not include a horse. (1983, c. 435, s. 24; 1989, c. 711, s. 2; 1993, c. 285, s. 1; 2006-253, s. 9.)

§ 20-138.2. Impaired driving in commercial vehicle.

(a) Offense. - A person commits the offense of impaired driving in a commercial motor vehicle if he drives a commercial motor vehicle upon any highway, any street, or any public vehicular area within the State:

(1) While under the influence of an impairing substance; or

(2) After having consumed sufficient alcohol that he has, at any relevant time after the driving, an alcohol concentration of 0.04 or more. The results of a chemical analysis shall be deemed sufficient evidence to prove a person's alcohol concentration; or

(3) With any amount of a Schedule I controlled substance, as listed in G.S. 90-89, or its metabolites in his blood or urine.

(a1) A person who has submitted to a chemical analysis of a blood sample, pursuant to G.S. 20-139.1(d), may use the result in rebuttal as evidence that the person did not have, at a relevant time after driving, an alcohol concentration of 0.04 or more.

(a2) In order to prove the gross vehicle weight rating of a vehicle as defined in G.S. 20-4.01(12e), the opinion of a person who observed the vehicle as to the weight, the testimony of the gross vehicle weight rating affixed to the vehicle, the registered or declared weight shown on the Division's records pursuant to G.S. 20-26(b1), the gross vehicle weight rating as determined from the vehicle identification number, the listed gross weight publications from the manufacturer of the vehicle, or any other description or evidence shall be admissible.

(b) Defense Precluded. - The fact that a person charged with violating this section is or has been legally entitled to use alcohol or a drug is not a defense to a charge under this section.

(b1) Defense Allowed. - Nothing in this section shall preclude a person from asserting that a chemical analysis result is inadmissible pursuant to G.S. 20-139.1(b2).

(c) Pleading. - To charge a violation of this section, the pleading is sufficient if it states the time and place of the alleged offense in the usual form and charges the defendant drove a commercial motor vehicle on a highway, street, or public vehicular area while subject to an impairing substance.

(d) Implied Consent Offense. - An offense under this section is an implied consent offense subject to the provisions of G.S. 20-16.2.

(e) Punishment. - The offense in this section is a misdemeanor and any defendant convicted under this section shall be sentenced under G.S. 20-179. This offense is not a lesser included offense of impaired driving under G.S. 20-138.1, and if a person is convicted under this section and of an offense involving impaired driving under G.S. 20-138.1 arising out of the same transaction, the aggregate punishment imposed by the Court may not exceed the maximum punishment applicable to the offense involving impaired driving under G.S. 20-138.1.

(f) Repealed by Session Laws 1991, c. 726, s. 19.

(g) Chemical Analysis Provisions. - The provisions of G.S. 20-139.1 shall apply to the offense of impaired driving in a commercial motor vehicle. (1989, c. 771, s. 12; 1991, c. 726, s. 19; 1993, c. 539, s. 363; 1994, Ex. Sess., c. 24, s. 14(c); 1998-182, s. 24; 2006-253, s. 10; 2010-129, s. 1.)

§ 20-138.2A. Operating a commercial vehicle after consuming alcohol.

(a) Offense. - A person commits the offense of operating a commercial motor vehicle after consuming alcohol if the person drives a commercial motor vehicle, as defined in G.S. 20-4.01(3d)a. and b., upon any highway, any street, or any public vehicular area within the State while consuming alcohol or while alcohol remains in the person's body.

(b) Implied-Consent Offense. - An offense under this section is an implied-consent offense subject to the provisions of G.S. 20-16.2. The provisions of G.S. 20-139.1 shall apply to an offense committed under this section.

(b1) Odor Insufficient. - The odor of an alcoholic beverage on the breath of the driver is insufficient evidence by itself to prove beyond a reasonable doubt that alcohol was remaining in the driver's body in violation of this section unless the driver was offered an alcohol screening test or chemical analysis and refused to provide all required samples of breath or blood for analysis.

(b2) Alcohol Screening Test. - Notwithstanding any other provision of law, an alcohol screening test may be administered to a driver suspected of violation of subsection (a) of this section, and the results of an alcohol screening test or the driver's refusal to submit may be used by a law enforcement officer, a court, or an administrative agency in determining if alcohol was present in the driver's body. No alcohol screening tests are valid under this section unless the device used is one approved by the Department of Health and Human Services, and the screening test is conducted in accordance with the applicable regulations of the Department as to its manner and use.

(c) Punishment. - Except as otherwise provided in this subsection, a violation of the offense described in subsection (a) of this section is a Class 3 misdemeanor and, notwithstanding G.S. 15A-1340.23, is punishable by a penalty of one hundred dollars ($100.00). A second or subsequent violation of this section is a misdemeanor punishable under G.S. 20-179. This offense is a lesser included offense of impaired driving of a commercial vehicle under G.S. 20-138.2.

(d) Second or Subsequent Conviction Defined. - A conviction for violating this offense is a second or subsequent conviction if at the time of the current offense the person has a previous conviction under this section, and the previous conviction occurred in the seven years immediately preceding the date of the current offense. This definition of second or subsequent conviction also applies to G.S. 20-17(a)(13) and G.S. 20-17.4(a)(6). (1998-182, s. 23; 1999-406, s. 15; 2000-140, s. 5; 2000-155, s. 16; 2007-182, s. 2; 2008-187, s. 36(a).)

Vision Books Order Form

Fax Orders:	1-980-299-5965
Phone Orders:	1-704-898-0770
E-mail Orders:	www.visionbooks.org
Mail Orders:	Vision Books, LLC P.O. Box 42406 Charlotte, NC 28215

Shipp To:
Name_____
Address_____
City_____State_____Zip_____
Phone_____Fax_____
Email_____@_____

Bill To: We can bill a third party on your behalf.
Name_____
Address_____
City_____State_____Zip_____
Phone____(_____)_____Fax_____
Email_____@_____

Pamphlet Number ($15.00 Each)	Qty	Total Cost
_____	_____	_____
_____	_____	_____
_____	_____	_____
_____	_____	_____
_____	_____	_____
_____	_____	_____
_____	_____	_____
<u>Full Volume Set 1-92</u>	<u>92 Pamphlets</u>	<u>1,380.00</u>

Free Shipping Shipping & Handling on Full Volume Orders
Add $1.00 Shipping & Handling per pamphlet $_____

Total Cost $_____

Thank You for Your Support. Management!

DID YOU ENJOY THIS BOOK?

Vision Books would like to hear from you! If you or someone you know has been falsely imprisoned, we would like to hear your story. If the 'North Carolina Criminal Law and Procedure' has had an effect in your life or if you have suggestions, we would like to hear from you. Send your letters to:

Vision Books, LLC
Attn: Staff Writers
P.O. Box 42406
Charlotte, NC 28215
Email: staff@visionbooks.org

Order Additional Copies:

Fax Orders:	1-980-299-5965
Phone Orders:	1-704-898-0770
E-mail Orders:	www.visionbooks.org
Mail Orders:	Vision Books, LLC P.O. Box 42406 Charlotte, NC 28215

www.ingramcontent.com/pod-product-compliance
Lightning Source LLC
Chambersburg PA
CBHW071403170526
45165CB00001B/162